WASHINGTON

THROUGH TWO CENTURIES

WASHINGTON
THROUGH TWO CENTURIES

A History in Maps and Images

JOSEPH R. PASSONNEAU

THE MONACELLI PRESS

First published in the United States of America in 2004 by
The Monacelli Press, Inc.
902 Broadway, New York, New York 10010.

Library of Congress Cataloging-in-Publication Data
Passonneau, Joseph.
Washington through two centuries : a history in maps and
images / Joseph R. Passonneau.
p.   cm.
Includes bibliographical references and index.
ISBN 1-58093-091-3
1. Washington (D.C.)—History. 2. Washington (D.C.)—
History—Pictorial works. 3. Washington (D.C.)—History—
Maps. 4. City planning—Washington (D.C.)—History.
I. Title.
F194.P37   2004
975.3—dc22   2003024057

Printed and bound in Italy

Edited by Stephanie Salomon
Designed by Abigail Sturges

Front cover
**The City of Washington, Bird's-Eye View from the
Potomac—Looking North, 1892.** Lithograph of a drawing by
Charles Parsons, published by Currier & Ives, New York. *LCPP*

Back cover
Aerial view of the Mall, looking west past the Capitol, 1985.
Dennis Brack, NGA

Frontispiece
**Scene at the Pennsylvania Avenue Entrance to the Capitol
Grounds on the Daily Adjournment of Congress.** Detail.
Harper's Weekly, April 1866.

Contents

About the Maps in This Book

The format for the maps in this book has its roots in a mapping project I managed in Chicago more than thirty years ago. By the mid-1960s, the first "urban extensions" of the Interstate Highway System had been completed. The reaction in many cities to proposals for further urban expressway building was negative, vocal, and sustained. In Chicago, citizen opposition halted the design of the Crosstown Expressway, planned to cut through the city's industrial heart.

Between 1967 and 1970, I served as director of the Chicago Crosstown Design Team, which was charged with designing an expressway and rail transit system that citizens would accept. We decided to start by mapping every building, color-coded by use, on the entire twenty-two-mile-long and half-mile-wide Crosstown Expressway corridor. We also prepared three-dimensional (axonometric) maps of critical areas. Unique to urban expressway design, these maps proved invaluable; citizens and community groups could use the maps to determine the impact of each of our many proposals on their houses and neighborhoods. By 1970, every federal, state, county, and city agency and most of the affected Chicago citizens had approved the design of what was named the Richard J. Daley Expressway.

Work on the maps of Washington, D.C., for this book began in 1973 when I was the Kea Distinguished Visiting Professor in the School of Architecture at the University of Maryland. The Kea Professorship included a $10,000 research grant. With an additional $10,000 from the National Endowment for the Arts, students were hired during the summer to draw color-coded maps, similar to the Chicago maps, and axonometric maps of the center of Washington in 1900 and 1970. That work provided base maps for a year-long studio, during which students prepared urban design proposals for central Washington.

The maps describing the center of Washington in 1900 were based on turn-of-the-century Sanborne Insurance Atlases. These atlases locate each building, listing its use, number of stories, and materials of construction. Most buildings on the 1900 axonometric maps were drawn in outline from Sanborne data; Jeffrey Wolf, a skilled student draftsman, drew in detail the monumental buildings existing in 1900 that remained in 1973.

The 1970 maps were based on photogrammetry from the D.C. Department of Transportation; the axonometric map was also based on oblique aerial photography, supported by the Kea grant. During the first four weeks of the fall semester, two-student teams surveyed every building in the center of the city. These surveys provided the database for the maps showing the patterns of urban activity, similar to the Chicago Crosstown maps in which colors identify the use of each building.

During the next several decades, my office continued this work, mapping the center of Washington with the help of young draftspersons from around the world: Azslina Abu Hassen, Elizabeth Blount, Janey Chan, Tamar King, Ying Kai Mu, Patricia Parola, and Jane Passman. Parts of the center were also mapped, on contract, for the D.C. Office of Planning, the Pennsylvania Avenue Development Corporation, and the Cassidy & Pinkard real estate firm.

The maps of Washington's center, and similar maps of Georgetown, have been completed and perfected since 1990 by Vitali Gevorkian and David Akopian, two experienced Armenian architects, and superb draftsmen, stranded in the United States by the breakup of the Soviet Union. By 1998, my office had completed the urban activities and axonometric maps, locating points of interest for the years 1800, 1860, 1900, 1940, 1970, and 2000. The choice of dates depended on the availability of data and, of course, on significant times in the city's history.

The foldout maps for each of the six periods, at a scale of approximately one inch to 750 feet, describe the area from P Street NW to Independence Avenue and from West Thirtieth Street in Georgetown to East Third Street on Capitol Hill. We have also mapped the Southwest neighborhood from Independence Avenue to M Street SW.

All the maps are laid out according to the 1803 Nich King surveys, the bases for the District of Columbia's square and right-of-way boundaries. The original 1800 axonometric map was prepared by T. Loften of the National Geographic Society. She drew the map looking south, as was the practice in the nineteenth century. With her permission, the map was rearranged to fit into a format focusing on central Washington.

The maps describing the center of Washington in 1860 are based on detailed maps created just before the Civil War by Albert Boschke, a German surveyor employed by the Coast Survey. The building uses were taken from the Business Directory of 1865. The 1860 axonometric map has as its basis the Boschke maps and a spectacular aerial sketch of the center of Washington during the Civil War (see pages 48–49). The 1940 maps are based on the Sanborne Atlases and the Baist Real Estate Atlases, on contemporary photographs, and on images from James M. Goode's book *Capital Losses* (1979). The 2000 maps are based on new surveys, on aerial and eye-level photography, and on notes and sketches from life. These last maps were the first we prepared on computer; using them as a basis, we will continue to record the history of the center of Washington as it occurs.

—J.R.P.

Georgetown and the Federal City. Engraving from a painting by George Beck, published in 1801. *LCPP*

Change and Continuity in the National Capital

Washington is a famously planned city. The idea of a "federal city" for the newly formed United States, and debates over its location, predated even the nation's Constitution. The first Congress met in New York in 1789, and New York citizens considered their city the logical choice for the capital; citizens of Philadelphia, which had served as a temporary capital, felt the same way about their city. The heart of the argument, however, was between the North and the South, each insisting it was the proper location for the capital city. This dispute became linked to another contentious issue of the time: Secretary of the Treasury Alexander Hamilton's plan for funding the national debt, opposed by the southern states. Finally, then Secretary of State Thomas Jefferson arranged a meeting between Hamilton and key southern congressmen; the southerners agreed to support Hamilton's plan in return for what Jefferson called a "sweeten"—northern support for a southern location for the capital.

With a southern location agreed upon, George Washington, as the first president, was authorized in 1790 to select a site on the Potomac River not more than ten miles square. The president chose a location centered on Georgetown, a tobacco port below the Great Falls of the Potomac River. At Washington's request, Congress added Alexandria, Virginia, just beyond the ten-mile square, to the proposed area. In September 1791, the capital's three appointed "commissioners" named the platted area the "City of Washington" and the ten-mile square the "District of Columbia."

The L'Enfant Plan

Earlier, in January 1791, Jefferson had written to the commissioners that "The president, having thought Major L'Enfant peculiarly qualified to make such a Draught of the Ground as well as enable himself to fix upon the Spot for Public Buildings; he has been written to for that purpose." Peter Charles L'Enfant—a French volunteer and brevet major in the Continental army known since the early twentieth century as Pierre L'Enfant—arrived in Georgetown in March 1791. In August, only five months after he first saw the site, L'Enfant presented to the president a document he described as the "Plan of the City, intended for the Permanent Seat of the Government of the United States."

During the eighteenth century, elaborate baroque city plans were proposed for a number of European cities; the American capital, however, was the only city in which these plans were realized. The plan that L'Enfant overlaid on an almost virgin landscape was extraordinary; there was nothing like it anywhere in the eighteenth-century world.

Panoramic View of Washington, 1856.
Drawn by Edward Sachse, published
by E. Sachse & Co., 1856. *LCPP*

In this frequently published view
of the early city the enlarged House
and Senate wings have been added
to the Capitol. The low dome
designed by Charles Bulfinch (which
some congressmen considered too
high) has been replaced by the much
larger dome designed by Thomas
Walter and Montgomery C. Meigs.
Maryland Avenue (visible in the left
center of the painting) and

Pennsylvania Avenue (on the right),
both 160 feet wide, converge on the
Capitol. On the Mall stands the
Washington Monument (finally
completed in 1885), with an elaborate base designed by Robert Mills
but never executed, and the just-
completed Smithsonian "Castle."
There is light industry on the Mall
(seen in the foreground). The city
is dominated by church steeples
and government buildings—
the White House, the Old State
Department, the Treasury, the
Post Office, and the Patent Office.

Broad avenues radiating from ceremonial public open spaces embraced
an area larger than colonial New York, Boston, and Philadelphia combined. That President Washington was able to persuade a fractious
Congress to adopt such a vast and unusual plan, with little or no
recorded dissent, and probably over quiet resistance from Thomas Jefferson, is a tribute to the president's stature. Although it would be
decades before a town and then a city would rise from the wilderness,
the L'Enfant plan would direct the growth of the city for one hundred
years and continue to shape the city into the twenty-first century.

The National Capital:
Two Hundred Years

In the first half of the nineteenth century, the city's energies were focused
on public building, aimed at securing a foothold for the capital on the
eastern edge of a country rapidly growing westward. Design and construction of the federal buildings did not go smoothly. The various architects battled each other and their federal employers. Money was scarce,

and in 1814, the British (during the War of 1812) burned both the still-
unfinished Capitol and the White House. Eventually, Boston architect
Charles Bulfinch brought order to the vast project and, in 1829, completed Washington's most important building, the Capitol.

Before the Civil War, the capital was not a city but a collection of
villages. Almost everything bought, sold, and used was made within
walking distance of one of four open markets. After the war, railroads
brought goods from all over America to new department stores. The
private city grew rapidly, transforming Washington by the end of the
nineteenth century into a modern, corporate city.

In 1895, L'Enfant's avenues were extended to the district line, the
borders of the ten-mile square, and by 1900, the built-up area was
about to expand beyond the L'Enfant center. In 1900, however, the
heart of the city had assumed a shape that L'Enfant would have had
trouble recognizing. The Mall was a landscaped English park, modeled
on a cemetery and featuring a railroad station and its marshaling
yard—an example of planning gone awry.

In 1902, the Senate Park Commission Plan, often called the
McMillan Plan after the senator who presided over it, returned the
direction of the city's growth to the principles of L'Enfant. In the words
of Frederick Law Olmsted Jr., who was a force in the plan's creation,
"In great undertakings, requiring centuries to mature, the one hope of
unity and harmony, the one hope of successful issue, is the establishment of a comprehensive plan and the consistent adherence to it." The
commission reorganized the Mall in ways that L'Enfant had indicated
and prepared a monumental framework for the growing federal government surrounding the Mall.

There is a symmetry between the two centuries during which the
city has existed. In the first half of the twentieth century, as in the first
half of the nineteenth, governmental Washington grew in size and
importance. After a brief primacy of private interests following World
War I, the administration of Franklin Delano Roosevelt, in response to
the Great Depression, populated the federal office buildings anticipated by the Senate Park Commission.

During World War II, the growth of the federal government again
accelerated, and "temporary" government buildings, many left over
from World War I, covered most of the Mall west of Seventeenth
Street. After World War II, as in the nineteenth century after the Civil
War, most of the important changes occurred in the private city. Many
of these changes were negative. By the 1970s, the flight of the middle
class, both white and black, to the Virginia and Maryland suburbs had
devastated the center.

By the year 2000, the center had again been transformed. Providing more than 450,000 jobs, it had become the second-largest employment center in America (roughly tied with Chicago), surpassed only by
central and lower Manhattan. During the last decades of the century,
the steadily increasing number of private and public office jobs and the
attractiveness of the many new federal museums played an important
role in the rebirth of the city center. Two other related factors also contributed to the economic success of the commercial center: the historic-

The Mall, looking west from the Smithsonian Castle, 1870s. *LCPP*

The Mall was described in the mid-nineteenth century by *Atlantic Monthly* magazine as a "marshy and desolate waste." Here the Department of Agriculture (in the nineteenth century an extremely important federal agency) is in the foreground. The stump of the Washington Monument is barely visible through the haze. The mall east of the Potomac's tidal flats would soon be covered with landscape architect Andrew Jackson Downing's informal "specimens of every American tree," to be replaced in the twentieth century by the Senate Park Commission's formal arrangement of American elms.

The Mall looking east, aerial view from above the Lincoln Memorial, 1946. *NA*

During World War II, the Mall west of the Washington Monument was covered with "temporary" buildings. The buildings north of the reflecting basin (visible on the left), which remained from World War I, were returned to active naval duty in 1942. Some thirty years later, the admirals, finally and reluctantly, moved across the Potomac River to the Pentagon—as instructed by President Richard M. Nixon—and the buildings were replaced by the Constitution Gardens in 1976.

preservation movement and the renaissance of the late-nineteenth-century residential neighborhoods within walking and short transit distance of downtown Washington. The Mall, described by an early resident as a "mere cow pasture," had become one of the world's most appealing and active public open spaces. Three elegant airport terminals, two on the National Register of Historic Places, connected the city to the global economy. By 2000, Washington had become one of the world's great cities.

Civic Planning

The history of physical change in the national capital is also a history of the interaction between public and private planning, and particularly a history of the effect of public investments in urban transportation. Not many people believe that cities are "designed." Most Americans argue that cities simply grow, and that this growth is formless, mindless, and often destructive. Cities do grow in ways that are sometimes destructive. This growth, however, is not mindless and the results are not formless. Cities grow and change as a result of multitudes of decisions by private and public planners as they locate and relocate houses, shops, factories, offices, and institutions. While these planners do not follow a simple blueprint, they are guided by widely agreed upon civic objectives, by what Joseph Hudnut, for many years dean of Harvard University's Graduate School of Design, called the invisible city—the city of law, custom, economic force, and human aspiration—that underlies and shapes the visible city.

Urban designer David Crane, in a luminous understatement, describes the consequence of this largely private, incremental planning as "the City of Ten Thousand Designers." As a practical matter, this is the way most cities have always been designed. Each of the private decisions that shape a city, however, is itself formed by large numbers of public decisions regarding lending policies, tax policies, zoning statutes, and the location of public buildings, as well as by public investments in water mains, sewers, and other utilities and in city streets. These public decisions molding the city's infrastructure dictate the range of choices within which private decisions may be made. The public actions most important in determining the character, efficiency, and quality of modern cities are massive public investments in urban transportation.

Urban Transportation

Transportation technology has always shaped cities. During the first few thousand years of urban history, travel was powered by foot, human or animal. Cities were small and more or less circular in plan. Except for churches, which dominated the centers of preindustrial cities, buildings at the edges of urban areas were about the same height as those at the centers. A city's radius was determined by the distance a person could travel in half an hour to an hour; its height was determined by the bearing strength of masonry and the number of stairs people were willing to climb.

The two centuries of the capital's existence have coincided—exactly—with a series of transportation revolutions. Historian Stephen Ambrose, in his book *Undaunted Courage* (1996), observes that starting in 1803, it took Lewis and Clark three years to get to the Pacific Ocean from St. Louis, Missouri, and back, and that it took two months or more for messages from Lewis (in St. Louis) to reach President Thomas Jefferson in Washington. Ambrose quotes Henry Adams as saying, late in the nineteenth century, that "great as were the material obstacles in the path of the United States, the greatest obstacle of all was the human mind. Down to the close of the eighteenth century no change had occurred in the world which warranted practical men in assuming that great changes were to come." As a matter of fact, people, goods, and information almost certainly moved around the Roman Empire faster than they moved around colonial America. Little more than a half century later, however, President Abraham Lincoln was following the western campaigns instantaneously, by telegraph, and the Union was moving men and matériel to the front, by railroad, at speeds and in quantities previously unimagined.

During the Civil War, Washington was still a pedestrian city. This changed in 1863 when the first horsecars connected the Navy Yard with the White House and beyond. By the last decade of the century, seventeen electrified streetcar lines linked the residential neighborhoods with the city center. The neighborhoods were compact; people generally lived in three-and-a-half-story row houses.

In the 1880s and 1890s, the first tall apartments were built, served by electric elevators. Construction of the Cairo apartments in 1892, almost 155 feet high, created bitter opposition to tall buildings. In 1910, the Act to Regulate the Height of Buildings limited the maximum height of commercial buildings, usually to the width of the street on which the building fronted. Lower heights were mandated for residential buildings. As a result, Washington has the low skyline once characteristic of, though now disappearing from, European cities.

During the first part of the twentieth century, people traveled in streetcars and, increasingly, in private automobiles. By the beginning of World War II, the District of Columbia was fully developed. In 1940, almost half of Washington's commuters traveled by public transit, and 15 percent of the commuters walked to work. After World War II that changed. People could travel at high speeds in their own automobiles in all directions where roads could be found. Washington spread out at very low densities into the surrounding Virginia and Maryland countryside.

The other new transport technology, the high-speed elevator, permitted people to concentrate some activities at densities not seen since ancient Rome. Even in Washington, despite the building-height limitations, an enormous concentration of activities exists in the center. The impact of the new freedom to travel both horizontally and vertically was profound, permanently altering the way people live in cities.

This familiar tale emphasizes the relationship between transportation technology and the size, shape, and internal organization of cities. Because the public, through the agencies of government, controls the design and management of travelways, public decisions have a direct

effect on the quality and efficiency of cities. In order to plan effectively for the future of the capital, not only individuals but citizens as a community must understand the possibilities and the limitations of urban transportation technology.

Washington in the Twenty-First Century

As the twenty-first century begins, Washington is the economic heart of the national capital region and the ceremonial heart of the country. Yet the city faces a number of problems, some of long standing, some new. From the point of view of transportation, the dense center, overrun by private automobiles, is no longer functional. The city has neglected some of its most valuable resources—the great L'Enfant avenues, the riverfronts, and some of the residential neighborhoods, which it almost abandoned. To their mutual disadvantage, the city and its suburbs have ignored many of the problems and the advantages they share.

Since the mid-1960s, however, a number of plans have been proposed by both public agencies and private civic groups that recognize these problems and suggest solutions. By 1800, the L'Enfant plan was in place; by 1902, the plans of the Senate Park Commission were complete. By acting on plans proposed, but never implemented, and on additional plans responding to the changing character of the city, Washington's centennial tradition of exceptional planning can be continued.

Aerial view of Washington, D.C., 1990. *Alex McLean, LBM*

The Potomac River (visible in the foreground) is bordered by the parks of the National Park Service. The Mall, along with the Lincoln Memorial, the Washington Monument, and the Capitol, dominates the center of the city. Unlike any other large American city, in Washington, buildings in the center are low and of a uniform height. Beyond the center are three-and-a-half-story-high residential neighborhoods, with taller apartment and office buildings along the avenues. Extending beyond the District of Columbia (here shrouded in haze) are the low-density Maryland suburbs, with occasional clusters of tall office buildings and apartments.

Chapter 1

Planning the National Capital

Reproduction of a nineteenth-century copy of L'Enfant's August 1791 plan. Detail.

L'Enfant Arrives

In March 1791, Major Peter Charles L'Enfant, a French volunteer in the Continental army who had served with General George Washington, arrived in Georgetown, a tobacco port on the Potomac River. He was charged by President Washington with locating sites for public buildings in the new nation's capital. L'Enfant interpreted his charge broadly and designed a city. His plan, for an entirely new national capital, was largely completed by August of that same year.

L'Enfant had trained as a painter at the Royal Academy of Painting and Sculpture in Paris, where his father was an instructor. While the younger L'Enfant had few credentials as an architect, and none as a city planner, John W. Reps suggests in his book *Monumental Washington: The Planning and Development of the Capital Center* (1967) that during a stay of several months in Paris in 1783–84, L'Enfant had the opportunity to study the latest developments in that city. On his return to America, he remodeled New York's old city hall into Federal Hall, the first capitol of the United States and the site of Washington's inauguration.

While he had been instructed to report to the new capital's three commissioners, L'Enfant recognized his real client. In a March 29 letter to President Washington he described his vision of "a direct and large avenue ... planted with double rows of tree ... a street laid out on a dimension proportioned to the greatness which ... the Capital of a powerful Empire ought to manifest," which would run from Georgetown to the Eastern Branch (the Anacostia River). That street became Pennsylvania Avenue, 160 feet wide, following L'Enfant's instructions; two hundred years later, it was finally planted with double and triple rows of trees. In subsequent letters to Washington the architect expanded on his views for the new city, describing Jenkins Hill, the future site of the Capitol, as "standing ready as a pedestal waiting for a superstructure ... [no other location] ... could bear a competition with this." In August 1791, five months after his arrival, L'Enfant presented Washington with the "Plan of the City, intended for the Permanent Seat of the Government of the United States." The plan continues to shape the nation's capital to this day.

Locating the National Capital

The battle over the location of the new capital city was one of the many controversies that plagued the Continental Congress of the new United States. Southerners wanted the capital in the South, while northerners wanted it in the North. *Monumental Washington* summarizes the dispute over the location of the new capital and its partial resolution as follows: "At one point in the fall of 1783, the Continental Congress approved a plan for two capital cities, one at Georgetown in Virginia and the other at the falls of the Delaware. This bizarre arrangement

Cartouche from L'Enfant's August 1791 city plan for "the Permanent Seat of the Government of the United States." *CUOL*

Detail of a map of the Potomac watershed, first printed c. 1753. *JWR*

One of the cartographers was Peter Jefferson, father of the future U.S. president.

was repealed the following year, but not before one delegate suggested that a single town on a wheeled platform could be built and moved from one site to the other as the need arose. The statue of George Washington, just authorized by the Congress, was also to be portable so it could accompany the mobile town!"

Other solutions were presented from time to time, but the Constitutional Convention in 1787 succeeded only in formalizing the impasse. Without debate, the delegates adopted a clause in Article 1 of the proposed Constitution giving Congress the power "to exercise exclusive Legislation in all Cases whatsoever, over such District (not exceeding ten Miles square) as may, by Cession of particular States, and the Acceptance of Congress, become the Seat of the Government of the United States, and to exercise like Authority over all Places purchased by the Consent of the Legislature of the State in which the Same shall be, for the Erection of Forts, Magazines, Arsenals, dock-Yards, and other needful Buildings." At last, in return for southern support of Alexander Hamilton's plan for financing the national debt, northern congressmen agreed to a southern location for the national capital.

The Residence Act of 1790 authorized President Washington to select a site not more than ten square miles on the Potomac River "at some place between the mouths of the Eastern Branch and the Connogochegue." Carrying out these instructions, in the fall of 1790 Wash-

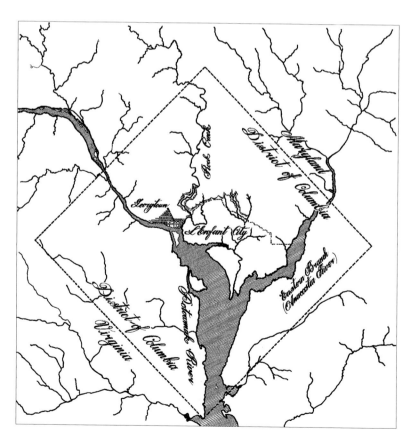

Present-day map of the ten-mile square comprising the original area of the national capital. *JRP*

ington rode up the valley of the Potomac, stopping at towns along the way, where he was wined and dined while citizens argued the advantages of each place for the location of the new capital city. By the end of the year he had settled on a location roughly centered in Georgetown, a port situated at the farthest point of navigation of oceangoing ships sailing up the Potomac River, and a convenient distance from his Mount Vernon home.

Georgetown was one of a number of Maryland and Virginia tidewater towns created as inspection stations and shipment points for tobacco. In Maryland, a 1745 law mandated official inspection of tobacco, the area's major crop. A group of merchants petitioned the Maryland General Assembly for the right to lay out a town—sixty acres bounded approximately by present-day N Street on the north, Jefferson Street on the east, and Thirty-fourth Street on the west— and a charter was granted in 1780. Georgetown became President Washington's base of operations as the plans for the new capital developed, and the town's merchants provided the president with his earliest support.

In November 1790, Thomas Jefferson, as secretary of state, wrote to the president that the Residence Act required the capital to move from New York to Pennsylvania, and then to its new location ten years later. At Washington's request, the act of 1790 was modified by Congress to include Alexandria, Virginia, just beyond the southern edge of the ten-mile square.

The president appointed three commissioners, as required by the Residence Act, on January 22, 1791. On March 29, after dinner at the Georgetown house of General Uriah Forrest, Washington, the newly appointed commissioners, and the principal landowners of the federal district met to discuss the disposition of land within the district. The next day Washington wrote in his diary:

> The parties to whom I addressed myself yesterday evening, having taken the matter into consideration, saw the propriety of my observations; and whilst they were contending for the shadow might lose the substance; and therefore mutually agreed and entered into articles to surrender for public purposes, one half the land they severally possessed within the bounds which were designated as necessary for the city to stand.
>
> This business thus being happily finished and some directions given to the Commissioners, the Surveyor and the Engineer with respect to the mode of laying out the district...Surveying the grounds for the City and forming them into lots...I left Georgetown, dined in Alexandria and reached Mount Vernon that evening.

In September the commissioners agreed "that the federal District be called 'The Territory of Columbia' and the federal City the 'City of Washington.'"

Washington appointed Andrew Ellicott as surveyor of the capital in January 1791, and in March delegated L'Enfant to assist Ellicott. At Valley Forge in the winter of 1777–78, Lafayette, likewise a French citizen who had volunteered to fight the British in the American Revolution, had L'Enfant draw a portrait of General Washington. During the war, L'Enfant prepared drawings for Baron von Steuben's manual *Order and Discipline for the Army of the United States*. Von Steuben recommended him for a commission, and in May 1783, Congress appointed L'Enfant brevet major of engineers. L'Enfant also designed the medal for the Society of Cincinnati, of which Washington was president-general, and in the winter of 1783–84, Washington commissioned him to arrange for the striking of the medal in Paris. On his return to America, L'Enfant began to practice architecture in New York.

In September 1789, L'Enfant wrote to newly elected President George Washington:

> The late determination of Congress to lay the Foundation of a city which is to become the Capital of this vast Empire, offers so great an occasion of acquiring reputation, to whoever may be appointed to conduct the execution of the business, that your excellency will not be surprised that my Ambition and the desire I have of becoming a useful citizen should lead me to wish a share in the undertaking.

> No nation perhaps had ever before the opportunity offered them of deliberately deciding on the spot where their capital should be fixed, or of combining every necessary consideration in the choice of situation—and altho' the means now within the power of the country are not such as to pursue the design to any great extent it will be obvious that the plan should be drawn on such a scale as to leave room for that aggrandizement and embellishment which the increase of the wealth of the Nation will permit it to pursue at any period however remote—viewing the matter in this light I am fully sensible of the extent of the undertaking and under the hope of the continuation of the indulgence you have hitherto honored me I now presume to solicit the favor of being Employed in this Business.

Washington's instructions to L'Enfant were conveyed by Thomas Jefferson:

> You are desired to proceed to Georgetown, where you will find Mr. Ellicott employed in making a survey and map of the Federal territory. The special object of asking your aid is to have drawings of the particular grounds most likely to be approved for the site of [a] federal town and buildings. You will therefore be pleased to begin on the eastern branch, and proceed from then upwards, laying down the hills, valleys, morasses, and waters between that, the Potomac, the Tyber [or Tiber] and the road leading from Georgetown to the eastern branch, and connecting the whole with certain fixed points of the map Mr. Ellicott is preparing. Some idea of the height of the hills above the base on which they stand, would be desirable. For necessary assistance and expenses, be pleased to apply to the Mayor of Georgetown, who is written to on the subject. I will beg the favor of you to mark me your progress about twice a week.

By directing work to start at a distance east of Georgetown, the president hoped to convince citizens that the city was likely to be built along the Eastern Branch, so that landowners near Georgetown would be persuaded to sell their property at reduced prices.

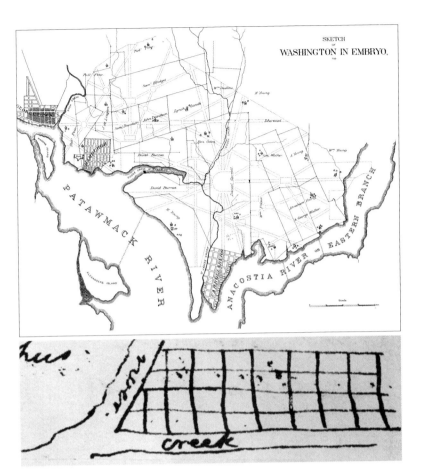

Sketch of the city of Washington in embryonic form, before its survey by L'Enfant. *LCGM*

Prepared in 1894, this map, although it contains errors, provides the best record of land ownership and town plans in 1791 for the area that was to become the "federal city."

Thomas Jefferson's plan for a capital city at Carrolsburg. *LCM*

Carrolsburg, between the Eastern Branch and the Potomac River, and Hamburg, between Goose Creek and Rock Creek, were platted but undeveloped.

L'Enfant's correspondence is laced with his prescient view of the future of the United States, a view clearly shared by Washington and Jefferson, but very likely not by many of their compatriots. Jefferson and L'Enfant had different views of the future capital city, however. Jefferson expressed in sketch plans his ideas of a small, compact town laid out on a rectilinear grid. In contrast, during his first weeks on the job, L'Enfant could only use rhetoric: "Capital of this vast Empire . . . that aggrandizement . . . which the increase of the wealth of the Nation will permit." Although he refused to act imperially in this matter, Washington provided the support that L'Enfant would need to design a capital city to match his rhetoric.

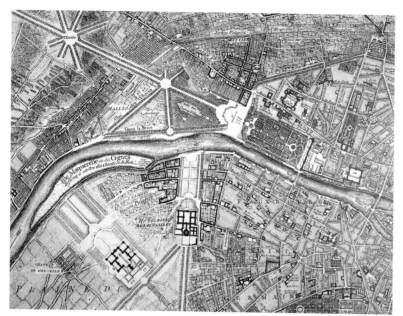

Paris

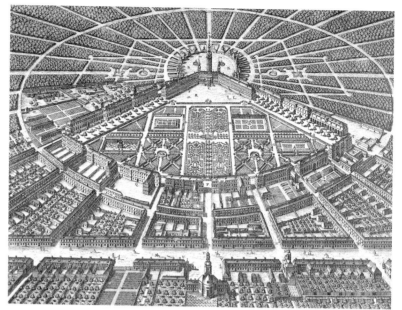

Karlsruhe

Eighteenth-century maps of Paris, Karlsruhe, Turin, and Amsterdam. *JWR*

L'Enfant asked Jefferson to send him copies of city plans from his library. Jefferson reported this to Washington, along with his preference for a grid plan: "I received last night from Majr. L'Enfant a request to furnish him any plans of towns I could, for his examination. I accordingly send him by this post, plans for Frankfort on the Mayne, Carlsruhe, Amsterdam, Strasburg, Paris, Orleans, Bordeaux, Lyons, Montpelier, Marseilles, Turin and Milan, on large and accurate scales…They are none of them however comparable to the old Babylon, revived in Philadelphia and exemplified."

L'Enfant at Work

In April, a few weeks after L'Enfant arrived on the scene, William Loughton Smith, a visitor from South Carolina, wrote: "As soon as I arrived at Georgetown, I rode with Major L'Enfant . . . over the greatest part of the ground; the Major pointed out to me all the eminences, plains, commanding spots, projects of canals by means of Rock Creek, Eastern Branch, and . . . Goose Creek . . . quays, bridges, etc., magnificent public walks, and other projects. The ground pleased me much; the Major is enraptured with it; 'nothing,' he says, 'can be more admirably adapted for the purpose; nature has done much for it and with the aid of art it will become the wonder of the world.'" In his notes Jefferson reflected on his own ambitions for the capital city:

> I propose that these [streets] be laid out at right angles as in Philadelphia, and that no street be narrower than 100. feet with footways of 15. feet . . . I doubt much whether the obligation to build the houses at a given distance from the street, contributes to its beauty. It produces a disgusting monotony. All persons make this complaint against Philadelphia, the contrary practice varies the appearance, & it is much more convenient to the inhabitants. In Paris it is forbidden to

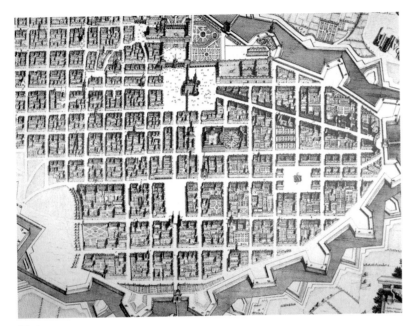

Turin

Amsterdam

build a house beyond a given height, & it is admitted to be a good restriction. It keeps down the price of ground, keeps the houses low and convenient, and the streets light and airy. Fires are much more manageable where houses are low.

Jefferson must have conveyed his ideas to L'Enfant, because in his own notes L'Enfant lashed out at plans composed with right angles:

> It is not the regular assemblage of houses laid out in squares and forming streets all parallel and uniform that . . . is so necessary . . . it never would answer for any of the spots proposed for the Federal City, and on that here held as the most eligible it would absolutely annihilate every [one] of the advantages enumerated and . . . alone injure the success of the undertaking. Such regular plans indeed . . . even when applied upon the ground the best calculated to admit of it become at last tiresome and insipid and it never could be in its origin but a mean continuance of some cool imagination wanting a sense of the real grand and truly beautiful only to be met with where nature contributes with art and diversifies the objects.

Early in April, L'Enfant reported to Jefferson that Washington had reviewed his work and told him, in so many words, to proceed:

> Great as were my Endeavor . . . the moment of the president's arrival at this place . . . I could present him with no more but a rough drawing in pencil of the several Surveys which I had been able to run . . .
>
> Nevertheless . . . I had the satisfaction to see the little I had done agreeable to his wish, and the Confidence which he has been pleased since to Honor me in ordering the survey to be continued and the delineation of a grand plan . . . of the City to be done on principle conformable to the ideas which I took the liberty to hold before him.

That spring of 1791, the thirty-seven-year-old L'Enfant set out to explore the almost untouched terrain between the Potomac River and its Eastern Branch, an area more expansive than was conveyed by any of the maps Jefferson had provided. On this landscape, he was charged with laying out the capital of a new nation. His vision, hugely ambitious, had the support of the country's most powerful individual. L'Enfant accomplished much of this daunting task in just six months.

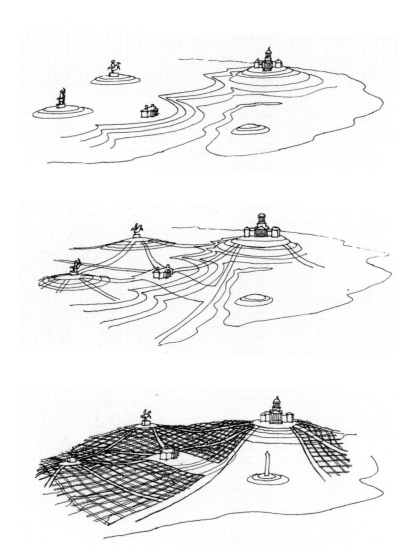

L'Enfant's "Observations" interpreted in present-day sketches.
Prepared by Laurie Olin.

Focal points.

In his "Observations explanatory of the Plan," L'Enfant noted: "I. The positions for the different Grand Edifices, and for the several Grand Squares or Areas of different shapes, as they are laid down, were first determined on the most advantageous ground, commanding the most extensive prospects, and the better susceptible of such improvements as the various intents of the several objects may require."

Radiating avenues.

"II. Lines or Avenues, of direct communication, have been devised, to connect the separate and most distant objects with the principal, and to preserve through the whole a reciprocity of sight at the same time. Attention has been paid to the passing of those leading Avenues over the most favorable ground for prospect and convenience."

Grid of streets.

"III. North and South lines, intersected by others running due East and West, make the distribution of the City into Streets, Squares, etc. and those lines have been so combined, as to meet at certain given points with those divergent Avenues, so as to form on the spaces 'first determined,' the different Squares or Areas, which are all proportional in magnitude to the number of Avenues leading to them."

The Structure of the L'Enfant Plan

The geometry of L'Enfant's plan is complex. Its structure is based on seventeenth- and eighteenth-century French principles of town planning, adapted to a demanding American terrain, and on L'Enfant's vision of a new, still evolving form of government. L'Enfant managed, in a few months, to assemble those disparate principles into a coherent city plan. His objectives were articulated in letters to Washington and Jefferson and in his notes on the plan itself, in imperfect English and using curious calligraphy.

Early critics of L'Enfant—and he had many—accused him of having an overblown notion of the appropriate scale of the new capital. Jefferson does not seem to have been a supporter, and his own sketch for the new city contrasts with L'Enfant's.

By late June 1791, L'Enfant had written a long memorandum to Washington, indicating that he had already settled on many of the characteristics of his final plan:

> Having determined some principal points to which I wished to make the others subordinate. I made the distribution regular with every street at right angles, North and South, east and west, and afterwards opened some in different directions, as avenues to and from every principal place, wishing thereby not merely to contract with the general regularity, nor to afford a greater variety of seats with pleasant prospects, which will be obtained from the advantageous ground over which these avenues are chiefly directed, but principally to connect each part of the city, if I may so express it, by making the real distances less from place to place, by giving them reciprocity of sight and by making them thus seemingly connected, promote a rapid settlement over the whole extent, rendering those even of the most remote parts an addition to the principal, which without the help of these, were any such settlement attempted, it would be languid, and lost in the extent, and become detrimental to the establishment.

Early in August, L'Enfant sent Washington another memorandum and a diagram, with streets appearing as dotted lines and with many open spaces.

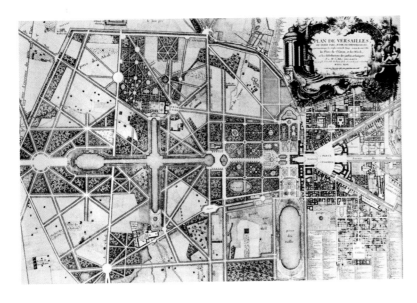

Plan of Versailles, 1746. *JWR*

L'Enfant's father painted ceilings at the Palace of Versailles, and L'Enfant's plan for Washington has been compared with the plan for Versailles.

Jefferson's plan for the national capital, c. early March 1791. *LCM*

Jefferson's grid plan for the capital was more practical than L'Enfant's plan. The "President" and the "Capitol," only four blocks apart, formed the nucleus of a compact development, with blocks for expansion denoted by dots on the sketch. A "public walk" connected president and Capitol. In Jefferson's plan the capital faced the "Tyber" (Tiber, or Goose Creek) and the Potomac, unlike L'Enfant's version.

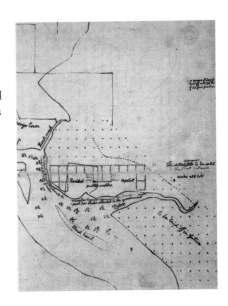

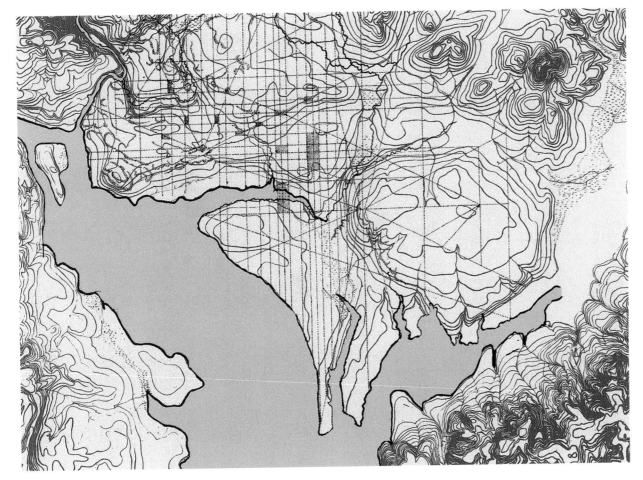

L'Enfant's map of dotted lines overlaid on a present-day topographic map. *Prepared by Don Hawkins. LCDH*

Based on Nich King's 1803 surveys, the overlay illustrates the fit of L'Enfant's city to its eighteenth-century terrain. L'Enfant placed the city inside the bowl formed by an arc of hills. The Capitol, located on Jenkins Hill, dominates the estuary that would later become the Mall.

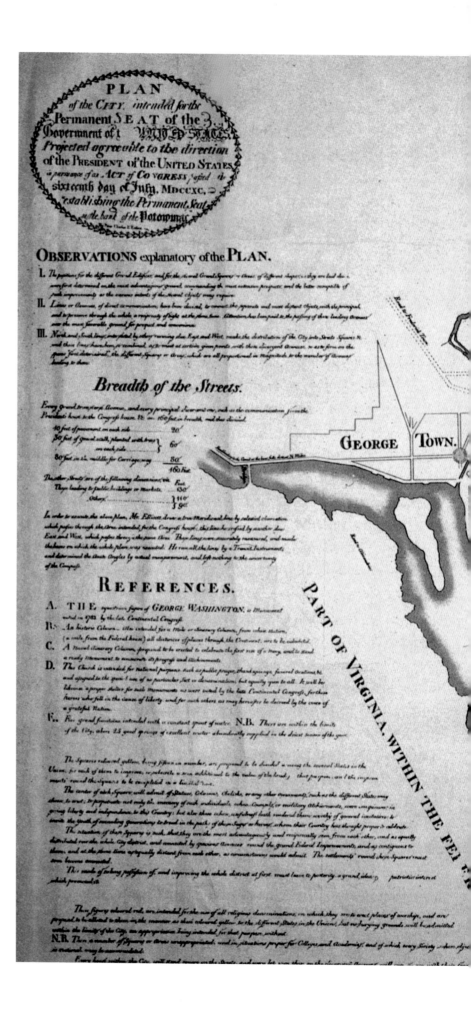

In pattern and imagery, L'Enfant's Washington was baroque—intricate variations within a repeating structure. Its parallel with baroque music is striking. There was nothing like it anywhere in the eighteenth- and nineteenth-century world (nor is there today). In the plans for baroque cities of the eighteenth century, arrays of avenues radiating from important ceremonial points were proposed, but it was in Washington that these ideas were realized. The "Great Triangle," the radiating avenues, and the rhythmic arrangement of north-south streets established the baroque framework of L'Enfant's plan.

In his August 1791 plan, L'Enfant specified the breadth of the streets: "Every Grand transverse Avenue, and every principal divergent one, such as the communication from the President's House to the Congress House . . . shall be 160 feet in breadth . . . The other Streets are of the following dimensions, viz. Those leading to the public buildings or market . . . 130'. Others . . . 110/90'." He even specified details of the Grand Avenues: eighty feet in the middle for the carriageway and thirty feet of gravel walk planted with trees and ten feet of pavement on each side.

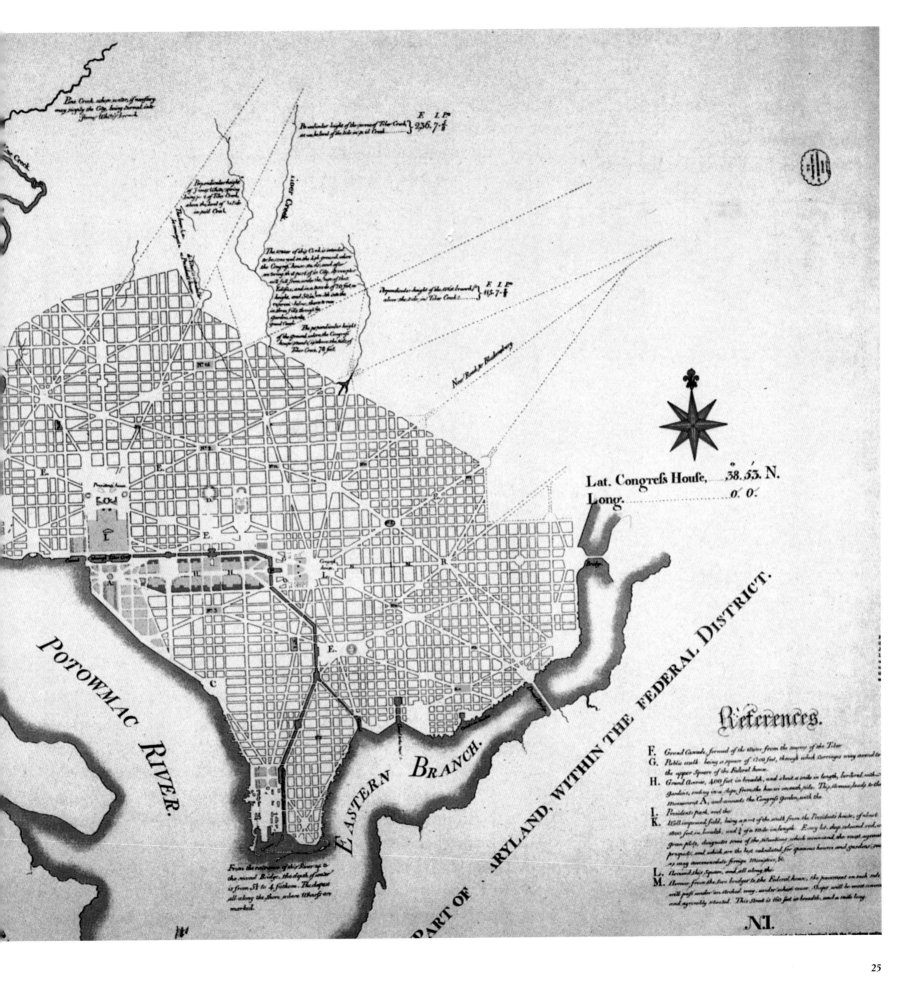

POTOWMAC RIVER.

EASTERN BRANCH.

PART OF ... ARYLAND, WITHIN THE FEDERAL DISTRICT.

Lat. Congress House, 38. 53. N.
Long. .... 0.' 0.'

References.

F. *Grand Canal, formed of the water from the spring of the Tiber*
G. *Public walk being a square of 1200 feet, through which carriages may ascend to the upper Square of the Federal house.*
H. *Grand Avenue, 400 feet in breadth, and about a mile in length, bordered with Gardens, ending in a slope from the houses on each side. They are most likely to the Monument A, and connect the Congress Garden, with the*
I. *President's park, and the*
K. *Well improved field, being a part of the walk from the President's house, of about 1800 feet in breadth, and ¾ of a mile in length. Every lot, deep coloured red, with green plots, designate some of the situations which command the most agreeable prospects, and which are the best calculated for spacious houses and gardens, such as may accommodate foreign Ministers, &c.*
L. *Around this Square, and all along the*
M. *Avenue from the two bridges to the Federal house, the pavement on each side, will pass under an arched way, under whose cover Shops will be most conveniently and agreeably situated. This Street is 160 feet in breadth, and a mile long.*

N.I.

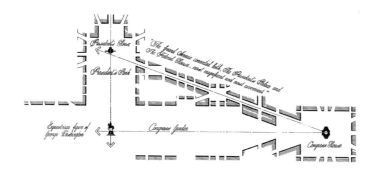

L'Enfant's plan rendered in present-day diagrams. *JRP*

Three ceremonial public open spaces, the basis of the plan.

The heart of L'Enfant's plan is a great triangle. The Mall is one side; the axis between the president's house and "the equestrian figure of George Washington" on the Mall is the other side; and Pennsylvania Avenue is the hypotenuse.

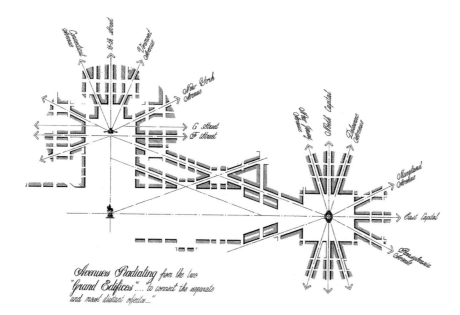

Avenues Radiating from the two "Grand Edifices"... to connect the separate and most distant objects...

The radiating avenues.

Two sets of avenues establish the primacy of the presidency and Congress. Pennsylvania, New York, Vermont, and Connecticut Avenues and Sixteenth Street radiate from the president's house. Pennsylvania, Delaware, New Jersey, and Maryland Avenues, North, South, and East Capitol Streets, and the Mall radiate from the Capitol.

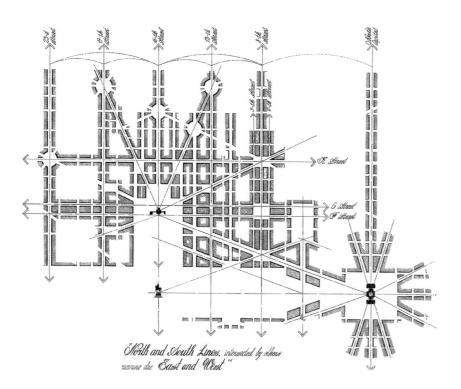

"North and South Lines, intersected by others running due East and West"

The harmonic framework of north-south streets.

North Capitol, Eighth, Sixteenth, and Twenty-third Streets are almost exactly equidistant. Against this baroque rhythm, Thirteenth Street forms the "subharmonic" between Eighth and Sixteenth Streets, and Nineteenth Street is the "subharmonic" between Sixteenth and Twenty-third Streets.

The Eighth Street axis is an important locus of places, including three of the "Squares . . . proposed to be divided among the several states" and the location of the National Church (now the National Portrait Gallery/Museum of American Art). The intersection of Eighth Street and Pennsylvania Avenue was to be adorned with "a grand fountain intended with a constant spout of water," now the Navy Memorial. The "Naval Itinerary Column" was to be located at the intersection of Eighth Street and the Potomac, suggesting that L'Enfant intended Eighth Street to be the American prime meridian. He later identified North and South Capitol Streets as the prime meridian. (This was a half century before Greenwich, England, was designated the universal prime meridian.)

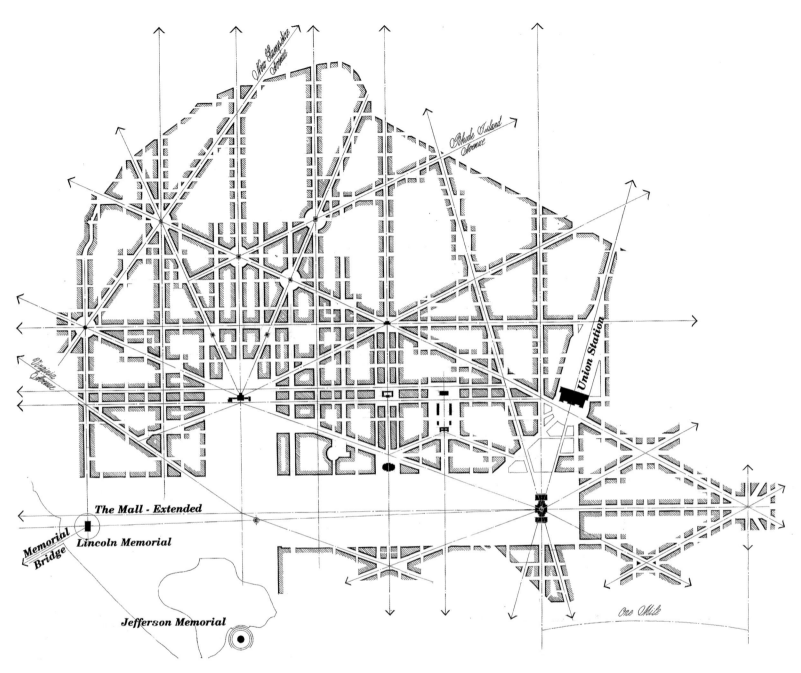

L'Enfant's plan as it existed in the capital in 2000. *JRP*

New Hampshire Avenue connects Washington Circle, at the intersection of K and Twenty-third Streets, with Dupont Circle, at the intersection of Connecticut Avenue and Nineteenth Street. Rhode Island Avenue connects Scott and Logan Circles. Ohio Avenue and most of Indiana Avenue were obliterated by the Federal Triangle, created early in the twentieth century by the Senate Park Commission to house federal agencies, but most of the principal elements of the L'Enfant plan are intact.

Florida Avenue (Boundary Street), at the northern edge of L'Enfant's plan, follows the base of the fall line, the same escarpment that creates the Great Falls of the Potomac and the location of Georgetown. The fall line, which runs from New Jersey to Georgia, is the fault line between the coastal plain (the Tidewater) and the Piedmont plateau. It provided water power for flour milling at Georgetown and, during the Civil War, for manufacturing armament at Richmond and other southern cities.

Massachusetts, Pennsylvania, and Virginia Avenues, each 160 feet wide and representing a powerful state, are arranged geographically in the plan as the states are in reality, from north to south. Because there is a "kink" where Massachusetts Avenue intersects New Jersey Avenue, Massachusetts intersects East Capitol Street at Lincoln Park, exactly one mile from the center of the Capitol dome. The "Itinerary Column," from which all distances in the United States were to be measured, was to be erected in what is now the center of Lincoln Park.

Surveying and mapmaking were among the most important applied sciences in the eighteenth century, and the great survey of France, completed only a few years before L'Enfant laid out the American capital city, remains unsurpassed in accuracy. (The French prime meridian ran through the Paris Observatory, and the French Itinerary Column was apparently located at Nôtre Dame de Paris.)

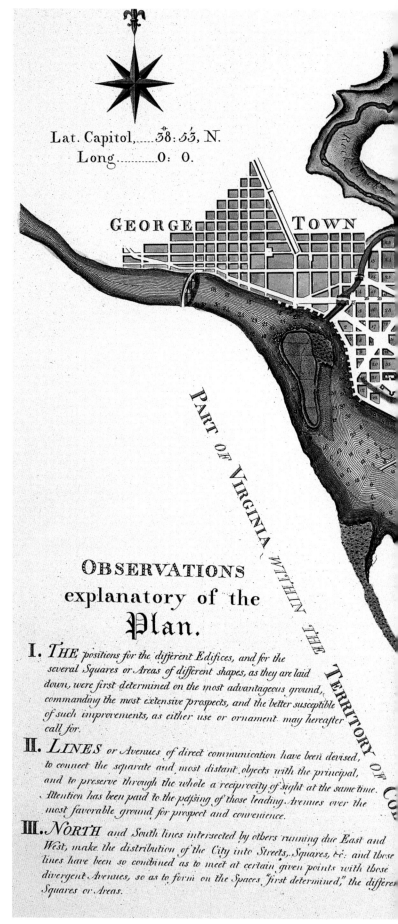

Engraving of Andrew Ellicott's
drawing of L'Enfant's plan, 1792.
JWR

Lat. Capitol,......38:53, N.
Long.............0: 0.

GEORGE TOWN

PART OF VIRGINIA WITHIN THE TERRITORY OF CO

OBSERVATIONS
explanatory of the
Plan.

I. *THE positions for the different Edifices, and for the
several Squares or Areas of different shapes, as they are laid
down, were first determined on the most advantageous ground,
commanding the most extensive prospects, and the better susceptible
of such improvements, as either use or ornament may hereafter
call for.*

II. *LINES or Avenues of direct communication have been devised,
to connect the separate and most distant objects with the principal,
and to preserve through the whole a reciprocity of sight at the same time.
Attention has been paid to the passing of those leading Avenues over the
most favorable ground for prospect and convenience.*

III. *NORTH and South lines intersected by others running due East and
West, make the distribution of the City into Streets, Squares, &c: and these
lines have been so combined as to meet at certain given points with these
divergent Avenues, so as to form on the Spaces "first determined," the different
Squares or Areas.*

L'Enfant was not easy to work with. He refused to submit to the authority of the three commissioners who had been directed by Washington to oversee the project. Daniel Carroll, nephew of one of the commissioners and an original landowner, began building a house on one of L'Enfant's mapped avenues; when Carroll was away L'Enfant had it torn down. Washington ensured that Carroll was compensated financially, but the avenue remained inviolate.

Washington must have been captivated by the grandeur of L'Enfant's ideas early on, since he apparently did nothing to interfere with, and in fact quietly supported, the architect's work. Once the plan was approved, Washington needed engraved copies so that buyers of lots for development could identify their property. Through intermediaries he ordered L'Enfant to prepare the engraving. L'Enfant ignored the order; increasingly acrimonious exchanges led to his refusal to answer questions about timing. This was too much for Washington, and he had L'Enfant dismissed, although L'Enfant may have first resigned. Thomas Jefferson, whose ideas L'Enfant had ignored, carried out the president's order. According to the historian Pamela Scott, the job of preparing the engraved map fell to Jefferson. He made some changes to L'Enfant's plan: for instance, he reduced the number of diagonal streets. Andrew Ellicott, who had surveyed the site, produced a drawing following Jefferson's revisions—a simplified version of L'Enfant's August 1791 plan. This was used by the engravers in 1792, and by Nich King in 1803 to map the city's streets, avenues, and public spaces. It is Ellicott's version that was laid out on the ground and that became the basis for the plan of the national capital.

This branch and that of the Tiber may be conveyed to the Presidents house.

above the level of the tide in said Creek. ....}

The water of this Creek may be conveyed on the high ground where the Capitol stands & after watering that part of the City: may be distined to other usefull purposes.

The Perpendicular height of the ground where the Capitol is to stand is above the tide of Tiber Creek 78 Feet.

Perpendicular height of the West branch above the tide in Tiber Creek } F L Lth 113. 7 . 18

PLAN
of the CITY of
Washington
in the Territory of Columbia,
ceded by the States of
VIRGINIA and MARYLAND
to the
United States of America,
and by them established as the
SEAT of their GOVERNMENT,
after the Year
MDCCC.

Engrav'd by Thackara & Vallance Philad.t 1792.

President's House

Capitol

POTOMAK RIVER.

EASTERN BRANCH

PART OF MARYLAND WITHIN THE TERRITORY OF COLUMBIA.

Breadth of the Streets.

THE grand Avenues, and such Streets as lead immediately to public places, are from 130 to 160 feet wide, and may be conveniently divided into foot ways, walks of trees, and a carriage way. The other Streets are from 90 to 110 feet wide.

IN order to execute this plan, Mr. ELLICOTT drew a true Meridional line by celestial observation, which passes through the Area intended for the Capitol; this line he crossed by another due East and West, which passes through the same Area. These lines were accurately measured, and made the basis on

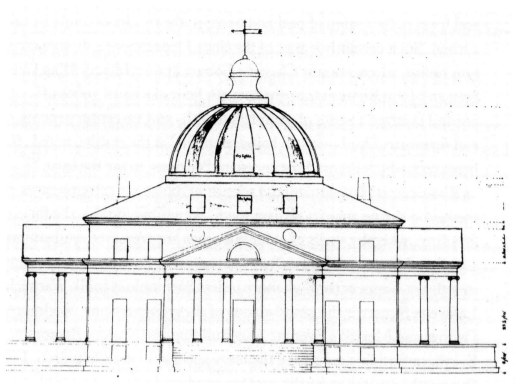

Thomas Jefferson's design for the president's house, 1792. *LCPP*

The north wing of the Capitol in 1800. Sketched by William B. Birch. *LCPP*

This sketch is very likely an accurate picture of the Capitol, its grounds, and local activity when the Congress first met in Washington in November 1800.

Preparation for the Capital City

Before 1792, the area that would become the national capital was used only as farmland. Descendants of the Rozier-Young-Carroll family had owned land in the future Capitol Hill location for almost a century, farming it with slave labor. Beginning in 1770, Daniel Carroll, of "Duddington" (as he called it), tried to attract developers, with no success. Philadelphia resident George Walker and other land speculators assumed there would be early development on Capitol Hill. Several Englishmen, who had become wealthy as a result of the East India trade, built wharves along the Eastern Branch in anticipation of development on the Hill. Thomas Law, who married one of George Washington's step-granddaughters, built at least ten houses on Capitol Hill, and Washington himself built at least one group of row houses near the Capitol. It would be decades, however, before there would be significant residential development in the new national capital.

Despite, or perhaps because of, problems in encouraging residential development, both Washington and Jefferson considered work on the new government buildings to be urgently important. They expected that L'Enfant would design the Capitol and the president's house. When Jefferson sent L'Enfant the European city plans from his collection he wrote: "Whenever it is proposed to prepare Plans for the Capitol, I should prefer the adoption of some one of the models of antiquity, which have had the approbation of thousands of years, and for the President's House I should prefer the celebrated fronts of modern buildings, which have already received the approbation of all good judges. Such are the

Gallerie du Louvre, the Gardes Meubles, and the two fronts of the Hotel de Salm. But of this it is yet time enough to consider." Later, when Washington wrote to L'Enfant to explain the reasons for his dismissal, he added: "In like manner five months have elapsed and are lost, by the compliment which was intended to be paid you in depending alone upon your plans for the public buildings instead of advertising a premium to the person who should present the best."

Jefferson wrote to the commissioners informing them that L'Enfant had been discharged, and pointed out the need to seek new plans for the buildings. The commissioners announced a competition for the design of the Capitol and the president's house, with the winner of the latter to receive $500 or "a medal of that value." A number of designs were submitted, including one by Jefferson, anonymously, based on Palladio's Villa Rotonda near Vicenza, Italy. Jefferson, who believed that neoclassicism would "improve the taste of my countrymen," would go on to design the library and central quadrangle of the University of Virginia, one of America's most distinguished architectural compositions. In 1792, the competition winner was selected—a Palladian design by James Hoban, a thirty-year-old Irish-trained architect practicing in Charleston, South Carolina. Construction on the president's house began immediately.

In the meantime, the notice announcing the competition for the Capitol read: "A premium lot in the city of Washington . . . and $500 shall be given by the Commissioners of the Federal Buildings to the

person who, before the 15th of July, 1792, shall produce to them the most approved plan for a Capitol to be executed in this city." Both Washington and Jefferson were disappointed by the designs submitted. Finally, William Thornton, a Scottish-born physician practicing in Philadelphia, asked to be allowed to offer ideas, although the deadline had passed. Having neither theoretical nor practical architectural experience, he had needed time to study the subject. After consulting books on architecture in the Philadelphia library, he delivered a design that Jefferson favored. Washington also was enthusiastic: "The grandeur, the simplicity, and the beauty . . . will, I doubt not, give a preference in your eyes as it has in mine."

The commissioners selected Thornton's concept but felt obligated to Stephen Hallet, who had been retained to produce a series of designs for the Capitol, following suggestions by the commissioners, the president, and Thomas Jefferson. Hallet's interior plans were chosen for Thornton's shell, and Hallet was hired to execute their design. On September 18, 1793, Washington laid the cornerstone of the Capitol. Hallet soon inserted so many of his own ideas that the architect James Hoban was appointed to supervise construction, with Hallet's assistance. The north wing was completed under Hoban's guidance.

Preparation for the arrival of the government was challenging. Francis Bailey, an Englishman, wrote in 1796: "The private buildings go on but slowly . . . in all I suppose about 200; and these constitute the great city of Washington. The truth is, that not much more than half the city is cleared—the rest is woods; and most of the streets which are laid out are cut through those woods, and have a much more pleasing effect now than I think they will have when they shall be built; for now they appear as broad avenues in a park, bounded on each side by thick woods."

President Washington retired after his second term in office in 1797, setting an example for every successor except Franklin D. Roosevelt a century and a half later. John Adams, who assumed the presidency in 1797, apparently intruded into the planning for the capital only once. During his first year in office he suggested to the commissioners that, for convenient communication between government officials, the executive departments should be near the Capitol, rather than next to the president's house. When landowners heard of this they protested to George Washington, who wrote to President Adams: "Where or how the houses for the president and other public officers may be fixed is for me as an individual a matter of moonshine; but the reverse of the president's reason for placing the latter near the Capitol was my motive for fixing them near the former."

Although there were many who did not believe the capital would ever move from Philadelphia, the official papers and office furniture began to be shipped to the new city in 1799. And despite the architectural conflicts, lack of funds, and shortage of skilled artisans, the Senate wing and foundations on the House wing were ready for the Congress and President Adams in the fall of 1800.

"Plan of the City of Washington, Laid down agreeably to the Surveyor's returns, by Nich King, L.C.W.," 1803. *NCPC*

While Andrew Ellicott's engraving is more accurate than L'Enfant's pencil drawing, the north-south streets are not accurately represented. Therefore, even the engraving does not reflect the structure of the plan. The dimensions and names of each street and avenue were first recorded and accurately drawn on the "Plan of the City of Washington," produced by Nich King in 1803.

Not many cities have more than a few streets over 100 feet in width; downtown Washington has over thirty miles of streets between 110 and 160 feet wide. New Jersey, Delaware, Massachusetts, and Virginia Avenues and Sixteenth Street (rights-of-way) are 160 feet wide, and K Street is 147 feet wide. The remaining "grand avenues" are either 130 feet or 110 feet wide. Overlaid on this elaborate but rigorously organized framework is a grid of streets generally 90 feet wide.

While the diagonal avenues were named after states, the important streets—Sixteenth and K Streets in particular, but also Eighth, Thirteenth, Nineteenth, and Twenty-third Streets—are not so distinguished. It is for this reason that the baroque structure of L'Enfant's plan resonates with so few of the capital's citizens. North and South B Streets were named Constitution and Independence Avenues, respectively, more than a century after King published his maps.

King's plan was accompanied by surveyed cross sections through the streets, which show changes in the height of the terrain.

Washington in 1800

Modified from a map drawn by T. Loften.

1. **The Capitol, North Wing***
2. **President's Palace (White House)***: No rooms were finished.
3. **Patsy Peter Home:** George Washington visited his granddaughter, Patsy, here.
4. **Stone House***: The earliest structure still standing in Washington.
5. **Untie Tavern:** Coach house with stables for fifty horses.
6. **Lear's Stone Warehouse:** Sloops bringing U.S. government furniture and official papers unloaded here.
7. **Key of Keys Quarry:** Foundation stones for the Capitol and president's house were taken from here.
8. **Camp Hill:** Temporary housing for the U.S. Marine Corps.
9. **Cockpit:** For cock fighting.
10. **The "Six Buildings":** Home of the State Department.
11. **The "Seven Buildings"***: The facades of two buildings remain on a parking garage at 2020 Pennsylvania Avenue.
12. **Pearce's Apple Orchard and Tobacco Farm**
13. **Tayloe's Octagon House***: President James Madison lived here temporarily, after the British burned the president's house. The Octagon is now part of the American Institute of Architects.
14. **Treasury Department Building**
15. **Rhodes Tavern:** Remnants demolished c. 1990.
16. **Blodget's Hotel** (unfinished)
17. **Tiber Creek, formerly Goose Creek:** "Great flocks of Mallards and geese stop here spring and fall, so many that the sound of their wings at takeoff is like the rumble of thunder." —T. Loften
18. **Large spring**
19. **Post Office Department and D.C. Post Office**
20. **Tom Jenkins's Farm:** Planted with corn, apples, and tobacco.
21. **Road to Frederick, Maryland**
22. **Dormitory for hired slaves**
23. **Irish workmen's shanties**
24. **Tuncliff's Washington Capitol Hotel:** Baltimore stagecoach stop.
25. **Daniel Carroll Rental Houses**
26. **George Washington Rental Houses**
27. **Duddington:** Home of Daniel Carroll.
28. **Stone bridge** (newly constructed)
29. **Robert Sewell House** (built 1750, addition 1790)
30. **Conningham Brewery**
31. **Seventh Street Bridge**
32. **Morin Hotel**
33. **Pennsylvania Avenue:** "A sea of mud when it rains, footpaths just cleared both sides (center 2 wagons wide cleared in 1792, all 160 feet cleared in 1800)." —T. Loften

Buildings and public projects existing in 2000 are identified with an asterisk.*

Until 1670, a large Indian village stood south of the Capitol site, and even as late as 1800, the "city" was still largely open landscape. Around 1800, Francis Jackson wrote: "I put up a covey of partridges, about 300 yards . . . from the Capitol . . . admired the beautifully picturesque appearance of the country. I have nowhere seen finer scenery than is caused by the Potomac and the woods and hills around it; yet it has a wild, desolate air from being scantily and rudely cultivated and for want of population."

An early resident gave the following account: "On November 21, 1800, during a very unusual (3-inch) fall of snow, the Congress met for the first time in the new Capitol building. The 106 representatives and 32 senators from 6 states, as well as President John Adams, 4 department heads and 131 clerks have recently and permanently removed to this new city as required by law.

"Our beloved first President, the late George Washington, chose the exact site in 1790 and directed the founding of the city for the next 6 years. Under his inspired leadership, Charles Pierre L'Enfant created the design for the city, which will become more visible as buildings rise on squares and all the streets and avenues are opened. Numbers of buildings at the moment: 109 brick, 263 wood, 2 sandstone.

"Population of the city is presently [in 1800] 3,210, or about 600 families . . . [Population in 1790] was about 75, being landowners, hotel and tavern keepers, farmers, laborers, and slaves . . . Population of adjacent Georgetown is 2,993, and of Alexandria on the west side of the Potomac River and downstream about 2 miles, is 5,000."

0 100   500   1000 ft

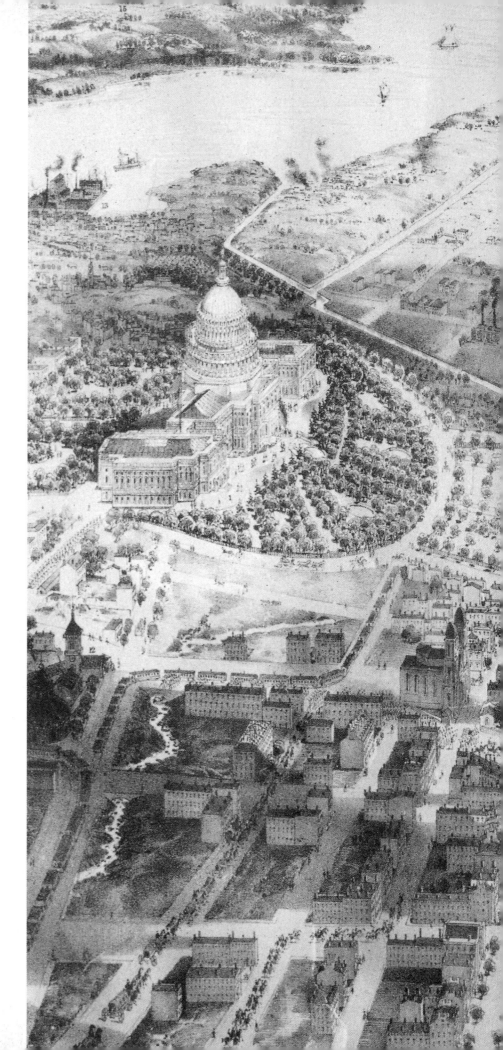

Chapter 2

1800 through the Civil War

Bird's-Eye View of the City of Washington, D.C.,
and the Seat of War in Virginia, **1862.** Detail.

Washington. Aquatint of a drawing by George Parkyns, published in New York, 1795. *LCPP*

This sketch of Washington, viewed from above and west of Georgetown, describes the site, not yet a city.

The National Capital in the Early Nineteenth Century

At the time of the first congressional meeting in the fall of 1800, work had stopped on the Capitol because of a lack of funds. Representative John Cotton Smith of Connecticut reported that "one wing of the Capitol only had been erected, which, with the President's house, a mile distant, both constructed of white sandstone, were shining objects in dismal contrast with the scene around them. Instead of recognizing the avenues and streets portrayed on the plan of the city, not one was visible . . . Pennsylvania [Avenue] . . . was then nearly the whole distance a deep morass, covered with alder bushes."

F Street at 15th Street NE, looking northwest, 1817.
Painting by Baroness Hyde de Neuville, wife of the French minister plenipotentiary. *NYPL*

The building on the left housed the State Department. In the foreground is the Bank Metropole, originally Rhodes Tavern, then Indian King Tavern, then Mrs. Sutter's boardinghouse. It was also an early home to Riggs Bank and the Press Club.

The "Seven Buildings" on Pennsylvania Avenue, 1865. Photographed by Mathew Brady. *LCPP*

The "Six Buildings," home of the State Department, originally with seven employees, and the "Seven Buildings" were constructed on Pennsylvania Avenue in the 1790s.

Washington City, **1821.** Painting by Baroness Hyde de Neuville. *NYPL*

In the view south from Lafayette Square, the Treasury and State Department are on the left, the White House is in the center, and the Departments of War and Navy are on the right.

When Congress and President John Adams and Abigail Adams arrived in Washington for the opening of the first Congress, "main street" was F Street, located on the ridge above Goose Creek (which would later be renamed Tiber Creek). On it were Rhodes Tavern, along with two Catholic churches and various early brick structures. The Treasury, the Post Office, and Blodget's Hotel (not yet finished) were a few steps to the south. "Shanties" for Irish laborers and dormitories for hired slaves working on the Capitol stood on what was to be Judiciary Square.

Also by this time, John Tayloe's "Octagon House," designed by William Thornton for a wealthy plantation owner and friend of the president, was completed and occupied. But while a number of blocks of imposing row houses—similar to the "Six Buildings" and the "Seven Buildings" erected on Pennsylvania Avenue in the 1790s—were built in Georgetown in the first quarter of the nineteenth century, there was little in the way of residential design in the capital during its first decades. Construction was focused on public buildings.

View of the Capitol of the United States after the Conflagration of the 24th August 1814. Engraving by W. Strickland from a drawing by George Munger. *LCPP*

The fire set by British soldiers destroyed the roof and interior of the south wing and badly damaged the older north wing. It was not until 1819 that Latrobe could restore the building to the point at which Congress could again meet in the Capitol.

The "Brick Capitol." Photographed by Mathew Brady in 1862. *LCPP*

Thirty-eight local citizens, including Daniel Carroll and Thomas Law, afraid of losing Washington as the capital city, used their own funds to quickly build a large brick building on the site now occupied by the Supreme Court. Donated to Congress, the "Brick Capitol" housed both the Senate and the House of Representatives until they could return to the rebuilt Capitol in 1819. The building became a boarding-house and, during the Civil War, a prison for southern soldiers, spies, and cashiered Union officers.

The Capitol and the President's House

In March 1803, President Thomas Jefferson appointed Benjamin Henry Latrobe, an English-born engineer-architect, as surveyor of public buildings. Latrobe completed the south wing of the Capitol for the House of Representatives, connecting it to the north Senate wing with a wooden arcade. He also made additions to the president's house.

Because construction of the early public buildings took years, sometimes decades, the work often required the collaboration of a series of architects. Architects have disagreed with each other since architecture began, but seldom has a group of collaborators been as vitriolic as the designers of the capital's earliest public buildings. William Thornton described Benjamin Henry Latrobe in the following manner: "This Dutchman in taste, this monumental builder, this planner of grand steps and walls, this falling arch maker, this blunder-roof gilder, Himself an architect calls." Latrobe, in turn, said of James Hoban, the Irish-born designer of the president's house: "The style he proposes is exactly consistent with Hoban's pile—a litter of pigs worthy of the great sow [the president's house] it surrounds." And George Hadfield, architect of Old City Hall, referred to all the others when he said: "This premium [for the best design for the Capitol] was offered at a period when scarcely a professional architect was to be found in any of the United States, which is plainly to be seen in the pile of trash presented as designs for the said building."

More than 170 years later, the American Institute of Architects (AIA), in its *Guide to the Architecture of Washington, D.C.*, expressed a different view: "Paradoxically, these men who hurled such violent criticism at one another lived in an age of harmonious urban architecture, for despite personal animosities and professional jealousies, they all worked within the limits of generally accepted standards of taste, and perhaps just as importantly, within fairly narrow limits of available construction materials and techniques." The AIA cited as exemplary Thornton's Octagon House and Tudor Place (in Georgetown); Latrobe's Decatur House and St. John's Church, both on Lafayette Square; the White House (president's house) central facade by Hoban and Latrobe; and Hadfield's Arlington House and Old City Hall.

The president's house was unfinished when John Adams moved in during November 1800. The first lady, Abigail Adams, wrote to her daughter: "The house is made habitable but there is not a single apartment finished . . . We have not the least fence, yard, or other convenience, without, and the great unfinished audience room I make a drawing room of, to hang the clothes in." By 1807, President Jefferson described the building as "big enough for two emperors, one pope, and the grand Lama." He collaborated with Latrobe to add a low pavilion at each side of the house; in 1814, James Hoban added the semicircular south portico.

East front of the Capitol, 1846.
Daguerreotype, attributed to John Plumbe Jr. *LCPP*

This is the earliest known photograph of the Capitol building. By 1829, architect Charles Bulfinch had finished the building much as William Thornton had designed it almost four decades earlier. Bulfinch added a wooden, copper-covered dome over the rotunda and smaller domes over the congressional chambers.

The president's house and the Capitol barely survived the War of 1812. In August 1814, when British soldiers invaded Washington, their first stop was Capitol Hill. They burned and looted the unfinished Capitol building, called by British Admiral Cockburn "this harbor of Yankee democracy," and camped on its grounds. The commandant of the U.S. Navy, on orders, burned the Navy Yard and the ships being built there. People living near the yard, angry about the government's inability to protect their houses and jobs, looted the buildings that were still standing.

British soldiers also burned the president's house. When the British withdrew, the building was painted white to conceal the scars left by fire and smoke. It became known as the White House around this time, although the name most likely derived from the white stone from which it was constructed, and on which contemporaries frequently commented.

Reconstruction of the Capitol was begun by Benjamin Latrobe, supervised by William Thornton. The two quarreled constantly, and Latrobe, no diplomat, was fired. Calling President James Madison "a little shriveled spider," he was equally contemptuous of his mentor and predecessor, Thomas Jefferson. In spite of this, Latrobe did manage to complete his corn-and-tobacco-leaf column capitals, an American version of Rome's acanthus leaves.

In 1818, the succeeding president, James Monroe, brought in the Boston-based architect Charles Bulfinch to take over work on the Capitol. According to biographer Harold Kirtker, "Not the least of Bulfinch's talents . . . was the extraordinary political tact that marked a sharp break from the almost 30 years of political strife . . . that had brought the construction of the Capitol to a standstill." Bulfinch filled the gap between the separate buildings for the two houses of Congress (which Latrobe had left connected by a wooden walkway) by adding a domed link in 1827. Congressmen and cabinet officers told the architect they wanted (according to Bulfinch) a "bold . . . picturesque . . . lofty dome"; the architect obliged by providing a fifty-five-foot-high dome, modeled on one he had added to the Massachusetts State House in the 1790s. Latrobe and Thornton, surprisingly, had both wanted a low structure and considered Bulfinch's dome too large.

Bulfinch also added steps, terraces, gatehouses, and fences. In 1832, Frances Trollope (mother of British novelist Anthony Trollope) was entranced, telling her English readers, "The beauty and majesty of the American Capitol might defy an abler pen than mine . . . the magnificent western facade . . . the elegant eastern facade . . . exceedingly handsome . . . most splendid." She particularly liked "the beautiful capitals . . . composed of the ears and leaves of Indian corn . . . [where] America has ventured to attempt national originality."

President Adams's view of the White House from the Potomac River. Unsigned and undated lithograph. *HSW*

While L'Enfant may have neglected the Potomac, President John Adams frequently found his way to the river for a morning swim, as did Theodore Roosevelt a century later.

More than simply striking buildings, the Capitol and the White House, prominently sited, underscored the fit of the city to its terrain as well as its location at the junction of two rivers, the Potomac and the Anacostia. A businessman as well as a general and a president, George Washington—a plantation owner and real estate speculator—cannily located the new capital at the center of eighteenth-century navigation and at the head of the Chesapeake & Ohio Canal, which he had surveyed. The capital was to be a transshipment point between ocean-going commerce, the rich hinterland of Maryland and northern Virginia, and the frontier beyond the Alleghenies. Washington, however, never capitalized on its strategic location as a port city. This was partly due to silting of the Potomac from deforestation above the Great Falls but primarily because of competition from the port of Baltimore, which had better docking facilities and, later, better rail connections.

During its first century, the capital city failed to take advantage of the aesthetic and recreational advantages of its prime riverside location. It was not until the twentieth century that the city began to turn its face to the Potomac River, and the Anacostia River was neglected even into the beginning of the twenty-first century.

City of Washington from Beyond the Navy Yard, **1834.** Engraving by W. Bennett from a painting by G. Cooke. *LCPP*

The view north across the Anacostia River shows the Capitol standing prominently on Jenkins Hill. Buildings line Pennsylvania Avenue; rising to meet the White House, they are exaggerated in size. Residential development on the crescent connecting the Capitol and the Navy Yard (which occupies the same location today) is visible.

The Arsenal (the twentieth-century site of Fort NcNair) is at the far left. The imposing covered dry dock suggests the early importance of the city's location on the Potomac and Anacostia Rivers, at the head of Potomac navigation and soon to be connected to outlying areas by the Chesapeake & Ohio (C & O) Canal.

View of the City of Washington. The Metropolis of the United States of America. Taken from Arlington House the Residence of George Washington P. Custis Esq., **1838.** Lithograph by F. H. Lane from a drawing by P. Anderson. *MMNN*

Home of the president's nephew, George Washington Custis, Arlington House and the Custis properties would become Arlington Cemetery for the nation's military dead. While the image of the city at this time is somewhat inaccurate, its portrayal as underdeveloped is realistic. In 1838, L'Enfant's city covered an immense area, marked by scattered public buildings and even more scattered homes and businesses.

The Treasury Building, looking southwest from Fifteenth Street and Pennsylvania Avenue, c. 1863. *NA*

The Greek Revival–style Treasury Building was begun in 1836; the Treasury Department moved into the unfinished building in 1839. Containing 488 rooms, it cost $6 million. The old State Department Building, visible in the foreground, was soon demolished to make room for the north wing of the Treasury, completed in 1869.

Federal Building
in the Decades before and during the Civil War

The restoration of the Capitol after it was burned by the British in 1814 had diverted work from other public buildings. In 1820, however, City Hall was begun; in the 1830s, the Patent Office and the General Post Office were designed or begun; and in 1847, construction commenced on the Smithsonian "Castle."

President Andrew Jackson ordered construction of the Treasury Building in 1836. Congress, unable to choose between several sites, turned the matter over to President Jackson. The president chose a site east of the White House, which projected into the axis from the White House to the Capitol, undercutting L'Enfant's "reciprocity of sight." Writer Joseph Varnum, and many others both at the time and subsequently, objected that the building blocked the Seventh Street vista of the White House and extended into the Pennsylvania Avenue axis between the White House and the Capitol. Jackson, however, paid no attention.

The Treasury, almost five hundred feet long, was built on a scale unequaled anywhere in the country at the time. The architect Robert Mills called himself the first "native-born American" to study architecture in the United States. He later lived briefly with Thomas Jefferson and studied Jefferson's books on architecture. Mills began as an assistant to Benjamin Latrobe, supervisor of public buildings in Washington, and also worked for James Hoban. In 1814, Mills had won a competition to design a monument to Washington in Baltimore—a Doric column 160 feet tall, topped by a seventeen-foot statue of Washington.

William Elliot, who had competed with Mills for the Treasury commission, joined him to design the other major pre–Civil War structure, the Patent Office, on L'Enfant's site for the National Church. The first wing was completed in 1840. The north wing, delayed by the war, was not finished until 1869. Mills also designed the Post Office, begun in the 1830s and only finished after the war in 1869.

Another pre–Civil War public building, City Hall, was designed by George Hadfield. Started in 1820, it was not completed until 1881.

***Present State of the Washington Monument
to be Erected in the City of Washington.***
Engraving by Frank Leslie for *New York Illustrated News*,
January 8, 1853. *KC*

Construction of the Washington Monument, which
began on July 4, 1848, was halted six years later
when funds ran out. The 152-foot-high stump was
an object of ridicule for residents and visitors until
1880 when construction finally began again, using
a stone of a slightly different color. The change in
stone color remained as testament to the financial
difficulties that beset the capital during the nineteenth century.

The delays, typical of public building and other public investments in
nineteenth-century Washington, were due primarily to the reluctance
of the federal government to contribute to city finances, although
much of the city land was and would continue to remain federal land,
not subject to local tax (a problem that would continue to plague the
capital). The city was also encumbered with the maintenance of the
L'Enfant rights-of-way, which occupied 50 percent of its area. Also,
widely dispersed building sites made urban services more expensive
than they were in more conventionally arranged compact cities.

The most conspicuously delayed project was the Washington
Monument. In 1783, Congress had decreed that "an equestrian statue
of General Washington be erected"; L'Enfant determined the location
in 1791. Fund-raising discussions began when Washington died in
1799, and the Washington National Monument Society was organized
in 1833, the year after the centennial of the first president's birth. In
1836, the society held a competition for the monument's design. The
winner, Robert Mills, proposed a granite obelisk surrounded at the

base by an elaborately decorated colonnade. For this project the society
attempted to raise $1,000,000 but managed to reach only $30,000.

In 1848, Congress approved construction of the monument on
public ground "not otherwise occupied" and finally, in 1876, appropriated construction money. The Washington Monument was completed in 1884, off center on the Mall because of foundation problems
and more than one hundred years after the authorizing congressional
resolution.

In 1829, James Smithson, an English scientist who had never visited the United States, made his nephew the beneficiary of his will. If
the nephew died childless, the bequest was to go "to found at Washington, under the name of the Smithsonian Institution, an Establishment for the increase and diffusion of knowledge among men."
Smithson's nephew died unmarried, and the United States received
$550,000. To house the establishment, the regents of the Smithsonian
Institution selected a design by James Renwick, one of Washington's
earliest architects to work in the Victorian style. A red sandstone

View of Washington, 1850.
Drawing by Robert P. Smith. *LCPP*

The Mall appears empty of trees
or structures, except for the just
finished Smithsonian Institution
and the Washington Monument,
shown complete. The east front of
the Capitol faces the part of the city
that L'Enfant, and speculators
(to their sorrow), assumed would
be the first to be developed.

***Bird's-Eye View of the City of
Washington with Capitol in
Foreground,*** **1862.** Drawing or
engraving by G. H. Andrew for *London
Illustrated News*, May 25, 1862. *KC*

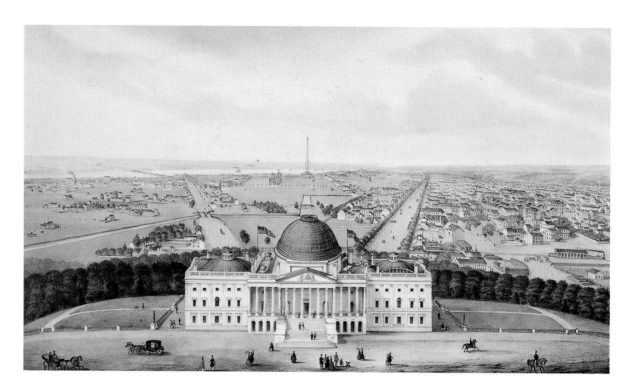

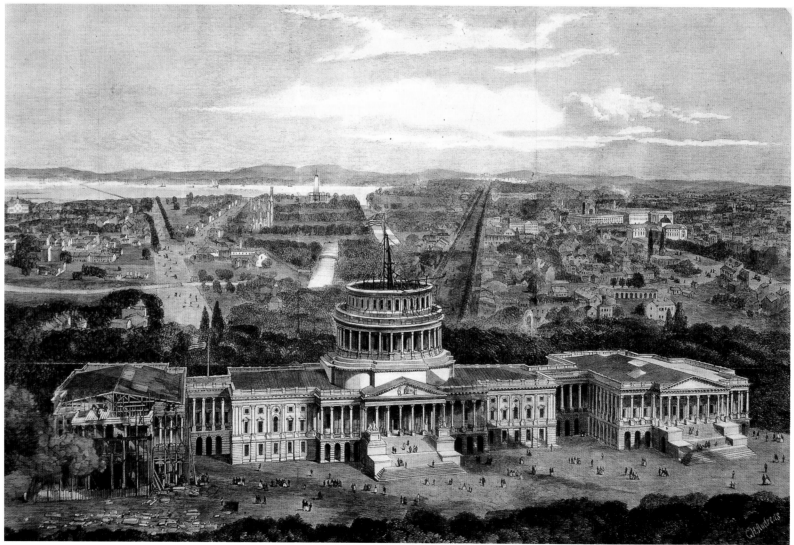

Romanesque "Castle," the building—despite criticism and subsequent attempts at demolition—became a centerpiece on the Mall, otherwise a model of French classicism.

In 1850, the Congressional Committee on Public Buildings recommended expansion of the Capitol following a plan by Robert Mills. After this proposal failed to win congressional approval, the committee offered a prize of $500 for the best expansion plan, selecting four designs of special merit. President Millard Fillmore finally chose Thomas U. Walter, one of the four architects who shared the committee's award. Overseen by engineer Montgomery C. Meigs, who also designed the Pension Building and other important public works, construction began immediately. Meigs and Walter began to quarrel, however, and finally Walter asked Congress to dismiss his "disobedient and rebellious assistant."

Walter expanded the Capitol, adding a new north wing for the Senate and a new south wing for the House of Representatives. The additions more than doubled the length of the building, from 351 feet to 746 feet, reducing Bulfinch's "too large dome" to insignificance. Walter, in fact, replaced the Bulfinch dome with a magnificent and technically advanced version that still towers over the Capitol and the capital city. Walter's (or possibly Meigs's) design comprises multiple exterior and interior classical shells, which disguise the prefabricated cast-iron structure supporting them. Its powerful architectural impact has obscured the fact that it is also one of nineteenth-century America's major engineering achievements.

Inside the structural dome, an architectural shell covers the 180-foot-high Capitol rotunda, one of the nation's great spaces. The interior shell opens to an oculus, with another shell above featuring Constantino Brumidi's fresco *The Apotheosis of George Washington.* In the fresco, classical gods and goddesses mingle with the country's Founding Fathers. Brumidi has been quoted as saying, "My one ambition and my daily prayer is that I may live long enough to make beautiful the Capitol of the one country on earth in which there is liberty." He died in 1880, however, before his work was finished. At eye level, the rotunda is embellished with historical paintings by John Trumbull, the "Artist of the Revolution," who has been described in the *AIA Guide* (2nd ed., 1974) as "a serious (if crotchety) artist who, to ensure accuracy, took the trouble to travel to London and Paris as well as throughout the United States to paint his subjects from life."

While Congress paid little attention to problems of the capital city, it lavished attention on the Capitol. Technological advances would produce a series of renovations and functional improvements to the building throughout the century: steam heat in 1865, elevators in 1874, fireproofing in 1881, and drainage in 1882.

Architect Thomas Walter's drawing of the cross section through the newly designed Capitol dome and rotunda, 1859. *LCPP*

Present-day view of the interior of the Capitol dome.

The structural interior of the dome—a very early example of prefabricated structural cast iron in a monumental building—is as elegant as it is efficient.

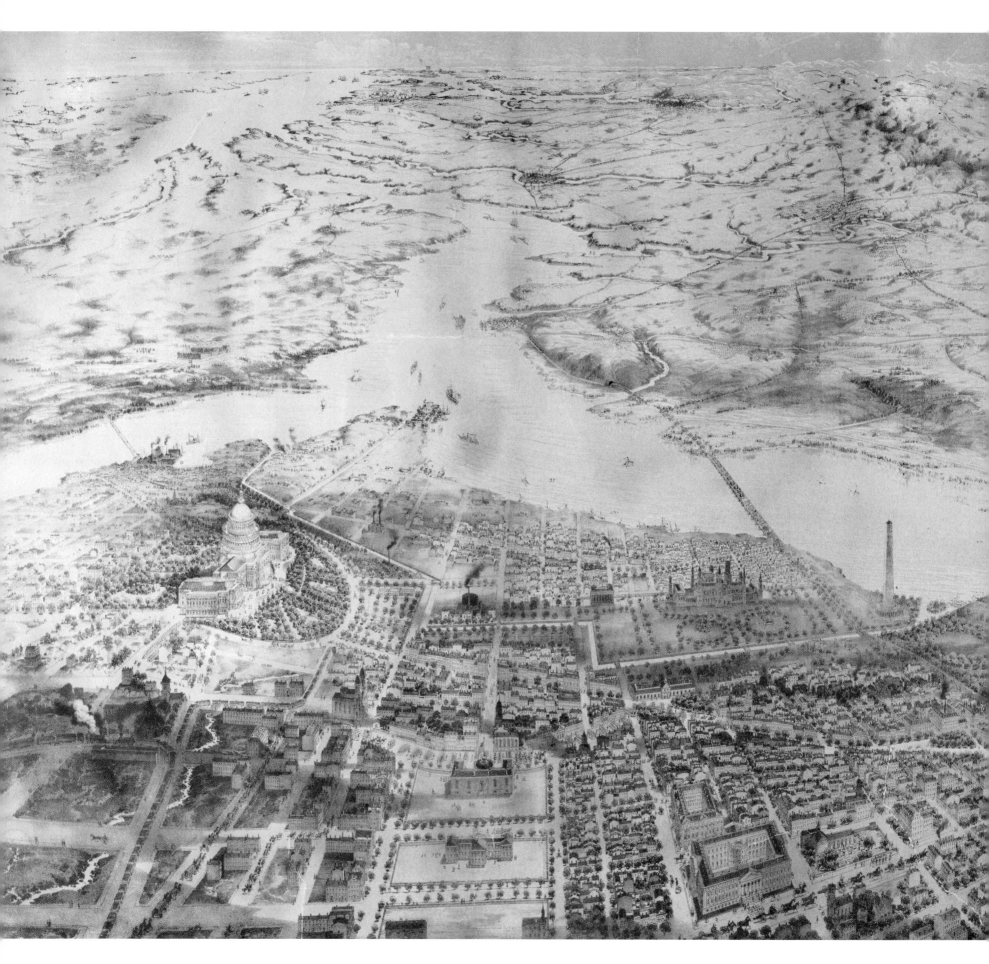

Bird's-Eye View of the City of Washington, D.C., and the Seat of War in Virginia, 1862. Drawing by John Bachmann. *HSW*

The capital city occupied a crucial position during the Civil War. The northern Virginia battlefields, where the war began and ended, lie across the city toward the south. Manassas and Bull Run are in the right foreground; to the far right is the Valley of the Shenandoah, an invasion route both south and north; and in the distance are Fredericksburg, on the Rappahannock River, and Richmond, the capital of the Confederacy, on the James River.

The Capitol dome, shown completed, was under construction throughout the Civil War. President Abraham Lincoln decided to continue construction as an important symbol of the permanence of the Union. In 1862, Tiber Creek still meandered through the eastern part of the town. Beyond and east of the Capitol is the Navy Yard and the bridge across the Anacostia River, John Wilkes Booth's escape route after he shot President Lincoln. The Arsenal, at the meeting of the Potomac and the Anacostia Rivers, is loading ships for the front.

A train nears the station on New Jersey Avenue, northwest of the Capitol. The first railroad entered the city in the 1830s, on Delaware Avenue, soon to be replaced by marshaling yards. (The railroads were important to the Union victory, and the war in turn boosted railroad development.) A military wagon train approaches the station on New Jersey Avenue; another train turns down First Street headed for the front, and a military wagon train follows it. A marching band and military parade in front of City Hall turn down Indiana Avenue to Centre Market and then turn up Pennsylvania Avenue.

The Patent Office, the Post Office, the Washington Monument, and the Smithsonian Institution, all exaggerated in size, dominate the view. Washington was not a manufacturing town; nevertheless, smoke rises from factories close to the Mall, along with the city's first "gasometer," a natural-gas storage tank. (Later in the century, every city of consequence commissioned an axonometric view, always full of smoking factories, the sign of a successful nineteenth-century community.) Like the Capitol dome, the then-unfinished Washington Monument is shown completed, including the planned but never added monumental base.

The Treasury Building, behind the old State Department Building, is still unfinished. Beyond the Treasury is the White House, and beyond the White House are the Army and Navy Buildings, soon to be replaced by a State, War and Navy Building. The Winder Building and Tayloe's Octagon House (both still standing in 2000) are just beyond. The Corcoran Mansion (later the Renwick Gallery) stands on the corner northwest of the White House. St. John's Episcopal Church, the traditional place of worship of presidents, and the Church of the Epiphany rise in the right foreground.

The Naval Observatory, the federal government's first scientific establishment, was placed on Camp Hill in 1844. Beyond the hill is the Georgetown waterfront.

Long Bridge, visible in the center of the drawing, crosses the Potomac River, connecting the city to northern Virginia. Georgetown is connected to Virginia by the Aqueduct Bridge and to Alexandria by the Aqueduct Canal. The C & O Canal follows the north bank of the Potomac toward Harper's Ferry, an important Potomac crossing.

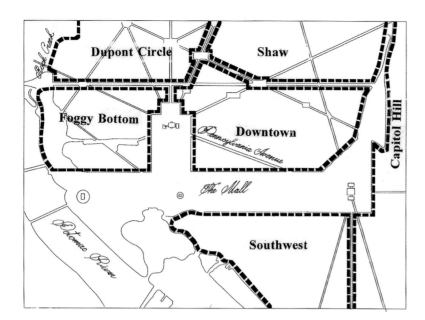

The neighborhoods of Washington. *JRP*

The Capitol Hill, Foggy Bottom, and Southwest neighborhoods were named before the Civil War. The names for Downtown, Dupont Circle, and Shaw date from more recent times. Georgetown (not shown) is west of Dupont Circle.

Neighborhoods

Before the Civil War, Washington was less a city than a collection of somewhat independent villages. Goods were produced and consumed within each neighborhood and sold from the places where they were produced. The Business Directory of 1865 includes coffee roasters, fishmongers, washerwomen, umbrella dealers, guano dealers, horse-shoe and harness sellers, "gents'" furnishings, coopers, ship joiners, bird-and-beast stuffers, bonnet bleachers, ink makers, and nail makers, to name only a few of the 120 trades listed.

When they were not at work, people went to communal places for recreation. The directory lists oyster saloons, lager beer saloons, billiard saloons, bathhouses, and porterhouses as well as other spots for relaxation scattered about the town.

The residential neighborhoods around the center of the city developed during the nineteenth century, each with a distinct identity and roughly defined boundaries. During most of its first hundred years, present-day Downtown, the area between K Street and the Mall, and between the White House and the Capitol, was the city's most densely populated residential neighborhood. Despite setbacks, Capitol Hill, east of the Capitol, also developed early because of jobs provided by the Capitol and the Navy Yard. What is today called the Shaw neighborhood is located east of Sixteenth Street and north of Massachusetts Avenue and K Street. The Dupont Circle neighborhood (which did not exist until the 1870s) lies west of Sixteenth Street and northwest of Downtown. Foggy Bottom is southwest of Dupont Circle and west of the White House; and Southwest lies south of the Mall and west of South Capitol Street. Georgetown, west of Rock Creek, was a town before the national capital existed.

Topographical Map of the District of Columbia, Surveyed in the Years 1856–59. Engraving by D. McClelland from a drawing by Albert Boschke, Washington D.C., 1861. *LCGM*

Albert Boschke was a German surveyor employed by the Coast Survey. This urban section of a survey of the entire District of Columbia shows the built-up area in detail, the large unbuilt parts of the L'Enfant city, and the farm- and woodlands beyond. Although the engraving is dated 1861, the plates were seized by the War Department after a few proof impressions had been made.

The rear of a group of substantial row houses facing the Patent Office, viewed from the southeast in 1846. Daguerreotype attributed to John Plumbe Jr. *MLKL*

The Patent Office was used as a hospital during the Civil War and later became the National Portrait Gallery.

F Street at Fifteenth Street, April 1865. *LCPP*

Row houses in west Downtown are typical of what was a fashionable residential neighborhood during the Civil War. At the far right is the Treasury Building; the house at the far left also served as a shop.

Downtown

L'Enfant's plan to locate the downtown along East Capitol Street never materialized. In 1801, Centre Market was built at Eighth Street and Pennsylvania Avenue NW, "probably the principal factor in drawing business away from the vicinity of the Capitol," according to historian Washington Topham. North Liberty Market was added in 1846 at Seventh Street and Massachusetts Avenue, and Western Market was built on K Street between Nineteenth and Twentieth Streets NW at about the same time. The most densely developed part of the city, between Pennsylvania Avenue and K Street and east of the White House, contained about four hundred acres, less than one square mile.

Downtown was also a fashionable residential neighborhood in the early and mid-nineteenth century. Commercial and residential buildings were similar in appearance—typically, two-, three-, or four-story brick buildings, two or three windows wide, with a gable roof (or by the 1850s, a flat roof). Often only a storefront sign would reveal the commercial purpose, and shopkeepers usually lived above their stores.

Merchants, such as William M. Shuster, who ran a dry-goods store at 38 Market Square and lived at 617 H Street, owned shops on the busier streets or in the markets. Government clerks worked in the government offices nearby. In 1853, Horatio King, a principal clerk in the Post Office, lived at 707 H Street. James Towle lived and worked at 807 H Street as a "measurer of carpenter's and builder's work in gen-

eral, and real estate agent." Not everyone was a homeowner. Because serving in Congress was part-time work, and because of uncertainty about the future of the capital, many people lived in boardinghouses.

Capitol Hill

In 1799, George Washington approved the location of the Navy Yard on the west bank of the Eastern Branch (the Anacostia River); later President Jefferson located Marine barracks near the Navy Yard. In the early 1800s, a neighborhood grew up on Capitol Hill between the employment centers of the Capitol and the Navy Yard. Capitol Hill attracted artisans from Europe—German, Irish, and southern European immigrants, including craftsmen who worked in the Navy Yard and on the expansion of the Capitol between 1850 and 1860. Among these was John Antonio Sousa, who came from Spain (though his parents were Portuguese), joined the Marines, and with his Bavarian-born wife, Maria Elisabeth Trinkhaus, became the father of Marine band director John Philip Sousa, one of America's first internationally known composers.

In 1807, three former slaves, George Bell, a carpenter, and Moses Liverpool and Nicholas Franklin, caulkers at the Navy Yard, established a school for black children. In 1808, the city founded Eastern Academy for poor white children living east of the Capitol. By 1810, gabled houses, shops, smithies, a farmer's market, Masonic Lodge

Military review in east Capitol Hill, fall 1861. *NA*

In the early years of Capitol Hill, as in most parts of the city, empty blocks outnumbered blocks containing even one building.

Carroll Row and Capitol Hill, looking toward the Navy Yard, c. 1880. *CFA*

Carroll Row, on First Street east of the Capitol, was a convenient home to congressmen (including Illinois Representative Abraham Lincoln), most of whom lived in Washington only when Congress was in session. These five Federal-style row houses were built about 1805. The large building on the left was also a tavern.

Number 4, and Episcopal, Presbyterian, and Methodist churches could be found on Capitol Hill. Residents formed a Roman Catholic Church, and Methodists split into black and white congregations.

Prior to the Civil War, land on Capitol Hill was available to anyone who had the money to buy it, regardless of race or creed. Families planted gardens on vacant lots and sold their vegetables at local markets. East Capitol Street, L'Enfant's proposed commercial center, remained so undeveloped before the war that it was used for horse races.

Shaw

The area known as Shaw acquired its name in May 1966, when the National Capital Planning Commission applied the title of Shaw Junior High School to the large, heterogeneous area around the school for purposes of urban-renewal designation. In 1791, land in the Shaw neighborhood was owned by only five men, including real estate developer Samuel Blodget and Robert Peter, the Georgetown tobacco merchant. By 1860, the area around Mount Vernon Square had been developed, but there were few structures beyond O Street. A development northeast of Massachusetts and New Jersey Avenues known as "Swampoodle"—Tiber Creek ran through the swampy area—was settled by Irish laborers.

On his map, published in 1861, the surveyor Albert Boschke platted five cemeteries, one designated "African." African-Americans lived north of N Street, around Iowa (now Logan) Circle, in areas known as Freeman's Alley, Crow Hill, and Nigger Hill. In contrast to urban settlement patterns in 2000, Shaw in 1860 mirrored the arrangement found in other American preindustrial pedestrian cities of the time. In this pattern, upper-class white inhabitants lived close to the center of the city, while poor white and black residents lived on the outskirts of town or, if they did live in the center, in alley dwellings.

Dupont Circle

Before the Civil War, there was no Dupont Circle neighborhood; in fact, there was no Dupont Circle. Located at the intersection of Massachusetts, Connecticut, and New Hampshire Avenues, the circle had been mapped by Andrew Ellicott but not laid out on the ground. In 1860, the area that was to become the Dupont Circle neighborhood consisted of open fields and swampland. It was drained by a creek, Slash Run, which by the end of the Civil War had become an open sewer.

Foggy Bottom

The origin of the name Foggy Bottom is unknown, but it was probably used first during this early period when so much of the area was swampy bottomland. Thomas Jefferson located his plan for the capital city in this part of Washington and placed the Capitol on Camp Hill, where troops were encamped during the War of 1812.

Foggy Bottom, looking south from Washington Circle, 1865. *LCPP*

Because large parts of Foggy Bottom were undeveloped, during the Civil War it was filled with military encampments. Camp Fry was located on both sides of Twenty-third Street. The western wharves are in the background on the right, at the foot of G Street. Camp Fuller, a giant depot for wagon trains, is in the background on the left.

Scribner's Flour and Feed Store at 119 E Street SW, October 1863. Photographed by Titus R. Peale. *SI*

A few well-to-do residents lived along K Street. In a development typical in Washington throughout the nineteenth century, Robert Peter built six three-story houses for his sons in 1797 on K Street between Twentieth and Twenty-seventh Streets. Similar houses were built on Pennsylvania Avenue about the same time. Beyond the White House grounds, however, Foggy Bottom was still largely vacant as late as 1862, except for military encampments. Despite the commercial activity along the water, city directories indicate that all of Foggy Bottom included only forty households in 1822, forty-one in 1830, and sixty in 1843.

The Naval Observatory (now part of the Bureau of Medicine and Surgery) stood on Camp Hill overlooking the Potomac. Light industry was located along the Potomac River and Rock Creek. In 1796, a brewery was opened on B Street between Twenty-first and Twenty-third Streets, beginning a long tradition of beer-making in Foggy Bottom, which continued well into the twentieth century. In 1807, George and Andrew Way started a glassblowing factory called Glass House. By 1850, the Chesapeake & Ohio Canal was completed, improving Foggy Bottom's industrial position. The number of households jumped from 58 in 1850 to 175 in 1860. Forty-two percent of laborers were described as unskilled, whereas in previous decades 9 to 18 percent were unskilled. The Ways' Glass House failed in 1833, but lampblack and roofing were soon being produced on its site. Three lime kilns, a shipyard, a wood yard, and an icehouse were in operation along the Potomac before the Civil War, and by 1860, they were joined by a factory producing plaster, ammonia, and fertilizer.

At the end of the Civil War, the Washington Gas Light Company built a gas-storage facility at Virginia and New Hampshire Avenues. The large, unsightly gas drum dominated the Foggy Bottom landscape for the next hundred years, contributing to the area's industrial character.

Southwest

Southwest Washington was a neglected, unfashionable neighborhood almost from the beginning. In 1815, the Washington City Canal cut off the area from Downtown and the more fashionable parts of the city. From then on, Southwest, known as the "island," was home to a mixed population that included many low-income residents. Trade in bulky, low-value goods such as fuel, building materials, and armaments, as well as foodstuffs and slaves, set the neighborhood apart from the seat of government north of the canal. The area provided work for tradesmen and laborers; households routinely kept chickens, pigs, and other livestock.

Before the Civil War, Southwest was home to many African-Americans. Enslaved and free blacks had coexisted in the capital since its inception, and by 1830, more than half the black residents were free. Besides free laborers, the black community included ministers, teachers, and businessmen. Anthony Bowen maintained a mission and day school at E Street SW, between Ninth and Tenth Streets. During the 1850s, he was part of the Underground Railroad, the network that helped slaves escape from the South.

Old Stone House, 3051 M Street, 1766.

The oldest building constructed in the District of Columbia, the Old Stone House was built by a Pennsylvania-born cabinetmaker, Christopher Layman, for use as a residence and a shop. (An older structure, Lindens, in Kalorama was moved to Washington from Danvers, Massachusetts, in 1935.)

Forrest-Marbury House, c. 1785. Designed by Uriah Forrest, remodeled 1988 by Grier Brown Renfrow.

The tobacco trade enriched a number of Georgetown merchants who built imposing homes. In 1791, Georgetown Mayor Uriah Forrest gave a famous dinner party for George Washington and the area's leading landowners. At dinner, the president persuaded the mayor's guests that the new capital served their interests and that they should sell their land at modest prices. Attorney William Marbury bought the house in 1800. In 1803, the Supreme Court, in *Marbury v. Madison*, established the principle of judicial review.

Georgetown

A thriving tobacco port since the middle of the eighteenth century, Georgetown predated the formation of the District of Columbia and the founding of the United States. The land north of the Potomac was granted in 1634 to Cecilius Calvert, the second Lord Baltimore, by King Charles of England. The first parcel of land in what is now Georgetown was granted to Ninian Beall in 1703; he called the 795 acres on the west bank of the present Rock Creek the Rock of Dumbarton. George Gordon bought three hundred acres along the Potomac River west of Beall's land and built a tobacco warehouse in 1745. A year later, a tavern was licensed near Rock Creek.

In 1751, a number of resident business owners petitioned the Maryland General Assembly for a town to be founded at the junction of the Potomac and Rock Creek, known then as "Town of George," after George II of England. The petition was granted, and sixty acres were acquired from Beall and Gordon and divided into eighty lots. Buyers were required to build on them within two years.

By 1800, Georgetown had 3,400 residents, divided almost equally between white and nonwhite, including 277 free blacks and 1,449 black slaves. The town comprised nearly one quarter of the new federal city's total population of 14,093. From the beginning, Georgetown consisted of a mix of middle-class row houses, many small workers' dwellings, fashionable residential neighborhoods, architecturally distinguished churches, and the city's few mansions.

Early in the nineteenth century, the most important economic development for Georgetown was the construction of the Chesapeake & Ohio Canal. The original plan, supported by George Washington, among others, was to extend the canal from Georgetown to Pittsburgh, connecting the Ohio River Valley with oceangoing traffic. On July 4, 1828, John Quincy Adams turned the first shovelful of dirt for the canal. Ironically, the Baltimore & Ohio Railroad was initiated on the same day in Baltimore, with Charles Carroll, a prominent resident, lifting the first spade for the railroad. The expansion of the railroad diminished the importance of the canal, eventually destroying it as a commercial artery.

The cost of the canal exceeded the estimates, and it was decided that it should be terminated in Cumberland, Maryland, rather than extended over the daunting traverse across the mountains. The total

Tudor Place, 1816. Designed by William Thornton. *Robert Lautman*

Using $8,000 left to Mrs. Peter by her grandmother, Martha Washington, Thomas and Martha Peter bought a sloping eight-acre site in 1805 and retained William Thornton to build this impressive Federal-style structure. Descendants of the Peter family continued to live at Tudor Place until the late twentieth century. The house was subsequently bequeathed to a trust and opened to the public.

Flour Mill, 1845. Designed by George Bomford.

Originally a cotton mill built by Colonel George Bomford, in 1866 this structure was converted to a flour mill by later owners. Of the many cotton and flour mills built in Georgetown during the middle of the nineteenth century, only Bomford's Flour Mill (converted to an office building) would remain by the end of the twentieth century.

View of Georgetown, D.C., 1855. Unsigned
lithograph published by E. Sachse & Co. *LCPP*

In *Monumental Washington*, John Reps quotes
a *New York Illustrated News* reporter in 1853,
who might have been describing the same view
as this lithograph: "The range of hills well
named 'Georgetown Heights,' overhang the
town of that name, which is built, as it were,
upon ranges of small precipices, increasing
in height until they find shelter under the
towering hills behind them. The noble aqueduct of the Chesapeake & Ohio Canal, with
its many massive piers, terminates the view on
that side. Still further to the right, perched
high among the 'heights' of Georgetown, is
seen the venerable college of the Jesuits where
the Superior of the order in the United States
has resided almost since the organization of
the government."

Holy Trinity Parish Church, 1846–49. Architect unknown.

The *AIA Guide* (3rd ed., 1994) provides the background for this early Catholic church: "Three different eras in religious history have produced three very different structures. The original brick church (1794, later the Convent of Mercy) was the District's first building erected for public Catholic worship, and its small scale and simple lines stand as the outward and visible sign of the tenuous state of Catholicism in eighteenth-century America. (Before the First Amendment guaranteed freedom of religion to all, the area's Catholic families, such as the Carrolls, had been forced to celebrate mass secretively in private chapels.)

"The tiny structure soon proved inadequate for the growing congregation; the handsome, Greco-Roman revival structure replaced it, and the building's larger size and attention to architectural style suggest American Catholicism's improved condition. Finally, the mansard roofed rectory, a splendid product of post–Civil War design, accurately manifests the financial stability that was at last insured when millions of industrial-era immigrants came from Ireland, Italy and elsewhere, swelling the ranks of the Roman Catholic Church in America."

St. John's Episcopal Church, 1804. Designed by William Thornton.

The town's oldest Episcopal parish was founded here, in 1796, by Reverend Walter D. Addison, Benjamin Stoddert, Francis Scott Key, and Thomas Jefferson. The church was remodeled in 1870 by Starkweather and Plowman.

cost was approximately 14 million dollars. Operation over the full 168 miles of the canal began in 1850, with coal from West Virginia the most important commodity to be shipped.

By 1834, after a mild depression in 1830, flour milling had become a major industry in Georgetown. Energy generated by the thirty-five-foot drop from the canal to the Potomac River made milling profitable. By 1850, there were five flour mills, a grist mill, and a cotton mill, in addition to a soap factory, an iron foundry, and kilns for producing lime along the waterfront. In the 1850s, the town's economy was based on small-scale manufacturing rather than shipping. Grain, flour, and coal warehouses and lumberyards had replaced the tobacco sheds.

Many wealthy citizens lived in the estates along "Georgetown Heights." They occupied most of the ridge north of Back Street (Q Street), which was cooler and healthier than the low-lying land along Rock Creek and the Potomac River. This pattern would be repeated at the turn of the century, as people who could afford to left the L'Enfant city for greener suburbs such as Cleveland Park.

By 1860, Georgetown had a population of 8,733, with about one quarter consisting of African-Americans, predominantly free (1,358 free blacks and 577 slaves); the District of Columbia's population nearly tripled between 1840 and 1860, growing to 75,000 in 1860. By this time, Georgetown had expanded to roughly its present-day boundaries, from Glover Archbold Park on the west to Rock Creek on the east, and from R and S Streets on the north to the Potomac River on the south. Georgetown, in "Washington County" beyond the L'Enfant city, was at once the capital's industrial and shipping center and its fashionable residential neighborhood.

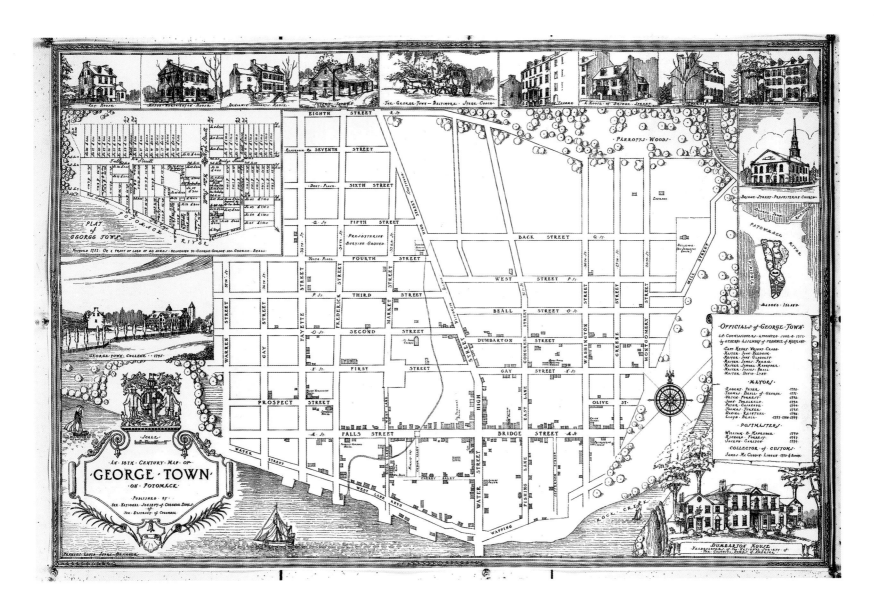

The Georgetown waterfront, early 1790s.
Aquatint by G.A. Parkyns.
LCPP

The illustration shows the waterfront shortly after it became part of the District of Columbia. Barely visible upstream in the middle of the Potomac are the rocks known as the Three Sisters, the focus of bitter and successful Georgetown resistance against the construction of an interstate freeway bridge in the 1960s.

Map of Georgetown in the late eighteenth century.
NSCD

The Forrest-Marbury House on Fall Street and the Lee-Ross-Getty Houses on Bridge Street were typical of a number of handsome dwellings built before 1800 along what is today M Street. In 1800, most of the buildings along Water Street (now K Street) were tobacco warehouses. The Dodge Warehouse, built in 1790, survives today on the northwest corner of Wisconsin Avenue and K Street.

Georgetown in 1860

Map redrawn by Nene Goulimarian based on an original by Albert Boschke.

Georgetown streets were laid out before the arrival of L'Enfant. In 1860, they retained their earlier names. Only Bridge Street (M Street) and Water Street (K Street) connect directly across Rock Creek to the L'Enfant streets of the capital.

In 1860, homes were scattered, with many small outbuildings, except for the more compact row buildings along Bridge Street and High Street (Wisconsin Avenue). Bridge and High Streets were commercial streets, and there were about three dozen shops sprinkled throughout the residential neighborhoods. The waterfront contained industry, mixed with residences, and cottage industries dotted the town. There were five livery stables on or near Bridge Street. Georgetown College was the capital's most important institution for higher education.

Based on a period map by Albert Boschke, the contours shown are impressionistic. Boschke probably intended to emphasize the high ground at the top of the map—the location of the estates of wealthy citizens. Crosses indicate cemeteries, regularly spaced circles stand for orchards, and short wavy lines indicate public open spaces. The land actually rose sharply north from the Potomac riverfront and west from Rock Creek. The C & O Canal, only a few hundred feet from the river's edge, is high enough above the Potomac River so that water falling from the canal to the river was able to drive the grinding wheels of Bomford's Flour Mill and other mills. East of Fishing Lane (Thirty-first Street), a series of locks lowered the canal to the level of Rock Creek near the Potomac.

1. Old Stone House*
2. Forrest-Marbury House*
3. **Tudor Place***
4. Georgetown College*
5. **Holy Trinity Parish***
6. **Convent of the Visitation***
7. **St. John's Episcopal Church***
8. **Washington Post Office and Custom House, Georgetown Branch***
9. **Georgetown Market***
10. **Bomford's Flour Mill***
11. Dodge Warehouse*
12. **Chesapeake & Ohio (C & O) Canal***
13. **Aqueduct Bridge***

Buildings and public projects constructed after 1800 are listed in **bold** type.

Buildings and public projects existing in 2000 are identified with an asterisk.*

Key

single-family residences

walk-up residences

elevator apartment

hotel

retail

private offices

federal offices

federal institutions

private & foreign institutions

local institutions

industrial

warehouse

transportation

0 100   500   1000 ft

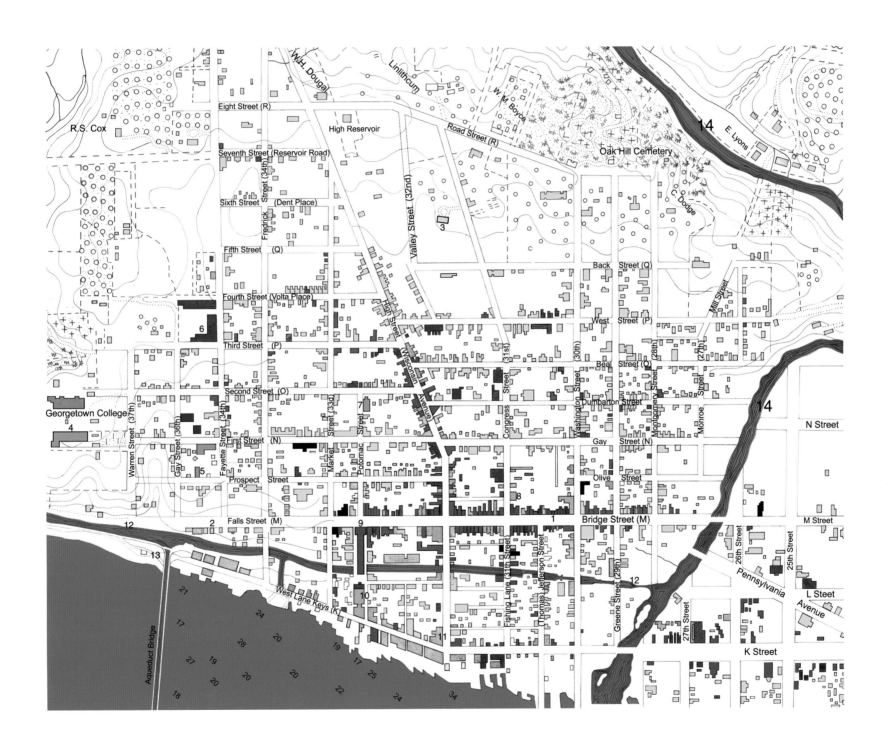

R.S. Cox

Eight Street (R)

High Reservoir

W. H. Dougal

Linlithcum

W. M. Boyce

Road Street (R)

Oak Hill Cemetery

E. Lyons

14

Seventh Street (Reservoir Road)

Sixth Street (Dent Place)

Fredrick Street (34th)

Valley Street (32nd)

Dodge

3

Fifth Street (Q)

Back Street (Q)

Mill Street

Fourth Street (Volta Place)

High Street

West Street (P)

6

Third Street (P)

Wisconsin Avenue (31st)

Street (31st)

Washington Street (30th)

Beal Street (Q)

(28th)

(27th)

14

Georgetown College

Second Street (O)

Market Street (33d)

7

Congress Street

Dumbarton Street

Montgomery Street

Monroe Street

N Street

4

Warren Street (37th)

Gay Street (36th)

Fayette Street (34th)

First Street (N)

Potomac Street

Gay Street (N)

5

Olive Street

Prospect Street

8

Bridge Street (M)

M Street

12

2

Falls Street (M)

9

1

26th Street

25th Street

13

Fishing Lane (31st Street)

Thomas Jefferson Street

Greene Street (29th)

12

Pennsylvania

L Steet

Aqueduct Bridge

21

West Lane Keys (K)

10

Avenue

24

17

28

20

19

17

25

27th Street

K Street

27

19

20

11

27

19

20

22

34

18

63

Washington, D.C., with Projected Improvements.
1853. Drawing by B. F. Smith Jr., published by
Smith & Jenkins, Lithographers and Engravers. *HSW*

Andrew Jackson Downing proposed a circular
parade ground south of the White House, which
he called Monument Park, with a suspension bridge
connecting Downtown across the Chesapeake &
Ohio Canal to the Mall. Around the Washington
Monument, the park would be planted "wholly
with American trees, of large growth."

Pennsylvania Avenue, 1857. *AOC*

The earliest known photograph of Pennsylvania Avenue, taken from Fourth Street looking toward the Capitol, shows the beginning of construction on the new dome.

President-elect Abraham Lincoln and President James Buchanan, March 4, 1861. *NA*

This view of President Buchanan and President Lincoln riding together to Lincoln's inauguration illustrates a continuing tradition. Many similar drawings and photographs of Pennsylvania Avenue record the Civil War's defining events.

Streets and Other Public Open Spaces

President Millard Fillmore initiated a major expansion of the Capitol Building and also took an active interest in the urban design of the capital city. In 1850, he hired Andrew Jackson Downing, America's most prominent landscape architect, to plan the Mall and the White House grounds. Downing had written about the absence of public parks in American cities and described the popularity of rural cemeteries. The Mount Auburn Cemetery area in Cambridge had become such a well-liked picnic area that its management had to prohibit refreshments and firearms within the grounds.

Downing had no interest in French formalism. He announced that his plans would provide "an example of the natural style of Landscape Gardening which may have an influence on the general taste of the Country. The straight lines and broad avenues" of L'Enfant's city "would be pleasantly relieved and contrasted by the beauty of curved lines and natural groups of trees in the various parks." Downing died in 1852 at the age of thirty-seven, before his work could be carried out. Only the White House grounds and the park in front of the Smithsonian Institution were completed. Today, the elliptical parade grounds south of the White House are all that remain; the rest of Downing's work was replaced by the French "bosques" of the Senate Park Commission.

Along with the Mall, Pennsylvania Avenue was the city's most important public open space. By the time of the Civil War, Pennsylvania Avenue had become the ceremonial center of the country, as L'Enfant had intended. The journey of newly elected presidents up and down the avenue, victory parades, and funeral marches for martyred heroes that began during the war would continue.

View of the Capitol at Washington, 1837.
Engraved by C. J. Bentley from a drawing by
W. H. Bartlett. *KC*

An unattractive characteristic of travel
in the capital, which would persist for
another half century, was that streets were
clogged with mud when it rained and
choked with dust when the weather
was dry. By 1837, the poplars Thomas
Jefferson had planted on Pennsylvania
Avenue had been replaced. With women
gossiping, families in carriages, and
children playing, the avenue appears to
have been a fashionable meeting place
as well as a travel artery.

Aqueduct of Potomac, Georgetown, D.C.,
1865. Lithograph from a drawing by
F. Dielman. *LCPP*

The Aqueduct Bridge across the Potomac
River was converted to a wagon bridge
during the Civil War. Here, the C & O
Canal disappears behind the brick warehouses and mills and elevated wharves
of the Georgetown waterfront. At the
end of the twentieth century, the masonry
abutment, between the canal and the
aqueduct, still stood.

Travel to and within the National Capital

Travel was a problem within L'Enfant's "city of magnificent distances," as one early visitor labeled the capital. In 1800 there were already three daily stagecoaches operating between the Capitol and Georgetown, but most citizens in the city had to travel long distances, walking or on horseback or in carriages, for simple tasks. In the early years, travel beyond the capital was by boat, horseback, or stagecoach. In 1800, a coach left the Capitol for Philadelphia, twenty-two hours away, at three o'clock every morning. By the time of the Civil War, the Chesapeake & Ohio Canal, surveyed and promoted by George Washington, had been completed. The railroads, however, were soon to make the canal obsolete.

When, in 1835, the Baltimore & Ohio Railroad trains entered the city, they were required to abandon steam locomotion in favor of horses, and the first station was a converted residence. During the Civil War, the tracks were extended across Pennsylvania Avenue along First Street, across the Mall just west of the Capitol, and on to Virginia across Long Bridge.

The midcentury arrival of tracked transportation was even more important to Washington than to other American cities. During much of the nineteenth century the capital city suffered from the grandeur of L'Enfant's vision. In 1860, it was a brisk half-hour walk from the northern edge of town to Centre Market; a walk from Georgetown to the Capitol took an hour and a half. In 1817, John Duncan, a visitor from Scotland, had written:

> To lay out the Plan of a city . . . is one thing, and to build it is another; of all the regularity and system which the engraved plan exhibits, scarcely a trace is discernible on the ground. Instead of beginning this giant undertaking in a central spot, and gradually extending the buildings from a central focus, they appear to have begun at once in twenty or thirty different places, without the slightest regard to concentration or the comforts of a good neighborhood.

This view would change. The penalties that the plan imposed on the pre–Civil War capital would lessen as Washington witnessed, and was shaped by, a transportation revolution. This revolution, like the city, began early in the nineteenth century; given impetus by the Civil War, railroads beyond the city and rail transit within the city would transform the national capital, and the use of L'Enfant's avenues, by the end of the century. The transportation revolution would continue on the ground through the nineteenth and twentieth centuries, and as the twentieth century ended, air travel would begin to determine the form of the capital city.

Baltimore & Ohio Station, completed on New Jersey Avenue in 1855. Photographed c. 1865. *NA*

President Lincoln arrived at the Baltimore & Ohio Station in 1861; it was also from here that the funeral procession bearing his body began in 1865. Behind the station is the four-chimneyed multifamily residence built by George Washington in 1798 and rebuilt after the British set it on fire in 1814. At the time it was demolished, in 1907, it was the Hotel Burton.

Horsecars on Pennsylvania Avenue during the Civil War. *RAT*

The first horsecar lines, completed in 1862, connected the Navy Yard with the Capitol and Georgetown along Pennsylvania Avenue and M Street, and N Street with the Potomac River along Seventh Street.

Scene at the Pennsylvania Avenue Entrance to the Capitol Grounds at Washington on the Daily Adjournment of Congress. Wood engraving from a drawing by F. Dielman, *Harper's Weekly*, April 28, 1866. *KC*

The railroad was built on East First Street during the Civil War to move military supplies to the waterfront. Four different types of transportation are in evidence—railroad, horsecar, horseback, and foot. In 1866, pedestrians appear to have had the right-of-way.

Washington, D.C., 1862. Lithograph by L. N. Rosenthal from an untitled, unsigned view. *LCPP*

This hand-colored depiction of Washington, D.C., seen from Arlington House, was drawn twenty-five years after an earlier view from the same location (see page 43). Over the course of two and a half decades, the look of the city center had changed from an almost rural landscape of isolated buildings to a compact townscape. What appear to be snow-capped mountains are misleading. L'Enfant had laid out the city in a natural bowl formed by the escarpment of the fall line, the break between the Piedmont plateau and the coastal plain.

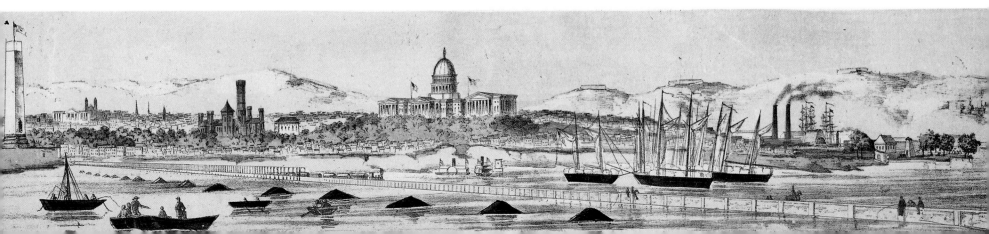

Washington in 1860

- The capital grew slowly, but by 1860 the population was sixty thousand. Even so, Washington in 1860 was not a city. Rather, it was a collection of villages, as contemporaries frequently noted. Stores and workshops were "cottage industries," and artisans and shopkeepers worked primarily out of their own residences.
- By 1860, most of the city's large, "fat" blocks had been divided by alleys. Snow's Court and Brown's Alley in Foggy Bottom still existed in 2000, as did Blagden Alley in Shaw; these became fashionable and historic landmarks. Shepherd Alley and Goat Alley in Shaw, Carroll's Place on Capitol Hill, State Alley, Corcoran Alley, Riggs Alley, Baptist Court, Baptist Church Alley, Temperance Alley in Downtown, and many others disappeared, swallowed up by denser development.
- Seventy-two houses of worship were scattered throughout the town. Fifty were Protestant, six Catholic, two Quaker, and one Hebrew; thirteen additional churches, also widely distributed, were identified as "colored." Most African-Americans lived in the alleys about the city. Shaw and Southwest were home to many black residents; otherwise, there was little geographic segregation.
- Centre Market was located on the Tiber Canal, a continuation of the recently completed Chesapeake & Ohio Canal. While there was no true "downtown," in the modern sense, there was a concentration of retail shops around Centre Market. There were similar markets on West K Street, on what is now Mount Vernon Square, and on Capitol Hill; the Capitol Hill market was still operating in 2000.
- Perseverance, Northern Liberties, and Union Fire Engine were fire stations for volunteer fire brigades. These were neighborhood centers, closely associated with the markets.
- While the Treasury, State Department, War and Navy Departments, and Patent Office had their own buildings, most government offices were housed in various smaller buildings. The Pension Office, for example, occupied the Winder Building, still standing in 2000.
- The offices of foreign countries were also located in scattered, modest buildings—the ministries of Great Britain and Sweden in Foggy Bottom; those of Russia and the Two Seychelles near the Treasury.
- Private offices were generally located in private houses. Larger offices were concentrated between the Capitol and the Patent Office, which was surrounded by lawyers' offices. (In 1865, there were already sixty such offices in Washington.)
- Seven newspapers are named in the Business Directory of 1865, all located between the White House and City Hall.
- Hotels were clustered on Pennsylvania Avenue between the White House and the Capitol. Because most congressmen returned home when Congress was not in session, hotels were important meeting places.
- Large "gasometers," or gas storage tanks, were located on West K Street and on Virginia Avenue at the east end of the Mall. Light industry operated along the Potomac River and the Mall and was concentrated in the triangle between Pennsylvania Avenue, the Tiber Canal, and Fifteenth Street. This triangle was also the location of what was probably the city's worst slum.

- The Mall, described by writer Joseph Varnum in 1848 as a "mere cow-pasture," and the White House grounds were laid out in the English tradition of romantic landscape, following generally, but not exactly, Andrew Jackson Downing's plan of 1851.
- The area that is now the Mall west of Fifteenth Street was a tidal flat, except for the knoll on which the Washington Monument was built. Low areas were drained by Slash Run, which surrounded the Dupont Circle area, Tiber Creek north and west of the Capitol, and Tiber Canal. These waters were all open sewers by 1860 and were avoided by citizens who could afford to live elsewhere. The land along Tiber Canal was particularly pestilent.
- The Baltimore & Ohio Railroad entered the city on Delaware Avenue in 1835, and the first horsecar lines were laid on Pennsylvania Avenue and Seventh Street in 1862, the beginning of tracked and mechanized transportation that would transform the city.

Key

- single-family residences
- walk-up residences
- elevator apartment
- hotel
- retail
- private offices
- federal offices
- federal institutions
- private & foreign institutions
- local institutions
- industrial
- warehouse
- transportation

0 100   500   1000 ft

1. **Iowa (Logan) Circle**: At the edge of the growing city.

2. **Centre Market**: Now the site of the National Archives.

3. **Tiber Canal**: Replacing Tiber Creek and serving Centre Market.

4. **Baltimore & Ohio Railroad**: First railroad to enter Washington, 1835.

5. **City Hall***: Begun in 1820 but not completed until 1881.

6. **Treasury Building***: Located by President Jackson, begun in 1836, completed after the Civil War.

7. **Patent Office***: Begun in the 1830s, completed after the Civil War.

8. **General Post Office***: Begun in the 1830s, completed after the Civil War.

9. **Smithsonian Institution "Castle"***: Begun in 1847, completed after the Civil War.

10. **Washington Monument***: Authorized in 1787, completed in 1884.

11. **White House grounds**: Designed by Andrew Jackson Downing.

12. **The Mall**: Designed by Andrew Jackson Downing.

13. **Expanded Capitol with monumental dome***: Completed during the Civil War.

14. **Naval Observatory***: Now the Bureau of Medicine and Surgery.

15. **War Department**

16. **Navy Department**

17. **St. John's Episcopal Church***

18. **Church of the Epiphany***

19. **Ford's Theater***: Site of Lincoln's assassination.

20. **Carroll Row:** Lincoln boarded here when he was a congressman.

21. **National Theater**

22. **Willard Hotel**

23. **William Wilson Corcoran Mansion**

24. **Lafayette Square**: In 1860, this was a fashionable residential neighborhood.

25. **"Murder Bay"**: "Here crime, filth and poverty seem to vie," commented a period police report.

26. **St. Patrick's Church and Gonzaga College**

27. **St. Paul's German Lutheran Church**

28. **Trinity Episcopal Church**

29. **Wesley Chapel**

30. **Friends Meeting Hall**

31. **First Unitarian Church**

32. **Asbury Chapel**: Identified as "colored" in early atlases.

33. **McKendrie Chapel**

34. **John Wesley Church**: Identified as "colored" in early atlases.

35. **St. Mary's Church**

36. **Metropolitan Methodist Church**

37. **St. Matthews R.C. Church**

38. **Riggs Bank**

39. **Bank of Washington***

40. **First Presbyterian Church**

41. **Second Presbyterian Church**

42. **Infirmary**

43. **National Hotel**

44. **Brown's (Indian Queen) Hotel**

45. **St. Charles Hotel**

46. **North Liberty Market**

47. **Western Market**

48. **Ringold House**

49. **Van Ness Mansion**

50. **Gas Works**

51. **Jail**

52. **Chesapeake & Ohio Canal***: A young George Washington surveyed the canal site.

Buildings and public projects constructed or laid out after 1800 are listed in **bold** type.

Buildings and public projects existing in 2000 are identified with an asterisk.*

0 100   500   1000 ft

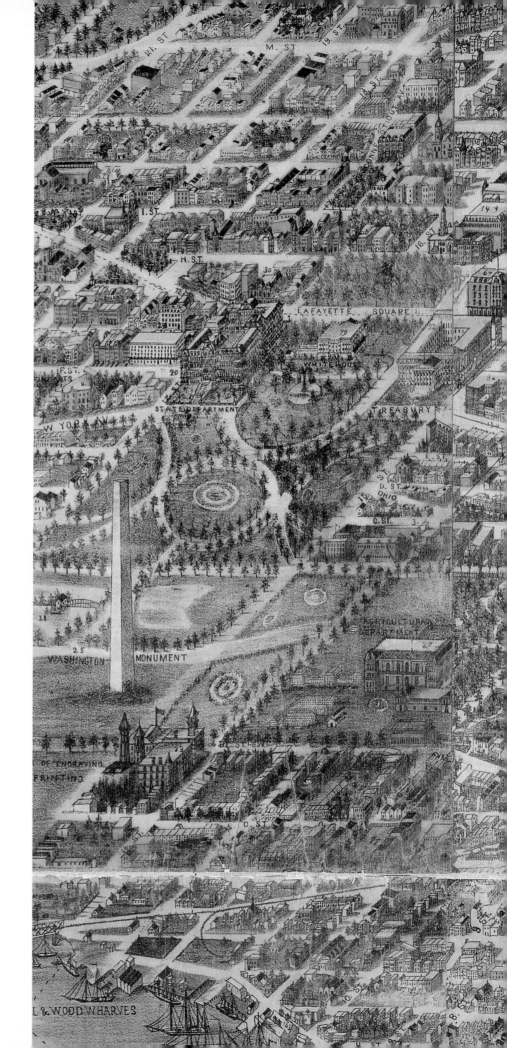

Chapter 3

The End of the Civil War to 1900

The National Capital Washington City D.C. Detail.

Changes between 1860 and 1900

Under construction at the same time, the Capitol dome and the Cabin John Bridge were symbols of the enormous changes that would mark the development of Washington between 1860 and 1900. The bridge embodied the end of an era; the dome, the beginning. The dome structure was made of standardized, prefabricated cast-iron sections and was typical of a flood of technological developments that would transform cities during the last half of the nineteenth century. The Cabin John Bridge, located a few miles beyond the District of Columbia boundary, was completed during the Civil War. With a 220-foot span, it remains one of the longest unreinforced masonry bridges in the world and was an anachronism even at the time of its construction. The engineer Thomas Telford had built longer spans in iron, at lower cost, earlier in the century, and in a few years, reinforced concrete would replace unreinforced masonry in masonry bridge construction.

The railroad and electric streetcar would change the way people and goods moved about the country and around their cities, reducing the densities and spreading out the distribution of urban activities. The other major nineteenth-century transportation innovation, the electric elevator, along with steel-and-reinforced-concrete building frames, would have the opposite effect, concentrating activities to a degree not seen since the days of imperial Rome. Sewer and water systems would do more to improve public health than all the doctors since antiquity. Electric lighting would expand and transform the way citizens spent their days. First the telegraph, then the telephone, and then an array of other new devices would create a continuing communications revolution.

As the Civil War ended, however, these events were just beyond the horizon. Descriptions of the capital by its own residents immediately after the war were more savage than what the writer Charles Dickens had penned some years earlier. Dr. William Tindall, for many years a Washington elected official, recalled that there were "in every part of the city . . . hog pens . . . many cow sheds . . . chicken, geese and cows roamed at large . . . Scavenger service offended both sense and sentiment, the most noisome kind of offal and refuse were dumped daily on the surface of the common." The city at war's end was primitive even by the standards of the mid-nineteenth century.

The unusual development pattern created by L'Enfant's plan, marked by many "fat" blocks, exacerbated the problems of sanitation and scavenger service. The interior of most blocks contained alleys, with both houses and shops, often in a degraded condition. Many alleys were populated by black residents only, and until World War II, alleys persisted as slum areas; those near the Capitol so incensed Eleanor Roosevelt that she began a crusade for better low-cost housing. Today, a few of these alleys, now private and shielded from traffic, are preserved as small, desirable residential neighborhoods (Blagden Alley and Snow's Court, for example).

Washington City, 1869. Wood engraving of drawing by Theodore Davis, *Harper's Weekly,* March 13, 1869. *KC*

This view from two blocks west of the White House, looking east, celebrates a fashionable part of town. The reproduction in *Harper's Weekly* was accompanied by text that read: "The view . . . shows in the immediate foreground many of the most interesting edifices of the city. The modest brick building at the right of the picture has been for some time the headquarters of General Grant. Across the street, at the left, is the Winder Building, occupied by the numerous offices of clerks of the different departments, which . . . could not be located in their proper edifices . . . At the extreme left of the picture is seen the building erected by the wealthy banker W. W. Corcoran, and by him dedicated to

art . . . Directly beyond this, and in the same block, is the 'Blair Home.' Vice-President Colfax has his present home also in this block, fronting on [Lafayette] square. Across Pennsylvania Avenue, to the right, is the War Department; still further to the right stands the Navy Department, and above and beyond is the White House with its conservatory . . . ; beyond lies the Treasury Department, from which looking down the Avenue is seen the Capitol with its extensive grounds. Beyond the Treasury, nearly half a mile distant, are the Patent and General Post offices. The large building at some distance to the left of these, and somewhat nearer the foreground, is the Franklin School, a large edifice located at the west [sic] of a fine square of the same name. A distant view of the Potomac is given on the right, where, too, may be seen the Navy-yard with its vari-

ous ship-houses and machine-shops. Across the eastern branch of the Potomac, upon which the Navy-yard is located, is seen the Insane Asylum, probably the finest in the country."

In addition, Seventeenth Street, with its 110-foot-wide right-of-way (in the foreground) unencumbered by vehicular traffic, is a public gathering place. Horsecars are operating on tracks in Pennsylvania Avenue, on the recently completed line connecting the White House and the Capitol. Visitors appear to have the run of the White House grounds. Lafayette Square is an attractive gathering place, as contemporary accounts indicated. Temporary structures around the unfinished Washington Monument are remainders from the Civil War. Beyond the monument is the Department of Agriculture and its gardens, and beyond the Depart-

ment of Agriculture are the Smithsonian Castle and the crowded east end of the Mall. The Tiber Canal still separates the Mall from the center of the capital, although it is no longer a useful channel for barges.

While the drawing is distorted, it emphasizes, accurately, L'Enfant's radiating avenues—New York Avenue, F Street, Pennsylvania Avenue—and shows how completely the Treasury cuts off the vistas of the White House. Church steeples dominate the mid-nineteenth-century capital, towering over even the government buildings. St. John's Church fronting on Lafayette Square and the Church of the Epiphany on G Street still exist. Andrew Jackson Downing's "greening" of the capital is evident.

The worst area appears to have been between Pennsylvania Avenue and the Mall, a part of the city described in a Civil War police report in the following way:

> Here crime, filth and poverty seem to vie in a career of degradation and death . . . whole families are crowded into mere apologies for shanties, which are without light or ventilation . . . In a space about 50 yards square I found a hundred families composed of 3 to 5 persons living in shanties one story high except . . . where tenements were actually built on top of others.

General Joseph Hooker housed his troops nearby, but what the locals called "Hooker's Divisions" were not frontline troops. While the source of the phrase is ambiguous, the general may have been immortalized in ways he had not anticipated when he was at West Point.

There was a consensus among Washington's private citizens and public officials that the city was in need of much attention. During the next decade, the capital would receive more public notice than many private citizens, and Congress, were prepared for.

After the war, Major Nathaniel Michler of the Army Corps of Engineers headed an office in charge of public buildings and grounds. He was also responsible for federal reservations (circles and squares in the city, as well as the oddly shaped street fragments resulting from L'Enfant's complex street layout), parks, including the Mall (except for the Smithsonian portion), the city's avenues and some of its streets, and the important parts of Washington's water supply. His office combined the work of the present-day Department of Public Works, National Capital Parks, National Capital Planning Commission, and Commission of Fine Arts.

Michler issued a report criticizing much of the area under his care in which he described the Tiber Canal as "nothing more than an open sewer." The market in Mount Vernon Square was "unsightly . . . an intolerable nuisance . . . on market days the most offensive matter accumulates in the adjoining streets, greatly detrimental to the health of the residents . . . vegetable matter . . . offal from the stall of the butcher . . . filth created by animals . . . causing a most disagreeable stench . . . engendering sickness." Michler noted "the dilapidated and unsightly buildings on Pennsylvania Avenue known as the Centre Market," and he also commented on the neglect of the Mall. The condition of public thoroughfares appalled him: "There is scarcely a street or avenue in the city over which one can drive with ease and comfort . . . [Parts of Pennsylvania Avenue] become almost impassable, either from the effects of weather, or being cut up by the immense amount of travel over them."

In his report, Michler made many recommendations. He argued that Tiber Creek be enclosed in a sewer. He also commented on the public places that add "so much to the appearance of the city [and] . . . to the health, pleasure and recreation of its inhabitants." Michler particularly liked Lafayette Square, "one of the most charming places for recreation," although he observed that its subsurface drainage needed improvement. He emphasized the importance to the city of Pennsylvania Avenue and argued for marked improvements. For the Mall, he

suggested a comprehensive plan with "carriage ways, paths for equestrians and pedestrians . . . the crossing of the streets between them being handsomely paved with flagging . . . [with the vexing problem of the north-south cross streets solved by] subterranean tunnelling," although he decided the land was too level. He also advocated improvements "ornamental as well as sanitary [and] the free introduction of water, as jets d'eau, fountains, miniature lakes into each and all [of the public grounds] with groups of statuary . . . as another evidence of enlightened taste."

It was not surprising that in the national capital these issues were politicized from the beginning. Many visitors agreed with Michler's criticism of conditions in the city and concluded that the capital should be relocated. At least one writer announced in 1867 that soon "the National Capital will be moved beyond the Mississippi River." Indiana, Illinois, Iowa, and Missouri petitioned Congress to remove the government from Washington, and in 1869, the city of St. Louis held a convention aimed at initiating its relocation to that city. There were even eastern supporters, including Horace ("Go West, young man, and grow with the country") Greeley, editor and owner of the *New York Tribune.* A series of events would quiet, but not eliminate, arguments to move the capital.

In January 1867 (a year and a half before the Fourteenth Amendment was ratified), the Republican-controlled Congress passed a bill granting black men the right to vote in the District of Columbia. In 1868, the abolitionist Sayles Bowen was elected mayor, supported by white Republicans and by African-Americans. Because he received no financial support from Congress, and because of the problems noted by Major Michler, Bowen raised the property tax by 40 percent.

Business and professional leaders, many of them Democrats and former slaveholders, met to plan changes in the city's government. The young businessman Alexander Robey Shepherd drafted a bill stipulating a territorial administration for Washington, Georgetown, and the District of Columbia, with a governor appointed by the president, an elected legislature, and a delegate to the House of Representatives.

A similar statute became law in 1871, giving a much increased federal presence in the affairs of the District. Among its other achievements, the bill created a board of public works with five members appointed by the president "to have entire control of and make all regulations which they deem necessary for keeping in repair the streets, avenues, alleys and sewers of the city and all other works which may be entrusted to their charge." Four months later, in June 1871, Shepherd, who had been appointed operating head of the board, presented to the new legislature a $6.25 million plan for street improvements, sewer construction, tree planting, and related projects. Subsequently, the board's former chief clerk described the plan as "improvements in every portion of the District . . . almost every street and avenue . . . as well as all the roads in the county," observing that the distinguished advisory committee was created "in order to guard against any criticism that might be made."

In his book *Monumental Washington,* John Reps notes that hundreds of laborers soon disturbed quiet neighborhoods and interfered with traf-

Our National Capital, Viewed from the South, 1882. Wood engraving of a drawing by Theodore Davis, *Harper's Weekly*, May 20, 1882. *JWR*

In the foreground of this view, on what is now Independence Avenue, Davis portrayed (from left to right) the Department of Agriculture building and gardens, the Smithsonian Castle, the Arts and Industries building (National Museum), and the Columbia Armory (where the first Union troops, arriving in 1861, were quartered). On the Mall opposite the Armory is the Baltimore & Ohio Railroad station, where a disgruntled office seeker shot President James Garfield. Beyond and to the left of the station is Centre Market.

Past the still unfinished Washington Monument is the White House, flanked on the left by the just completed State, War and Navy Building and on the right by the Treasury Building. The Capitol dominates the picture; the size of each building in the drawing indicates the artist's view of its importance rather than its actual size.

Davis also identified other buildings important to the city in 1882: the General Post Office; the Patent Office; the Army Medical and Surgical Museum; Ford's Theater, where President Abraham Lincoln was shot; the Government Printing Office; the Orphan Asylum; and in the distance, Howard University; Columbian College (later George Washington University); and the Soldiers' Home (the summer residence of several presidents, including Lincoln).

Washington, D.C.—The Inauguration of President Garfield. From *Frank Leslie's Illustrated Newspaper,* March 10, 1881. *HSW*

This drawing and the two photographs opposite were made at twelve-year intervals and from the same location, looking up Pennsylvania Avenue from the Capitol. The skyline of this fashionable pre–Civil War neighborhood was dominated by churches: the First Unitarian Church on Sixth and D Streets by Charles Bulfinch, Trinity Episcopal Church on Third and C Streets by James Renwick, the soaring tower of Metropolitan Methodist Church on 4½ and C Streets, First Presbyterian on 4½ Street above C Street, and Trinity Evangelical Lutheran Church on Fourth and E Streets.

fic, and that much of the city began to resemble a battlefield. By 1872, "Boss" Shepherd had completed seventy-six miles of newly paved streets, with forty-two more miles added in 1873. Workmen had built ninety miles of brick and three miles of concrete sidewalk by the end of 1872, completing more than two hundred additional miles of sidewalk by the end of 1873. In 1872, the Board of Public Works began three large interceptor sewers and eight miles of brick main sewers and had finished or begun seventy miles of smaller sewers and thirty-one miles of water mains. The board reported that "the waste places formed by the intersection of our broad streets and avenues had been laid off in small parks, with fountains." Old market buildings had been destroyed and replaced by new ones, streets were lined with hundreds of trees of different varieties, and obsolete bridges had been replaced. On a mid-November evening in 1872, Shepherd ordered two hundred men to spend the night tearing up the tracks and regrading portions of Maryland Avenue and First Street that had been preempted by the Washington and Alexandria Railroad during the Civil War.

This extraordinary array of enterprises, all undertaken simultaneously and rushed to completion, was not accomplished without considerable waste and confusion. Cost overruns in Shepherd's work and the national financial panic of 1873 created a certain amount of alarm in Congress. Two congressional investigations failed to prove that Shepherd had personally benefited illegally from construction contracts, but it became clear that associates had done so. Shepherd defended himself, pointing out the inequitable allocation of costs to local and national governments for public works in the capital. The *New York Times* provided numbers, stating, "Total expenditures by citizens since 1803, $24,762,117. The amount expended by the United States the same period . . . $4,476,706."

In 1874, Shepherd was dismissed from his post (as L'Enfant had been dismissed before him). Congress abandoned the territorial government of the District and replaced it with a government controlled by three commissioners appointed by the president.

Shepherd's short tenure was impressively productive, but during the last half of the nineteenth century, federal construction in the city barely equaled building during the first half of the century. The State, War and Navy Building and the Department of Agriculture housed important offices; the Library of Congress, the Government Printing Office, and the Pension Building (for Civil War veterans) addressed special federal functions; the Post Office Department and the City Post Office occupied the same building. The National Museum, the Botanical Garden greenhouses, and the Army Medical Museum (eventually demolished) were early tourist attractions. Most federal activities, however, were scattered about the city in modest buildings. Instead, the bulk of construction after the Civil War was by private citizens for commercial use.

At least one federal building did attract attention: the State, War and Navy Building. President Ulysses S. Grant reviewed the plans, which used the same footprint as the Treasury, before he left for a European tour. On his return, he was startled to see that a Victorian rookery had been erected over the footprint.

View northwest along Pennsylvania Avenue from the Capitol, 1893. *LCPP*

View northwest along Pennsylvania Avenue from the Capitol, 1905. *RAT*

The new Post Office towers over the city. Except for its projection into the Pennsylvania Avenue right-of-way, the Treasury has disappeared behind eight- and ten-story private office buildings. In the years since 1893, the increasing scale of building in the center had begun the change that would transform the skyline of the national capital. The Virginia hills are visible to the west; to the north is the escarpment beyond Florida Avenue that forms the bowl in which L'Enfant set the city.

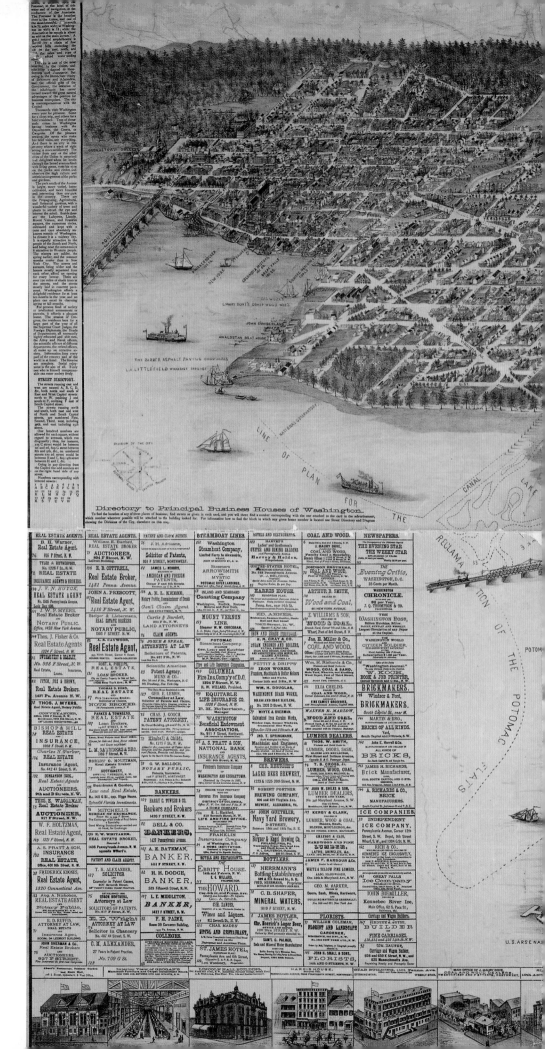

The National Capital Washington City D.C.

Sketched "from nature" by Adolph Sachse, 1883–84.
Lithographed and printed by A. Sachse & Co.,
Baltimore, Maryland. *LCGM*

This fairly accurate isometric drawing is the
most detailed map of nineteenth-century Washington in existence. As with a modern telephone
book, part of the cost of printing the map was
covered by advertisements for Washington businesses. The column at the left of the lithograph
is a contemporary description of the advantages
of the national capital: "Situated upon the
Potomac . . . the broadest river in the Union,
and one of the most beautiful . . . A grand natural amphitheater is formed by a chain of low
wooded hills encircling the city on the east
north and south and at the sides and tops of
which afford commanding views."

Also in the left-hand column, Sachse
describes the city: "Thousands visit Washington
every year for pleasure . . . Some for a short trip,
others for a brief residence. Tens of thousands
come to Washington having business with the
Departments, the Courts or Congress . . . And
there is no city in the country where a week of
sight seeing is more satisfactory. The visitor . . . is
surprised and delighted when he strolls through
the broad avenues lined with living green, rests
his eyes on the parks and circles, and observes
the high culture and artistic arrangements of the
parks and gardens . . . over 120 miles of shade
trees in the streets . . . For persons fond of society
or intellectual amusements or pursuits, it affords
a pleasant home. The sessions of Congress . . . the
Supreme Court Justices, the foreign diplomats,
the heads of Departments, all necessarily highly
educated and able men, the Army and Naval
officers . . . all make up an attractive society."

Centre Market, 1881.
AOC

In 1870, Centre Market burned down but was immediately rebuilt. Designed by the prominent German-born architect Adolph Cluss, the enormous, turreted brick structure filling two city blocks opened in July 1872. After its expansion in the 1880s, the market had indoor stalls for one thousand vendors and outside space for three hundred farm wagons and was open six days a week from dawn until noon. Centre Market continued to offer fresh meat, fish, and vegetables until it was demolished for construction of the National Archives in 1932.

North Liberty Market, at Fifth and K Streets NW, 1874. *MLKL*

A market had existed near this site since 1814. In 1874, North Liberty Market, near Mount Vernon Square, had the largest unsupported roof in America. The immense interior held 280 vendor stalls. An auditorium was added in 1891, and the name was changed to Convention Hall Market. When Centre Market was dismantled in 1932, its vendors moved here and renamed the spot New Centre Market.

Woodward and Lothrop department store, c. 1885. *LCPP*

The city markets were replaced by a late-nineteenth-century innovation— the department store. The railroads that laced America after the Civil War brought goods from all over the country; streetcars brought shoppers from all over the city.

Seventh Street, looking north from D Street, c. 1895. *MLKL*

At the turn of the century, Seventh Street just north of Pennsylvania Avenue was the shopping hub of the city. By the time of this photograph, the streetcars had been electrified and the cables put underground, via an act of Congress. Soon after the photograph was taken, the telephone poles were removed and the lines placed in an underground conduit.

Neighborhoods

Out of necessity, nineteenth-century shopkeepers and clerks lived close to their places of work. Consequently, during the nineteenth century and the first half of the twentieth, today's Downtown was a residential neighborhood. With the introduction of horsecars in the 1860s and electric streetcars in the 1880s, however, people who could afford to began to move away from their workplaces to quieter locations.

Downtown

The cottage industries scattered about the city in 1860 were gradually replaced, and commercial activities coalesced where access was most convenient—in the center. By 1870, more than one hundred businesses operated in Centre Market, with approximately another forty in the immediate vicinity. The sidewalks near the market generally measured thirty feet in width to accommodate the vendors and shopkeepers. Market days were Tuesdays, Thursdays, and Saturdays. Yokes of oxen brought farm products from the east by way of Pennsylvania Avenue, while farmers bringing goods down Seventh Street often stopped overnight at James Shreve's Livery Stable on Seventh between H and I Streets. A commercial thoroughfare from the start, Seventh Street remains so, and retains some of its historic ambience.

One estimate of immigrants in Downtown in 1889 put the number of German and Eastern European Jews at 700, other Germans at 1,000, and Irish at 1,050. The Irish, often day laborers, settled in the marshy area northeast of Massachusetts Avenue called "Swampoodle." Many German-run businesses congregated near Seventh Street. In 1850, only 11 percent of Washington's population was foreign-born, of which nearly 30 percent was German. By 1860, the number of foreign-born inhabitants had risen to 17 percent, 26 percent of which was German and Austrian. There were also thriving communities in Foggy Bottom, Southwest, and Capitol Hill, but because German residents tended to be dry-goods merchants and craftsmen, their enterprises flourished in Downtown.

St. Mary's German Catholic Church (extant in 2000) was built at Fifth and H Streets, with a German-language school, rectory, and orphanage next to it. The Church of the Epiphany at Fourteenth and G Streets, St. John's Episcopal Church at Sixteenth and H Streets, and New York Presbyterian, St. Patrick's, and First Congregational Churches (which all still stand) recall the original importance of the center as a residential neighborhood.

A growing Jewish minority lived and worked in the Downtown area, and three synagogues were built within six blocks of the Patent Office. In 1860, there were fewer than two hundred Jews in Washington; by 1910, there were more than five thousand, mainly from Germany. In 1860, twenty-nine of the fifty-one employed Jewish men were merchants, accounting for their settlement near Seventh Street. Albert Small, whose father, Isador, had a hardware store at 713 Seventh Street, described the area: "Seventh Street was a wide street. It had streetcar

F Street at Fifteenth Street NW, looking east, 1905. *NA*

Because F Street was located on high ground, above Tiber Creek, it was one of the earliest passable streets. A fine residential street until the 1880s, F Street did not reach its prime as a commercial thoroughfare until the 1920s.

In this photograph, the transition that vehicular traffic was undergoing can be seen. An electric delivery wagon, at left, and a gasoline-powered car, in front of the wagon, mingle with horse-drawn carriages and wagons. In the far right foreground, a streetcar on Fifteenth Street is climbing from Pennsylvania Avenue at E Street to Pennsylvania at New York Avenue. A bicyclist in the foreground pedals north.

Across the street from Rhodes Tavern, on the northeast corner of F and Fifteenth Streets, is the Corcoran Building (1875), on the southeast corner. At sidewalk level is a long-distance telephone center, the Delmar Cafe, and Lowdermilk's Bookstore. Beyond the Corcoran on Fourteenth Street is the mansard roof of the eleven-story Willard Hotel. On the near side of the Willard is the Union Trust and Storage Company building (1900). Across Fourteenth Street, with flags flying, is the Ebbitt House Hotel, and beyond stands "Julius Garfinkel Bros., Cloaks, Suits, Neckwear, Imported Novelties." Garfinkel's would soon move west, to the northwest corner of F and Fourteenth Streets.

The City of Washington, Bird's-Eye View from the Potomac—Looking North, 1892. Lithograph of a drawing by Charles Parsons, published by Currier & Ives, New York. *LCPP*

This interesting, but much distorted, view of the city between the Civil War and the end of the century reflects the artist's sense of the importance of various elements. The Capitol dominates the entire countryside. The White House, Treasury and State, War and Navy Buildings, Patent Office, General Post Office, and City Hall are significant, but less so than the Capitol. Church steeples rise above their surroundings, as they did in reality. The government buildings on the Mall and two commercial properties—Centre Market and the Baltimore & Potomac Depot—are depicted. The L'Enfant diagonals are prominently displayed; Pennsylvania Avenue is shown as the most important street in the national capital, as it indeed was.

The drawing offers one of the best early views of southwest Washington and the Potomac River. In the nineteenth century, the southwest waterfront was important, handling both freight and passengers. During the Civil War, it was a major transshipment point, delivering troops and supplies to the Army of the Potomac. In 1884, the Washington Monument was finally completed, and during the next two decades the Army Corps of Engineers filled in the Potomac shallows west of the monument. The Potomac and the Mall were lined with the industry that existed in the national capital.

Gallaudet University (formerly Gallaudet College), Main Hall, Florida and Seventh Street SE, designed 1867. *JRP*

The Main Hall is described in the *AIA Guide* (3rd ed., 1994) as "possibly the earliest Ruskinian Gothic college structure in America."

tracks . . . The temple played a very predominant part in [our] lives. Almost all of the merchants were Jewish." He noted that the area around St. Mary's was predominantly German, except for Washington Street, an alley through the block between Fourth and Fifth Streets at G and H Streets, where residents were African-American.

Some Jewish merchants were immensely successful. Max and Gustave Lansburgh, sons of one of the Washington Hebrew Congregation's first cantors, started a dry-goods store on Seventh Street between H and I Streets, moving to 406 Seventh Street in 1866, then up the block to develop one of the major department stores. Other German and German-Jewish department stores included Saks & Co. at Seventh Street and Market Place (1867–1932), Kann and Sons at Eighth Street and Market Place (1886–1975), and the Hecht Company at Seventh and F Streets (1896–1985).

Capitol Hill

At the beginning of the Civil War, most Capitol Hill residents lived in the crescent between the Navy Yard and the Capitol. Almost all of modern Capitol Hill was developed during the last half of the nineteenth century. During the early 1870s, the city built a market on open land halfway between the Capitol and the Navy Yard. Known as Eastern Market (and still extant), it became the center of the locales that changed Capitol Hill after the Civil War. The Capitol and the Navy Yard, both growing in importance, required more workers. With the Civil Service Reform Act of 1883, the worst aspects of the spoils system were ended, and government employment became more secure.

By 1900, the Navy Yard had become the world's largest ordnance production and engineering research center, and it would remain one of the city's largest employers for almost fifty years. Its demand for unskilled labor helped a new immigrant group establish a foothold in America, and the old buildings near the yard provided affordable housing. Capitol Hill's new Eastern European Jewish population sold kosher food, opened haberdashery stores, and formed the Southeast Hebrew congregation, all within four blocks of the Navy Yard's main gate.

While northwest Washington increasingly attracted the most affluent residents, Capitol Hill appealed to the city's burgeoning middle class. Toward the end of the century, the western and southern sections of Capitol Hill filled up with modest but comfortable two- and three-story row houses, often in groups of three to five or more. These Queen Anne–style buildings were made of hard red brick, often with stone trim, and frequently featured stained-glass window and door transoms and slate roofs.

After the Civil War, Capitol Hill became sprinkled with churches. German Catholics led the way in 1868 with St. Joseph's (still extant), two blocks from the Capitol. In 1882, Calvin Brent, Washington's first African-American architect, designed Mount Jezreel Baptist Church for a black congregation living in the crescent between the Capitol and the Navy Yard. African-American members of St. Peter's Catholic

Church, excluded from full participation, were granted their own parish, St. Cyprian's, in 1893. Most churches in the city had separated into black and white congregations long before.

The campus of the first institute of higher education for the deaf in America, Gallaudet College, was laid out on Florida Avenue by Frederick Law Olmsted in 1864. In 1867, Calvert Vaux designed the university's Main Hall. Named after Thomas Hopkins Gallaudet, a pioneer educator for the deaf, Gallaudet's campus and buildings maintain a presence in the Capitol Hill neighborhood.

Shaw

Shaw began to develop during the Civil War. In 1862, horsecars on Seventh and Fourteenth Streets made the southern area more accessible. This accessibility, combined with the growing numbers of military men, civilian government employees, black refugees from the slave states, and others looking for housing, attracted developers. On Eleventh Street between R and U Streets, a brick manufacturer, builder, carpenter, contractor, real estate broker, and clerk in the Land Office were among landowners who had subdivided their property for the first time by the early 1870s.

The District's territorial government made many improvements in its southern section between 1871 and 1874 under "Boss" Shepherd. Several roads were surfaced; some streets were included in the city's sweeping schedule; shade trees were planted; gas lamps, water mains, fireplugs, and sewers were installed; and telegraph lines were erected.

Shaw's African-American residents—civil servants, small businessmen, skilled and unskilled laborers, and a few professionals—bought lots and built houses or rented those already built. Some new residents were housed, at least temporarily, by social-welfare agencies such as the Freedmen's Bureau, charged with assisting people displaced by the Civil War. The black churches in Shaw also helped to provide housing for the needy.

A number of factors brought African-Americans to Shaw. For black refugees, Civil War encampments at the Wisewell Barracks at Seventh and P Streets, Campbell Hospital on Boundary Street (now Florida Avenue) between Fifth and Sixth Streets, and Camp Barker with its Freedmen's Hospital near Thirteenth and R Streets were early drawing points. Howard University, established in 1867 on Seventh Street just beyond Boundary Street, was an additional magnet for black residents.

By the mid-1880s, African-Americans in Shaw had formed building associations such as the Industrial Building and Savings Company, realty companies such as Oak Park Realty Company, and financial institutions such as the Capital Savings Bank of Washington, the first African-American-operated bank in the United States. These businesses promoted home building and purchase among blacks, though most still rented and some of the poorest found shelter in alleys that had been designed to provide service access to houses on the main streets. As housing pressures increased, some entrepreneurs capitalized on the profits to be gained from small alley dwellings. Many were orderly and well maintained; others were cramped and unsanitary.

Undated sketch of Tiber Creek, between H and G Streets in "Swampoodle." *MLKL*

After the Civil War, Tiber Creek, located in the swampy land between Capitol Hill and Shaw, had become an open sewer. In 1874, the bridges were removed and the creek was put in a closed underground sewer, part of Alexander "Boss" Shepherd's improvements.

African-American businesses, forced out of Downtown by increasing segregation, moved north into Shaw. A bank, printing company, drugstore, and many other black-owned enterprises prospered between Seventh and Fifteenth Streets. Edward E. Cooper published the periodical *Colored American* in the vicinity, and architect William Lankford had his office here. In 1892, Andrew Hillyer established the Union League, an organization through which black businesses could work cooperatively. There were at least a dozen black churches and public schools, as well as private schools such as Frelinghuysen University and Washington Conservatory of Music and Expression. The black Twelfth Street YMCA, later renamed for Anthony Bowen; the first YWCA in Washington; Howard University's dental infirmary; and the True Reformers Hall were all established in Shaw during this period.

By the end of the century, fine houses were being built to the west, around Logan Circle. But large blocks of another kind of housing were found along the freight yards in eastern Shaw and north of the Capitol. People here lived at densities of over two hundred families per acre, in one-story shotgun flats (so called because a shot could be fired through the front door all the way to the back door without hitting any walls) stacked in two-story tenement buildings.

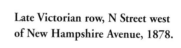

Sixteenth Street, looking north from Florida Avenue, 1888. *LCPP*

Florida Avenue was the northern edge of development until the end of the nineteenth century. Senator John Brooks Henderson (who drafted the Thirteenth Amendment, which abolished slavery) built a grand, Richardson Romanesque mansion for his wife, Mary Newton Foote, with the goal of making Sixteenth Street the location of foreign embassies. "Henderson's Castle" can be seen at left; Meridian Hill, at right.

Connecticut Avenue, looking north from Farragut Square, 1895. *DCDHT*

In 1873, when he had become head of the District's territorial government, "Boss" Shepherd built this row of three grand stone houses on Connecticut Avenue and K Street. "Shepherd's Row" was a typical Dupont Circle development. An investor would build his own house as one of a row of three or five or more, occupying one and selling or renting the rest. Shepherd's house is the turreted building on the right.

Late Victorian row, N Street west of New Hampshire Avenue, 1878.

This handsome late Victorian, or Second Empire, row covers the entire block between New Hampshire Avenue and Twenty-first Street. Common in England but unusual in Washington, the center row house has a special, more imposing facade, to create the impression that the row is a single, monumental building.

Queen Anne row houses, corner of Q and Seventeenth Streets, 1885.

This fine row covering the block between Seventeenth and Eighteenth Streets was built by Thomas Franklin Schneider, also the architect of the Cairo apartments. While the standard row house plan had persisted in Washington since the city's beginning, residential facades followed architectural fashion: Federal (early nineteenth century), early Victorian (pre–Civil War), Victorian Second Empire (post–Civil War), and Victorian Queen Anne (late nineteenth century).

Heurich Mansion, New Hampshire Avenue south of Dupont Circle, 1890.

The German-born Christian Heurich, for whom this mansion was constructed, owned a brewery that became Washington's leading private industry.

Dupont Circle

Early in the 1870s, the Board of Public Works put Slash Run—essentially an uncovered sewer—underground. This opened up the Dupont Circle neighborhood (named for the Civil War admiral Samuel Francis Dupont) for construction. The board's fortunes were tied to Alexander Shepherd, its de facto head, who built his own house on vacant lots in the area. His critics claimed he favored his new neighborhood over Georgetown and Capitol Hill, which already had streets that were graded, paved, and lit, as well as sewers and trees. The board did, however, add many improvements to this undeveloped land: it drained the marshes along the course of Slash Run when it was covered, replaced a low bridge to Georgetown with a new steel-truss bridge, fenced and planted trees in the park area around Dupont Circle, and paved Connecticut Avenue north to Boundary Street. In 1874, the Metropolitan Railroad Company laid streetcar tracks along Connecticut Avenue, making the neighborhood more accessible and desirable.

Shepherd's improvements to the Dupont Circle neighborhood immediately attracted wealthy investor-speculators, among them a member of the "California Syndicate," which profited after the Civil War from western mining investments and included Curtis Hillyer, Thomas Sunderland, and Nevada senator William M. Stewart. Stewart built an elaborate Second Empire mansion on the circle in 1873, when it was still remote. The house was designed by Adolph Cluss after he had completed the new Centre Market. Stewart and his wife were extravagant in an extravagant era; a newspaper reporter wrote that attending receptions at the couple's home "makes one feel like Marco Polo at the Court of Kublai Kahn."

Cairo apartments, Q Street east of Sixteenth Street, 1892.

The first modern elevator apartment buildings appeared about 1880. The Cairo apartments, completed in the spring of 1892, were built by Thomas Franklin Schneider, an architect and developer who also erected the Queen Anne–style row on Q Street west of Seventeenth Street. At twelve stories (almost 155 feet high), the Cairo dominated the neighborhood of three-and-a-half-story row houses. Violent local reaction led to legislation limiting the height of buildings.

Foggy Bottom viewed from the Washington Monument, 1894.
WGLC

Landfill operations using mule-drawn wagons can be seen in progress. Above the lockkeeper's house (right center), which still existed in 2000, are the YMCA athletic fields and the Van Ness Mansion, designed by Benjamin Latrobe in 1813–17. The mansion would soon be demolished to make way for the Pan-American Union. The just completed Christian Heurich Brewery stands on the Potomac River (left), with Georgetown and the Aqueduct Bridge beyond.

In 1872, British Minister Sir Edward Thornton built a residence for the British Legation at Connecticut Avenue and N Street, like Stewart's mansion in the Second Empire style. These two elegant buildings were flanked for years primarily by vacant lots, crude shanties, and a few modest frame houses. According to local historian Walter Albano, of the population of 3,100 in 1889, just over half were working-class people described in the census as black or mulatto. About 250 of the white residents were immigrants from Ireland, Germany, and Great Britain.

In 1885, realtors were promoting the area as the "West End," a place of wealth and fashion, and the Dupont Circle neighborhood gradually began to reflect that description. Albano points out that in 1880, only 10 percent of the families had live-in help; in 1900, that number had increased to 40 percent. By 1900, Dupont Circle had earned the reputation of a fashionable, upper-middle-class residential neighborhood and included the missions of China, Austria-Hungary, Spain, and Switzerland, which had joined that of Great Britain.

On Meridian Hill, at Eighteenth Street just north of Boundary Street, is the site of the first building of Columbian College, built in 1817. Columbian moved to Foggy Bottom in 1870 when it became George Washington University. Meridian, originally called Peter Hill after the mayor of Georgetown, was unsuccessfully proposed as the site of the Lincoln Memorial and, alternatively, as the location of a new White House.

Foggy Bottom

Simon Newcomb, who worked at the Naval Observatory, recalled the tents of soldiers and the sound of guns across the Potomac from Foggy Bottom during the Civil War. He remembered the two-mile walk from his house through the area's streets: "After a rain, particularly in the winter and spring, some of the streets were like shallow canals...night-swarms of rats, of a size proportioned to their food supply, disputed the right-of-way with the pedestrian."

After the Civil War ended, however, the industrial development that had begun before the war increased, drawing both skilled and unskilled workers to Foggy Bottom. Many were new immigrants, and contemporary accounts describe Foggy Bottom as a German and Irish area, with the members of each group trading and socializing only with people from their own countries. A large number of the German residents worked at the two breweries at the south end of Foggy Bottom. The Irish worked at the Washington Gas Light Company, which was enlarged between 1887 and 1903 to include the gasometer at Twenty-sixth and G Streets. Many Irish workers settled south of Virginia Avenue in a section called Connaught Row. They fielded their own baseball team, the Emerald Athletic Club, and football team, the Irish Eleven. By the 1880s, there was a West End Hibernian Society at Pennsylvania Avenue and Nineteenth Street.

Along with breweries and gasworks, Foggy Bottom's businesses included Godey's Lime Kiln, established in 1864 on Rock Creek at Twenty-seventh Street. Knott and Moler also converted limestone, which was carried on the C & O Canal from Harper's Ferry. There were the coal dealers J. Maury Dove at the foot of F and G Streets and James A. Tunelty at Pennsylvania Avenue and Twenty-sixth Street. Littlefield Alvord Movers was located at Twenty-sixth and D Streets, and Arlington Bottlers stood at Twenty-seventh and K Streets. All of these depended on the Potomac River and the canal for cheap freight transportation.

The congregation of St. Stephen the Martyr Church at Pennsylvania Avenue and Twenty-fifth Street was predominantly Irish. German Catholics attended a church farther away. In 1867, Foggy Bottom's black community established St. Mary's Episcopal Church on Twenty-fifth Street between G and H Streets. Membership of the African-American Church of the Epiphany, east of the White House, had grown enough and become wealthy enough to afford the services of James Renwick, architect of the Smithsonian "Castle," who designed the church that still occupies the site today.

Neighborhood housing was modest. Narrow brick row houses, typically one room wide and two rooms deep, with no basement, predominated. Some were built on alleys. Central Washington had many inhabited alleys, such as those in Foggy Bottom, where hundreds of families lived in narrow row houses inside large city blocks, often accessible only by a narrow passageway. In 1892, Congress banned construction of houses on alleys less than thirty feet wide without sewers, water, or light, as well as on blind alleys. By that time, however, approximately 1,500 people were already living in Foggy Bottom alleys.

Southwest

During and after the Civil War, the Southwest neighborhood flourished, growing from ten thousand to about eighteen thousand people between 1860 and 1870. From its docks hundreds of shiploads of arms, supplies, and troops were launched down the Potomac River to fight in the battles before Richmond. A gun and powder factory operated at the armory at Greenleaf's Point. Thousands of newly freed slaves settled in Southwest: while 18.5 percent of the population was black in 1860, that figure rose to 37.5 percent in 1870. Southwest's population nearly doubled between 1870 and 1900, and thousands of new row houses were built and commercial enterprises expanded. Many tiny, low-rent row houses sprang up along alleys hidden within the larger city blocks; they were like small villages, occupied by black families and hardly known to outsiders. Although impoverished, many communities nourished strong protective institutions and rich African-American folk traditions.

Although the Tiber Canal was abandoned and filled in the 1870s, the area of Southwest remained set apart by another physical barrier, the Baltimore & Potomac Railroad, built along Maryland and Virginia Avenues between 1856 and 1870. About the same time, however, new streetcar lines began to connect Southwest to the rest of the city.

As in other parts of Washington, racial segregation developed during the last half of the nineteenth century. Black residents, formerly living in several sections of Southwest, were increasingly concentrated east of 4½ Street, with whites dominating the area west of 4½. Geographer Paul A. Groves argues that Southwest was one of Washington's first fully segregated neighborhoods: "The development of a black residential area in Southwest was a fait accompli by 1897 . . . the Southwest was residentially divided."

The 900 block of 4½ Street SW, about 1900. *LCPP*

The shops along this primarily Jewish commercial street would be demolished by 1960 by the Redevelopment Land Agency, the federal urban renewal agency.

Cooke's Row, 1868. Designed by Starkweather and Plowman.

A number of rather grand double houses were built after the Civil War, with high ceilings and floor-to-ceiling windows. They stood on lots wider than the standard row house lot, with one side of each house exposed to natural light. Cooke's Row consists of a set of four Victorian double houses, two Italianate, two Second Empire. These were advertised as having, among other selling points, "tasty porches." The porches were later stripped away, but, modernized, these houses continue to provide gracious urban living on a one-eighth-acre lot close to the center of the national capital.

Queen Anne row houses on P Street near Rock Creek, c. 1890.

During the last quarter of the nineteenth century, houses like these filled in Georgetown's remaining vacant land. About one third of Georgetown houses have Queen Anne facades; about one third are earlier Victorian; and slightly more than one third are Federal style, similar in appearance to the Lee-Ross-Getty houses built in 1794. The facades changed as styles changed, and the scale of Georgetown row houses varied from two-story, two-window-wide workers' dwellings to four-story, three-window-wide mansions. The underlying fenestration pattern persisted, however, as did the standard row house plan. This has been partly because architects have honored the building context, since the standard row house is amenable to continuous modernization while generally retaining its functional plan.

Mount Zion United Methodist Church, 1876. Architect unknown.

The Mount Zion congregation was the first African-American congregation in the District. The original church, built around 1814 on Twenty-seventh Street above P Street, served as a station on the Underground Railroad.

Georgetown

During the Civil War, many people in Georgetown were sympathetic to the South. The war strained the relationships within the town between the "Yankees" and the Secessionists, or the "Secesh" (southern sympathizers), and even those southerners who favored retaining the Union. After 1862, when Lincoln emancipated the slaves in the District of Columbia, many African-Americans found lodging in the back streets and alleys of the District and Georgetown. There was an influx of thirty to forty thousand freedmen into the District of Columbia by 1864, and the black population of Georgetown increased from 1,935 to 3,271.

After the Civil War, much to the dismay of many of its citizens, Georgetown was annexed by the capital city. Following the example of Alexandria, which had seceded from Washington in 1846, Georgetown petitioned Congress in 1875 to secede from the District of Columbia. The petition was denied.

Soon after the Civil War, a housing boom occurred in many northern cities, including Georgetown, and by the end of the century almost all of Georgetown had been developed. In 1870, there were a dozen

Healy Hall, Georgetown University, 1879. Designed by Smithmeyer & Pelz.

Patrick F. Healy, president of Georgetown University from 1873 to 1882, was the first black president of a major, predominately white American university. He was one of fourteen children born to a white Irish planter from Georgia and a free black woman. Healy received his doctorate from Louvain University in Belgium and returned to teach at Georgetown in 1864. He expanded and upgraded the university, adding Healy Hall and other buildings to the campus.

The architects brought to the design of Healy Hall the same Victorian exuberance they lavished on the Library of Congress. Like the library, the hall has grand interior spaces, and its exterior dominates both the university campus and the Georgetown skyline.

Georgetown University Hospital, c. 1890.

At a 1993 Historic Preservation Review Board meeting, resident Jeffery Kilpatrick described the structure: "The building [proposed for renovation] is the old Georgetown University Hospital… a significant departure in American medicine from what had gone previously. The building went up in about 1890, and it was a rather bold statement by a religious college as to what they believed in… Whereas nursing previously had been done at home, this was a teaching hospital… where the best care of its time could be provided."

Georgetown churches, three of which were for African-Americans. In 1878, however, only one bank, the Farmers and Mechanics Bank (later a branch of Riggs Bank), remained in Georgetown.

There also continued to be a large working-class population, both black and white. In 1993, at a Historic Preservation Review Board (HPRB) meeting, Jeffrey Kilpatrick, a resident of the Georgetown University area, gave this testimony: "When the Georgetown University Hospital was built east of the University, the area was known as 'Hungry Hill.' It was populated largely by whites of very modest means, many of them Irish, and the houses consequently were very small. These houses are often only two rooms deep, they occupy most of the lot and, frankly, they are substandard; they could not be built today." A staff member of the board, David Maloney, added to Kilpatrick's testimony: "Georgetown [is not] a residential historic district. What makes Georgetown important and unusual as a historic district is that it is a complete town . . . It has commercial buildings, industrial buildings, residential buildings, institutional buildings—it has an entire college campus within its boundaries."

In the 1880s, the District wanted to fill in Rock Creek and place the water in a conduit, in part to rid the valley of dumps, breeding grounds for pests, and the hovels of the poor. Congress ultimately purchased Rock Creek Valley and the Glover-Archbold properties to the west, however, and made them both into National Capital Parks. These parks articulated the Georgetown boundaries and heightened the distinctiveness of the village.

After the Civil War, industries expanded on the waterfront. There were flour mills, barrel makers, iron foundries, lumberyards, and coal companies, along with houses for about 1,500 residents. On May 31 and June 1, 1889, the same weather that had caused the infamous Johnstown flood earlier that year brought floodwaters into Georgetown, breaching the canal walls and destroying boats. The C & O Canal Company became bankrupt, and the operation of the canal was taken over by its competitor, the B & O Railroad. The canal never again operated at a profit. The flood was the catalyst for changes in the waterfront. Its first effect was to drive the industries that were dependent on waterpower, such as flour milling, out of business, which left space for small entrepreneurs.

The Georgetown waterfront, 1890. *LCPP*

Visible along with the warehouses and docks on the Georgetown waterfront is the last elevated railway of the Georgetown Barge, Dock, Elevator and Railway Company, which carried coal from barges on the C & O Canal to ships on the Potomac River.

Metropolitan horsecar on Wisconsin Avenue, 1893. *HSW*

Soon after 1862, when the first horsecar left the Navy Yard for the White House, horse-drawn streetcars were traveling to Tenleytown through Georgetown on Wisconsin Avenue. The streetcars were electrified in 1888, and in the 1890s, electric streetcar lines extended north from Georgetown to Rockville and Great Falls, south to Rosslyn and Arlington Center, and west to Ballston, Falls Church, and Vienna, in Virginia.

A Georgetown resident, Herman Hollerith, devised a way to mechanize information, using punched cards to tabulate data from the 1890 census. By 1891, he had set up his experimental business, the Tabulating Machine Company, in the former barrel-making establishment of Horace Jarboe on Thirty-first Street. In 1911, the business was purchased by the company that would become International Business Machines (IBM). It remained a waterfront employer until just before World War II.

Streetcars provided an early escape from the city center for middle-class residents; they also provided access to Georgetown markets for Maryland and Virginia farmers. In 1900, only the very center of downtown Washington was more accessible to and from the surrounding neighborhoods than Georgetown. Two streetcar lines connected Georgetown with the center of Washington; one crossed Aqueduct Bridge to Virginia, turning west at what is now Rosslyn; one went west

beyond Georgetown University and then north to Cabin John Bridge; and one went north on Wisconsin Avenue to Tenleytown and on to Rockville and western Maryland. These converged in the unusual three-level Union Station Terminal on Thirty-sixth Street between M and N Streets, later an office building.

Originally, individual companies operated the streetcars on separate routes. The first company, Washington & Georgetown Electric, took the most profitable route—on commercial M Street. Metropolitan, an upstart, had to settle for residential O and P Streets. The principal maintenance facility for the streetcars was located on P Street near Rock Creek. Another repair shop stood on the south side of M Street west of Wisconsin Avenue. By 1962, the streetcars were gone, and at the end of the twentieth century, the M Street repair shop was filled with several dozen boutiques.

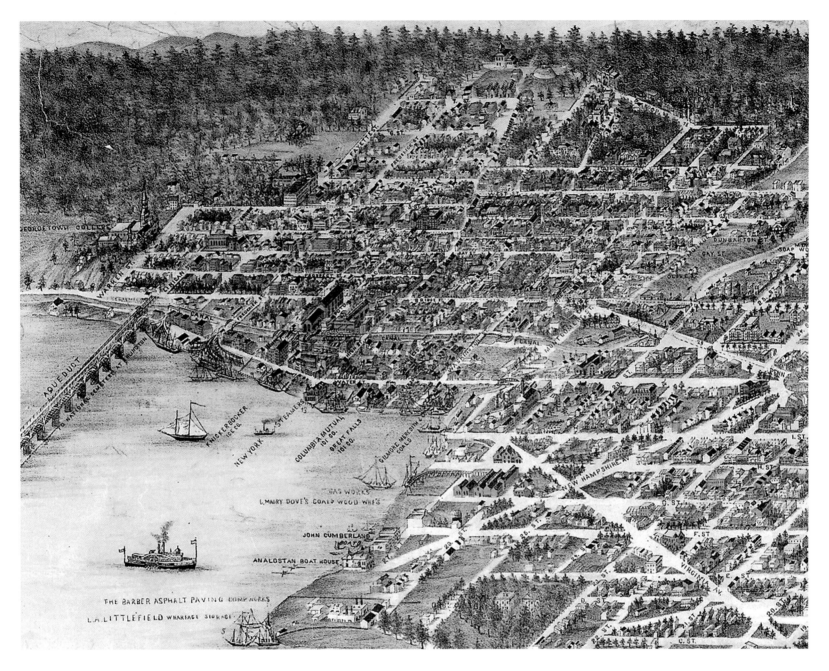

Bird's-eye view of Georgetown, 1884.
Drawn by Adolph Sachse. *LCGM*

In *Port Town to Urban Neighborhood* (1989), historian Kathryn Schneider Smith describes the changes on the Georgetown waterfront occurring toward the end of the nineteenth century: "The old wharves lining the river-banks, central to an earlier trade in tobacco, were enlivened by a new east coast trade in coal and ice. Coal had been the staple of the canal trade since the 1850s. In the 1880s Georgetown coal companies found new markets for their soft Cumberland coal in New England. Rapid population growth in the large east coast cities created an increased demand for ice and food preservation that nearby rivers and ponds could not meet.

"A series of warm winters exacerbated the problem and in 1880 a New York ice famine brought matters to a head. Maine ice companies . . . began shipping enormous quantities of ice in Maine-built schooners . . . They made the return trip loaded with coal for New England . . . many with soft coal brought in on the C & O Canal."

Georgetown in 1900

By 1900, about 90 percent of Georgetown lots had been developed. Densely built Georgetown contrasts with the empty blocks beyond Sheridan Circle on the opposite side of Rock Creek. Mixed in with Georgetown residences, primarily row houses, were schools, churches, shops, and stables. Most of the buildings on M Street and Wisconsin Avenue south of P Street were local retail shops, with some light industrial structures. Industry was concentrated mainly between the C & O Canal and the Potomac River, or bordered the north side of the canal.

The most dramatic change in Georgetown during the last half of the nineteenth century was the addition of the closely spaced streetcar lines. The lines to downtown Washington were on M and P Streets; the line to Rosslyn crossed the Potomac on the Aqueduct Bridge; the line beyond Great Falls followed Potomac Street and Canal Road; and the Rockville, Maryland, line followed Wisconsin Avenue.

1. **Cooke's Row***
2. **Dodge Mansion***
3. **Mount Zion United Methodist Church***
4. **Healy Hall, Georgetown University***
5. **Georgetown University Hospital***
6. **P Street streetcar maintenance shop**
7. **M Street maintenance shop**: Remodeled as retail shops.
8. **Union Station (streetcar) Terminal***: Remodeled as office space.

Buildings and public projects constructed after 1860 are listed in **bold** type.
Buildings and public projects existing in 2000 are identified with an asterisk.*

Key

- single-family residences
- walk-up residences
- elevator apartment
- hotel
- retail
- private offices
- federal offices
- federal institutions
- private & foreign institutions
- local institutions
- industrial
- warehouse
- transportation

0 100   500   1000 ft

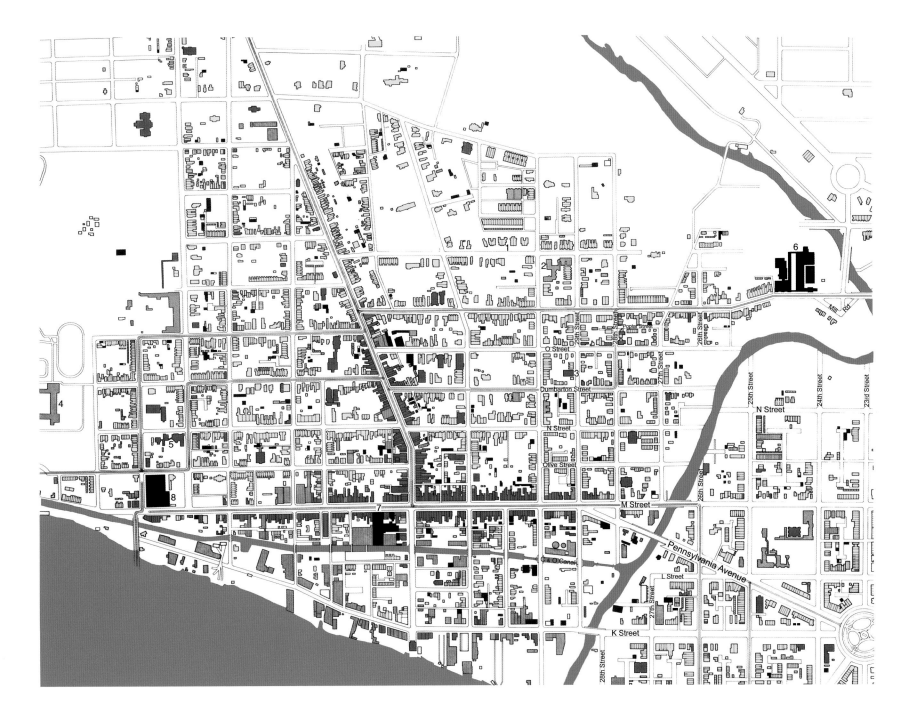

O Street

Dumbarton Street

N Street

Olive Street

M Street

C & O Canal

Pennsylvania Avenue

L Street

K Street

28th Street

28th Street

28th Street

27th Street

26th Street

26th Street

25th Street

25th Street

24th Street

23rd Street

27th Street

27th Street

N Street

N Street

Mill Rd

Pennsylvania Avenue NW, looking east from the terrace of the Treasury Building to the Capitol, 1871. *LOK*

This popular view of Pennsylvania Avenue shows the original streetcars of the Washington and Georgetown line. The crowd is gathered for a carnival to celebrate the reopening of the avenue after it had been paved with wood blocks.

Although Pennsylvania Avenue was still a street of Federal-style row houses dating from around 1800, it was changing. The Solaris Hotel and the first Willard Hotel can be seen in the foreground, on the north (left) side of the avenue.

Pennsylvania Avenue, view from the Treasury Building terrace, 1885. *NA*

Here, the Solaris Hotel is clearly visible. The building with the mansard roof on the north (left) side of the avenue is Shepherd's Centennial Building. The south side of the avenue remained basically unchanged in the years from 1871 to 1885. The urbanist Fritz Gutheim was fond of pointing out that horse-cars needed a "hill horse" to help them up the Fifteenth Street grade. After pulling a car uphill, the horse would return to the bottom, unattended.

Pennsylvania Avenue, view from the Treasury Building terrace, 1895. *LCPP*

By 1895, the horses were gone and buildings at the west end of the avenue next to the Treasury had become larger. The new Willard Hotel, the Post Office, the Hotel Occidental, and the Grand Army of the Republic building still stand; the Federal-style buildings have largely disappeared.

Streets and Other Public Open Spaces

Franklin Howe, chief clerk of the Board of Public Works in the 1870s, stated the board's plan to provide "for the improvement of the streets . . . by lessening the widths of the carriageways and paving and sewering them." A controversial aspect of the board's street improvements was the setting of proper street grades, which at that time still followed the rolling terrain that existed when L'Enfant prepared his plan. This required hills to be cut down and hollows filled. Howe described the reaction of residents: "It was not pleasant for a man who owned a house to find his street cut all the way from 5 to 20 feet down, and his dwelling left up in the air, as it were. On the other hand, the man who owned a house upon a street which was filled for several feet found himself way below grade, so that possibly he could have stepped from his second story window to the pavement . . . The board considered the general good, and not the effect . . . upon individual property holders."

During the last decades of the nineteenth century, a logical relationship between the density of urban activities, the width of the

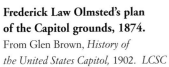

**Frederick Law Olmsted's plan
of the Capitol grounds, 1874.**
From Glen Brown, *History of
the United States Capitol,* 1902. *LCSC*

**Present-day views of Olmsted's
details for the Capitol grounds.**

Among the fixtures Frederick
Law Olmsted designed were light
standards in the Capitol forecourt, a Capitol streetcar stop,
and combined bench, light standard, and retaining wall. Olmsted
handled simple details—curbs,
gutters, outdoor furniture, a
variety of light standards—with
Victorian exuberance and
consummate skill.

streets, and the impact of travel developed in the L'Enfant city. Connecticut Avenue, with a 130-foot right-of-way, was an elegant neighborhood open space; the narrower (but still 90-foot-wide) residential
streets served the same purpose in more modest neighborhoods. The
hustle and bustle of streetcar, wagon, and pedestrian traffic on F Street
and Seventh Street was appropriate to a commercial center; the wide
ceremonial streets, such as Pennsylvania Avenue, provided a gracious
setting for a variety of activities.

By 1900, the Washington Monument was completed, Andrew
Jackson Downing's landscape plans for the Mall were expanded, and
the Capitol grounds were elegantly landscaped by Frederick Law Olmsted. Shortly before the Civil War, Olmsted had designed Central Park
in Manhattan, and by the 1880s, when he prepared the designs for the
Capitol grounds, he had already planned parks for many of the largest
American cities. The grounds and details showed the assurance of an
experienced and talented designer.

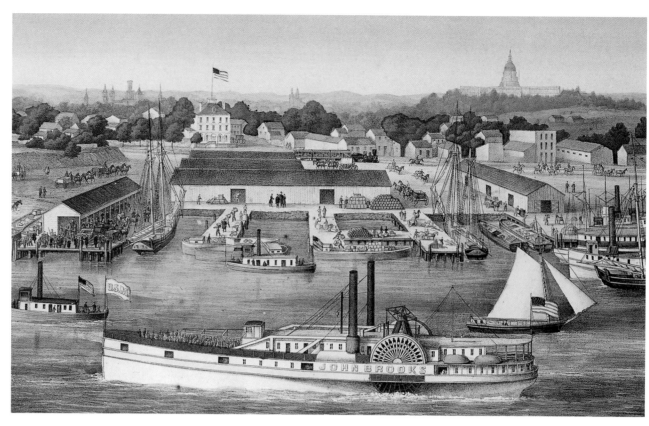

Bird's-Eye View of Sixth Street Wharf, 1862. Unsigned drawing published by Charles Magnus, Washington, D.C. *KC*

During the Civil War, the Richmond campaigns were supplied from southwest Washington's waterfront in ships powered by both sail and steam. By 1900, commercial shipping would be steam-driven and sailing would become a form of recreation.

Travel to and within the National Capital

Washington's extraordinary transformation from a collection of self-contained villages in 1860 to membership in a nation of cities in 1900 was driven by changes in travel. Before the Civil War, America consisted of somewhat independent urban economies with a rural base. A few decades after the war, however, that had changed: a national economy existed, created in large part by the increasing speed and decreasing costs of moving people, goods, and information around the country and its cities.

In 1800, travel on water was in wooden ships, powered by the wind. In 1807, Robert Fulton's *Clermont* steamed from New York City to Albany, 150 miles in thirty-two hours. The Yankee clipper ships, under full sail, traveled faster. But by 1900, steel ships powered by steam traveled at double the speed of the clipper ships; in 1850, the last Yankee clipper made the voyage around Cape Horn.

In 1830, the first American railroad was built and operating. By 1835, there were approximately one thousand miles of U.S. railroads, and in 1869, the final spike was driven in the first transcontinental railroad. In 1800, the journey from Washington to Philadelphia took twenty-two hours; in 1900, the trip took two hours.

Because the new transportation technologies reduced the cost and time of travel between cities, the relationship between the cost of production and the cost of distribution was turned on end. Goods could be produced where site costs were low and then shipped rapidly and inexpensively about the country.

The effect of the railroad on the city was not entirely benign. The railroad marshaling yards gouged vast, noxious holes into the fabric of industrial cities, unequaled in their consequences until the urban extensions of the Interstate Highway System appeared a century later. Washington was spared the worst effects of railroad construction; however, Delaware Avenue north of the Mall and Virginia and Maryland Avenues south of the Mall were sacrificed to rail travel by the end of the nineteenth century.

In 1862, Washington's first three horsecar lines were opened. One ran from the Navy Yard to the Capitol to the White House. Another ran on Seventh Street; this line was converted to cable cars in 1890, running from Fort McNair in Southwest to Boundary Street (present-day Florida Avenue). Period photographs show that Washington rapidly adapted to electric rail transportation.

Steam and electricity did not immediately replace the horse, and livery stables dotted the city in 1900. For delivery of merchandise the Woodward and Lothrop department store had stables in Blagden Alley, near Tenth and M Streets; for service to residents, the Cairo apartments had stables on M Street between Sixteenth and Seventeenth Streets. Because the new transportation technologies also reduced the cost and time of travel within cities, citizens (if they were middle-class and white) could live in attractive neighborhoods far from where they worked, and workplaces with concentrations of heavy industry could be isolated.

Herdic cabs, c. 1884. *MLKL*

Named for its inventor, Peter Herdic, the Herdic cab was popular in Washington during the 1880s and 1890s. In 1884, Joseph West Moore suggested, "Take a carriage with an intelligent driver, and leisurely ride through the center of the city. A ride like this will enable a stranger to obtain a general view of the prominent locations in a short time through the central portions of Pennsylvania Avenue, Seventh, Ninth and F Streets, and afterwards through the fashionable West End."

The League of American Wheelmen on Pennsylvania Avenue during a Washington meet, c. 1880. *LCPP*

Bicycles were invented in England in 1868 and introduced to America at the 1876 Centennial Exposition. The beginning of personal transportation, they became popular in Washington in a variety of styles.

Before the Civil War, neighborhoods tended to include citizens of all races and classes, and in parts where residents were middle- and upper-class white, there were always nearby areas where black servants lived. During the last half of the nineteenth century, in all American cities, residential areas began to be segregated by race and class, and neighborhoods became more racially and economically uniform. Throughout the twentieth century, this separation and homogeneity increased in tandem with and in response to the increasing speed of urban travel.

At the same time, white-collar workplaces could be concentrated efficiently. In the second half of the nineteenth century, workplaces were increasingly separated from residences. The streetcar lines were the instrument of that separation. Access from residential neighborhoods to what is today known as the Central Business District was provided by streetcar lines from the west and north on Pennsylvania Avenue, Connecticut Avenue, Fourteenth Street, Ninth Street, and Seventh Street. Access from neighborhoods to the north and east was via lines on Fifth Street, New York Avenue, and North Capitol Street; from the south and east, by lines on Fourteenth Street, Seventh Street, Sixth Street, and Pennsylvania Avenue.

This mutually beneficial relationship would become more pronounced as travel became faster and cheaper: the residential starting points for trips became ever farther from the center; as accessibility to downtown destinations became greater, downtown locations became more attractive, which further encouraged improvements in travel.

Copeland steam tricycle, 1888. *SI*

Bicycles remained popular in America through the end of the nineteenth century, but they never became a primary mode of urban travel. Bicycles were supplanted by the progeny of the "steam tricycle," shown here in front of the Smithsonian's porte cochere.

For centuries, the horse was the only available personal form of transportation, and only the very wealthy could afford to keep horses and vehicles for their private use. To get about town people hired a coach and driver, the forerunner of the modern taxicab. It was for this reason that the bicycle, introduced in the United States in 1876, became immediately popular. For the first time, ordinary Washingtonians could own a personal means of transportation.

The Mall, looking east to the Capitol, 1901. *SI*

Taken from the top of the Washington Monument, the photograph shows the Smithsonian "Castle" in the right foreground. Beyond it is the National Museum, which provided the setting for President Garfield's inaugural ball in 1881. The Baltimore & Potomac Railroad station is in the left middle distance. West of the Capitol, the Mall is pinched in by development along Pennsylvania and Maryland Avenues.

The Mall and Its Surroundings in 1900

Andrew Downing's arrangement of trees and paths on the Mall would soon be reexamined. With the approach of 1900—the centennial of Washington as the national capital—civic leaders, members of Congress, and federal officials looked for ways to celebrate the anniversary. Many considered improvements in the capital, particularly in its monumental center, to be the most appropriate commemoration, and officials and citizens made a number of proposals.

Franklin L. Smith, a Boston manufacturer and amateur architect who earlier had prepared a plan for central Washington, revised his plan in 1899 and again in 1900. His ideas included a parkway weaving down the center of the Mall and leading onto a new bridge over the Potomac, a museum, and land to be cleared for public buildings. Chicago architect Henry Ives Cobb proposed a "great avenue" lined with government buildings for the center of the Mall and a "magnificent union station" on the north side of the Mall, with marshaling yards south of it.

Senator James McMillan, chairman of the Senate Committee on the District of Columbia, had earlier arranged with the railroads to eliminate grade crossings (where some thirty people were killed or injured each year). In return, the Pennsylvania Railroad would be allowed to build a major station on the Mall, with the railroad crossing elevated on a viaduct. McMillan's committee supported Cobb's plan, along with additions by McMillan. Many people opposed McMillan, including Colonel Theodore Bingham, head of the Office of Buildings and Grounds, who in 1900 proposed moving the station to the south side of the Mall and clearing "Murder Bay," between Pennsylvania Avenue and the Mall, in preparation for construction of government buildings. Glen Brown led architects' opposition to McMillan. Brown, author of a two-volume history of the capital, was secretary of the American Institute of Architects, which had just moved its offices to Washington. He had studied the L'Enfant plan and knew members of Congress, including Senator McMillan and his secretary, Charles Moore. Brown proposed a plan of his own, which was published in the August 1900 issue of *Architectural Review*.

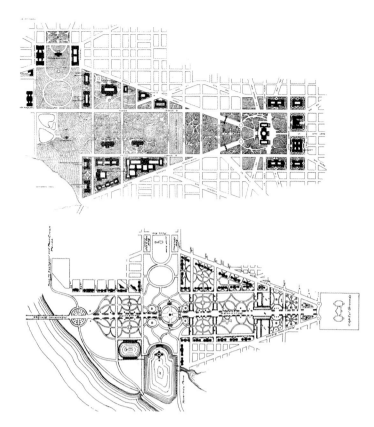

Automobile in front of east facade of the Capitol, c. 1900.

Two seminal events at the turn of the century were to influence the growth of the national capital. The City Beautiful movement, as represented in Washington by the Senate Park Commission Plan, was to have the most immediately obvious impact. It was the invention of the automobile, however, that would eventually have a more pervasive effect.

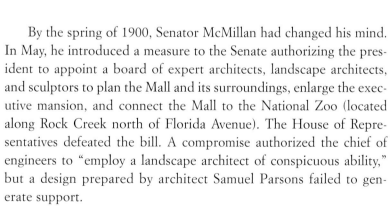

Study for the Grouping of Public Buildings in the City of Washington. Plan for central Washington by Paul J. Pelz, 1900. *CUFAL*

In his plan, Pelz favored a Mall in the tradition of Andrew Jackson Downing.

Plan for Grouping Government Buildings Landscape and Statuary on the Mall and Pennsylvania Ave. Washington, D.C., 1900. By Glen Brown. *CUFAL*

By the spring of 1900, Senator McMillan had changed his mind. In May, he introduced a measure to the Senate authorizing the president to appoint a board of expert architects, landscape architects, and sculptors to plan the Mall and its surroundings, enlarge the executive mansion, and connect the Mall to the National Zoo (located along Rock Creek north of Florida Avenue). The House of Representatives defeated the bill. A compromise authorized the chief of engineers to "employ a landscape architect of conspicuous ability," but a design prepared by architect Samuel Parsons failed to generate support.

In December, the annual meeting of the AIA, held in Washington, focused on the design of the center of the capital. Four papers were presented on December 13. Frederick Law Olmsted Jr., son of the great American landscape architect, suggested the following principle:

> Great public edifices must be strongly formal, where they are perfectly symmetrical or not, and this formal quality ought to be rec-

ognized in the plan of their surroundings if the total effect is to be consistent . . . the axis of the Capitol should neither be ignored by the use of a wiggling road and confused informal planning, nor should it be marked by a mere commonplace boulevard G . . . [The Mall should be treated as] a sort of compound "boulevard" marked by several parallel rows of trees with several pavements and turf strips.

An AIA committee met with the Senate Committee on the District of Columbia, and on December 17, McMillan introduced Senate Resolution 139 to create a commission. The House refused to pass the resolution, but Senator McMillan obtained approval from an executive session of the Senate, directing his committee to "report plans for the development and improvements of the entire park system of the District of Columbia . . . to secure the services of such experts as may be necessary for a proper consideration of the subject . . . paid from the contingent fund of the Senate." The stage was set for the Senate Park Commission Plan, the most ambitious proposal for planning the capital since 1791.

Washington in 1900

- By 1900, with a population of 278,700, the city was beginning to expand beyond its L'Enfant boundaries. It was more compact than in 1860, with average densities of about fifty people per acre.
- The 1860s town of small shopkeepers and artisans had become a corporate city. Commerce was concentrated in Downtown with a retail core on F Street and Seventh Street. Developed in tandem with this Central Business District were the multistory "cage-type" building and the high-speed elevator. The department store, a late-nineteenth-century mercantile innovation, helped concentrate commercial activity in the center.
- While there were still hotels on Pennsylvania Avenue near the Capitol, the newer hotels had moved west, closer to what was becoming a more fashionable neighborhood. Residential hotels were replacing transient hotels.
- Residential neighborhoods north of Downtown had become desirable. The first multistory apartment buildings appeared in the 1880s; by 1900, there were a dozen elevator apartments listed in the Sanborne Atlas.
- In 1900, there were 283 places of worship in the capital, including eighteen Catholic churches, three Quaker meetinghouses, and two Hebrew synagogues. One hundred two churches were designated as "colored."
- The area between the Mall and Pennsylvania Avenue was the red-light district, as it had been for decades.
- At the turn of the century, neither the Mall nor the Potomac River was seen as an amenity; most of the surrounding buildings were factories or warehouses, along with lumberyards, millworks, and furniture factories. There was already an "automobile livery" building east of the White House grounds.
- Most buildings serving transportation were livery stables, which had an impact on the environment. (In 1900, two and a half million pounds of horse manure was dropped on Manhattan streets every day.)
- More than one hundred miles of streetcar tracks laced the city, carrying development beyond Boundary Street, which had become Florida Avenue by the end of the nineteenth century.
- Railroads had expanded explosively after the Civil War and brought to the city bulk goods that had previously been produced locally in small quantities. Corsets were made in Baltimore, nails in Richmond, and umbrellas in Philadelphia, and all were shipped by rail to markets around the country. Most freight still arrived at the Baltimore & Ohio Depot, along Delaware Avenue, bound for its yards and station north of the Capitol. Passengers arrived at the Baltimore & Potomac Depot, located on the Mall.

Key

- single-family residences
- walk-up residences
- elevator apartment
- hotel
- retail
- private offices
- federal offices
- federal institutions
- private & foreign institutions
- local institutions
- industrial
- warehouse
- transportation

0 100   500   1000 ft

1. **State, War and Navy Building***

2. U.S. Treasury Building*

3. **Pension Building***: For Civil War veterans.

4. **U.S. Government Printing Office***

5. **Department of Agriculture:** Later replaced by new buildings on the same site.

6. **National Museum***: Built for the Centennial Exposition of 1876.

7. **Jefferson Building of the Library of Congress***

8. Department of Justice Library*: Now the Renwick Gallery.

9. **U.S. Weather Bureau**

10. **U.S. Botanical Garden**

11. **U.S. Fish Commission**

12. **Army Medical Museum**

13. **U.S. Museum of Hygiene**

14. Winder Building*

15. U.S. Land and Indian Office*: Former City Post Office.

16. U.S. Patent Office*

17. **City Post Office***: Construction began in 1892. Only the Capitol is taller.

18. **Columbia Hospital***: In 2000, the Columbia Hospital for Women.

19. **Franklin School***

20. **Carnegie Library***

21. **Corcoran Art Gallery***

22. **Stevens Public School***

23. **Little Sisters of the Poor***: Now the Capital Children's Museum.

24. **Christian Heurich Brewery**

25. **Heurich Mansion***: For many years (until 2000) the Historical Society of Washington.

26. **Stoneleigh Court apartments**

27. **Luther Memorial Church***

28. **St. Patrick's Roman Catholic Church***

29. **New Willard Hotel***

30. **Woodward and Lothrop department store***

31. **Woodward and Lothrop livery stable**

32. **Centre Market** (rebuilt) and **National Guard Armory**

33. **National Bank of Washington***

34. **Central Washington Bank***

35. Riggs National Bank: The site in 2000 was still home to a Riggs branch.

36. **North Liberty Market Convention Hall**

37. **Automotive Livery Building**

38. **Gasometer**: One of many.

39. **U.S. Electric Lighting**

40. **Baltimore & Ohio Railroad Station**

41. **Baltimore & Potomac Railroad Station**

Cairo apartments*: Just beyond the boundaries of the map, the Cairo is located on Q Street, east of Sixteenth Street. In 2000, at 155 feet high, it was still the tallest residential building in Washington.

Buildings and public projects constructed after 1860 are listed in **bold** type.

Buildings and public projects existing in 2000 are identified with an asterisk.*

0 100   500   1000 ft

Chapter 4

1900
to
1940

**Perspective painting of the Senate Park
Commission Plan, 1902, looking east.** Detail.

Changes between 1900 and 1940

During the first part of the nineteenth century, Washington was shaped by the struggle to establish a federal foothold; during the last half, it was molded by the emergence of the nation's mercantile and industrial economy. In the early twentieth century, the forces shaping the city became more complex. The Spanish-American War and World War I increased the international stature of the United States, and the responsibilities of the national capital grew accordingly. Federal employment swelled from fewer than 6,000 people in 1879 to more than 25,000 in 1903 to 65,000 in 1927.

As it began to evolve into a major American city at the turn of the century, built Washington focused increasingly on civic architecture, a response to the City Beautiful movement, which grew out of the 1893 World's Columbian Exposition in Chicago. This ended the hold of Victorian architecture on American building and established classicism as the dominant architectural style. Its most dramatic expression was in the work of the Senate Park Commission, which transformed the center of the national capital. The movement energized many business communities; in Washington, the Board of Trade took a special interest in expanding the city's extraordinary parks system.

The country and the capital prospered during the decade after World War I, and in the early days of the Great Depression, President Herbert Hoover continued major government building projects—a building for the Supreme Court, a new office building for the House of Representatives, an extension of the Senate office building, and an administration building for the Department of Agriculture. According to *Washington Seen: A Photographic History* by Fredric M. Miller and Howard Gillette Jr.:

> The Great Depression, which began with the October 1929 Wall Street crash, had a relatively mild impact on the area initially. Just as the slump began to tighten its grip locally, in 1932–33 the advent of Franklin D. Roosevelt's New Deal administration radically transformed the city. In a short period of time, tens of thousands of new employees joined the government work force, construction accelerated, and public relief programs blossomed. The extension of government activity into every area of national life kept the city prosperous and exciting until the even greater expansion that came with the approach of World War II in 1940–41.

The number of government employees grew from 93,000 in 1934 to 140,000 in 1940. *Washington Seen* adds:

> By the end of the decade, there were . . . double the number of civilian employees when FDR took office. This expansion of government . . . stimulated the public building boom in the city . . .
>
> Finally, Washington had its own share of the kind of relief projects sponsored by New Deal agencies around the country. The Public Works Administration (PWA) employed 350 men to clear the last trees from the Mall . . . another PWA crew cleaned the Washington

Monument for the first time in its history . . . the Works Progress Administration (WPA) put hundreds to work in libraries and museums and on a variety of literary and artistic projects.

Private employment increased in tandem with mounting public employment. The private building industry, which accounted for $7 million worth of business in 1934, was responsible for $24 million in 1936. The New Deal also encouraged the growth of the associations, lobbies, and news agencies that were to be so active in the capital throughout the remainder of the century. *Washington Seen* describes two problems that continued to plague the city, however:

> Some ten thousand residents—the vast majority black—still lived in several hundred dilapidated houses on alleys and small streets in the older part of the city . . . Drawing on reform efforts dating back decades, the New Dealers addressed the local problem through the 1934 creation of the Alley Dwelling Authority . . . [but] by the end of the 1930s the Alley Dwelling Authority and associated New Deal agencies had erected only about three thousand dwelling units.
>
> The second problem, linked to but far more intractable than the housing issue, was racial segregation and discrimination. Even the New Deal reformers rarely addressed the local situation directly . . . The reformist atmosphere of the New Deal stimulated some changes in segregation, but they were not profound.

In fact, while Eleanor Roosevelt was an effective lobbyist for racial justice, her husband was too dependent on southern congressmen to back his ambitious, controversial legislative agenda to give her much support.

By 1940, the city's monumental core had been re-created according to the Senate Park Commission's plan. *Washington Seen* describes the private downtown, north of Pennsylvania Avenue, as

> complex and highly specialized . . . pool halls and arcades lined 9th Street; first run movie houses concentrated between 12th and 15th Streets; while 15th Street from E to K Streets, was known as Little Wall Street . . . Linked closely to the downtown were the rows of embassies, offices, churches, and association headquarters which stretched up 16th Street to Park Road and from Dupont Circle west along Massachusetts Avenue.

Washington Transformed: The Work of the Senate Park Commission

Andrew Jackson Downing, Major Nathaniel Michler, and—toward the end of the nineteenth century—many other architects, both amateur and professional, prepared (or fantasized about) ambitious plans for the Mall and its surroundings. In 1900, at the annual convention of the American Institute of Architects, Frederick Law Olmsted Jr. had argued that the city should return to L'Enfant's plan: "In great undertakings, requiring centuries to mature, the one hope of unity and harmony, the one hope of successful issue, is the establishment of a comprehensive plan and the consistent adherence to it." Olmsted, whose father had designed the great mid-nineteenth-century urban parks as well as the Capitol grounds as they appear today, joined Senator James McMillan and architects Daniel ("Make no little plans; they have no power to move the minds of men!") Burnham and Charles McKim, along with sculptor Augustus Saint-Gaudens, to produce the Senate Park Commission Plan for central Washington.

At the commission's first meeting in April 1901, Burnham, the coordinating architect behind the World's Columbian Exposition of 1893, announced to his colleagues that they were to visit Europe "to see and discuss together parks in their relation to public buildings—that is our problem here in Washington and we must have weeks in which we are thinking of nothing else." Before leaving for Europe, Burnham met with Alexander J. Cassatt, president of the Pennsylvania Railroad (and brother of painter Mary Cassatt). Burnham reported that Cassatt had been receptive to McKim and his conviction that the railroad station should be removed from the Mall. The group, except for Saint-Gaudens, sailed in June, working on plans during the voyage. In Europe, they photographed, sketched, and discussed the great urban places in Paris, Rome, Venice, Vienna, Budapest, Versailles, and London. It was on this trip, particularly in Paris, that they developed the outline of their plan, which was refined in studios in Washington, New York, and Boston.

In the meantime, McMillan and Cassatt reached an agreement, later formalized in legislation, for the Pennsylvania Railroad to give up its rights to the location on the Mall and build a station north of Pennsylvania Avenue for the merged Baltimore & Potomac and Baltimore & Ohio Railroads. In return, the government agreed to build a tunnel for the Pennsylvania Railroad under First Street east of the Capitol, connecting the southern lines with what would be the new Union Station.

Senator McMillan and Charles Moore, the commission's secretary, who had accompanied the members of the Senate Park Commission to Europe, arranged to exhibit the plan at the Corcoran Gallery, which was completed in 1897 on Seventeenth Street across from the White House. The exhibition included models, rendered plans, and a number of large perspective paintings, complete with press releases. This material was part of an illustrated report, prepared by the Park Commission for the Senate, that described the proposals. The report and press releases were written by Charles Moore with help from Olmsted; Moore became an essential participant in the struggles over the plan's implementation.

On January 15, 1902, the exhibition was reviewed by President and Mrs. Theodore Roosevelt, members of the cabinet and the Congress, and other important citizens. Viewers looked from above at two huge models, one of their city as it existed, the other displaying the commission's proposals. They then stepped down to view the models at eye level and to examine large colored renderings illustrating details of the plan.

The commission made a number of proposals. It would remove the railroad station from the Mall and replace it with a monumental station north of the Capitol. The Mall would be laid out with a broad center lawn, flanked on each side by four rows of American elms, with buildings beyond the elms on each side for "scientific purposes and for the great museums" from First Street below the Capitol to Fourteenth Street east of the Washington Monument. The Capitol would be surrounded with imposing government buildings forming a Capitol square, and the triangle formed by Pennsylvania Avenue, Fifteenth Street, and the Mall would be cleared for government buildings. The Mall itself would be extended west to the Potomac River, and a "reflecting basin" in front of a memorial to Abraham Lincoln would be created, along with a new bridge crossing the Potomac from the Lincoln Memorial to Arlington Cemetery. The White House axis would be extended south beyond the Mall to a memorial to a national hero (the present location of the Thomas Jefferson Memorial).

Reactions to the commission's proposals were enthusiastic. *Century* magazine published an illustrated article by Charles Moore. Many laudatory articles in national periodicals followed, and historian John W. Reps concludes in *Washington on View* (1991):

> All this favorable publicity encouraged citizens and public officials in many cities to expand their efforts to improve their own communities, programs that had begun with the park and municipal art movements and that the Chicago World's Fair had done much to stimulate. The Washington plan of 1903 thus provided an inspiring example of how civic design principles developed for a temporary exposition could be applied to a real city.
>
> More than any single event, the Senate Park Commission Plan for Washington created the environment in which modern American city planning took root and began to grow.

Several more formal modifications to the Mall were proposed, but these were never implemented. Each of the essential elements of the Senate Park Commission Plan, however, was completed or under construction by 1940.

Urban planning was—as it is today—a political art. The Senate Park Commission did not have a George Washington who could serve as an advocate in Congress and with the public. While Presidents Theodore Roosevelt and William Howard Taft were both helpful, the commission had to create its own political support, and battles over the implementation of the plan lasted many years.

Senator McMillan had personally escorted the presidential party around the Corcoran exhibition and was soon busy lobbying the press. On January 16, 1902, the *Washington Post* published photographs of the presidential review, accompanied by an enthusiastically supportive editorial that ended: "Hitherto our public improvements have had no definite scheme including the entire system and making each feature harmonious with the rest. Now, however, we appear to have done with the haphazard and fitful and to have started on a scheme that time cannot render obsolete. The exhibition at the Corcoran Gallery of Art

Model of central Washington as it existed in 1900, prepared by the Senate Park Commission. *CFA*

is tangible proof of good work accomplished and a bright promise of great results to follow."

The *Washington Evening Star,* the *Philadelphia Press,* and other influential newspapers published articles commending the work, generally calling on Congress to adopt the plan. Montgomery Schuyler, architectural critic for the *New York Times,* wrote a scholarly review on January 19 that described the rationale for using a baroque plan and addressed the issue of costs:

> The point is to have a plan that you believe in, that is based upon study of what has been found most admirable in its kind in the world, in those examples of the art of city making which "have pleased many and pleased long" . . . Whatever it may cost Uncle Sam to do all this, it will cost him nothing to say now that he believes in it, that he means to do it in good time, and that in the meantime whatever he does in the way of public architecture or public embellishment he will do in accordance with it.

Schuyler added an important suggestion—"that the commission which have devised such a plan shall be perpetuated to supervise its execution."

While the plan was widely supported in the press and in official Washington, the commission had a formidable enemy. Representative Joseph Cannon of Illinois resented Senator McMillan's strategy of bypassing the House of Representatives by financing the work from Senate contingency funds. When McMillan died in the summer of 1902, the plan lost its most powerful, knowledgeable, and dedicated supporter. Cannon became Speaker of the House in 1903, and he dominated that body for more than a decade, a time during which the acceptance of the plan was in doubt.

A number of federal departments needed new space, and the planning for some of these had preceded the Senate Park Commission's report. Congress had authorized the purchase of a site between E and F Streets and Eighteenth and Nineteenth Streets for a "hall of records." At the request of the president, correspondence followed between Daniel Burnham and Secretary of the Treasury Leslie Shaw. Burnham argued for one of the sites laid out by the commission:

> If the Executive [President Roosevelt] yields now, it will be much more difficult to refuse in the future, because it will then have not

Model of central Washington proposed by the Senate Park Commission. *CFA*

alone the urgency of personal interest, but precedent as well to contend with . . . Therefore, I believe that unless you now adhere to the general plan it will be lost and the work done upon it thrown away. It will never again be so easy as it is now to stem the tide.

Shaw pointed out that Congress had authorized the building and the site; the president could abandon the building but could not change the site. He told Burnham, "Personally, I do not believe that any Congress will ever pay the least attention to the report of the Commission. Personally, I would follow any plan rather than erect buildings with no general plan, but Congress is a practical not a theoretical body." The issue was tabled and eventually resolved. The National Archives was built on a site on axis with Eighth Street on the south side of Pennsylvania Avenue.

A more serious dispute arose over the location of a new building for the Department of Agriculture near the older Agriculture building on the Mall. The Commission had established a building line set back four hundred feet from the center line of the Mall. The department's building committee, supported by Senator Jacob Gallinger of New Hampshire, successor to Senator McMillan as chairman of the

Senate Committee on the District of Columbia, recommended a three-hundred-foot setback. At a well-attended hearing of the District Committee, Burnham, McKim, Olmsted, Saint-Gaudens, eight members of the American Institute of Architects, and several senators explained the reasons for the four-hundred-foot setback. Burnham described the four rows of trees, fifty feet apart in each direction, that would line each side of an eight-hundred-foot Mall and showed the commission's original drawings. The committee finally agreed to support a Senate resolution calling for the eight-hundred-foot Mall.

The architects, individually and through the AIA, campaigned to obtain the president's support for the plan. Roosevelt was invited to speak at the AIA's annual dinner in January 1905, along with Senator Elihu Root (a supporter and adviser for the plan from the beginning), Justice John Harlan, and Speaker Cannon. The remarks Roosevelt gave that evening were repeated whenever the plan was in danger:

The only way we can hope to have worthy artistic work done for the Nation, State or municipality is by having such a growth of popular sentiment as will render it incumbent upon successive administrations, or successive legislative bodies, to carry out steadily a plan chosen for

Perspective painting of the Senate Park Commission Plan, 1902, looking west. *JWR*

The great plaza that was proposed to provide a monumental forecourt to the Capitol would have mirrored the plaza at the base of the Washington Monument. This became a particular bone of contention as the plan was implemented, because it replaced a grove of fine trees and the Botanical Gardens. The *Washington Evening Star* railed against it, editorially and in cartoons.

them, worked out for them by such a body of men as gathered here this evening.

What I have said does not mean that we shall go, here in Washington for instance, into immediate and extravagant expenditures on public buildings. All that it means is that whenever hereafter a public building is provided for and erected, it should be erected in accordance with a carefully thought-out plan adopted long before, and that it should not only be beautiful in itself, but fitting in its relation to the whole scheme of public buildings, the parks and the drives of the District.

Controversy over the implementation of the plan continued. One of Roosevelt's last acts as president was the creation of the Council of Fine Arts through an executive order. After fiery debate in the House, and less divisive discussion in the Senate, Senator Root steered through Congress a bill creating the Commission of Fine Arts, to be composed of seven "well-qualified judges of the fine arts"

Perspective painting of the Senate Park Commission Plan, 1902, looking east. *JWR*

appointed by the president for four-year terms. The role of the commission was "to advise upon the location of statues, fountains, and monuments in the public squares, streets and parks of the District of Columbia, and upon selection of . . . artists for execution of same . . . The commission shall also advise generally upon questions of art when required to do so by the President, or by any committee of either House of Congress." Executive orders by Presidents Taft, Woodrow Wilson, and Warren G. Harding widened the charge to the commission to include review of all federal buildings affecting the appearance of the city, improvements of public grounds, and design of medals, insignia, and coins.

Resolving the problem of where to locate the Department of Agriculture building was significant because it established the dimensions of the center of the Mall. The location of the Grant Memorial was also important in determining the future of the work of the Senate Park Commission. Congress had authorized a memorial to Grant to be

The painting underscores the overwhelming importance of the axis planned by the commission—from the Capitol through the Washington Monument to the Lincoln Memorial—in response to the dilemma presented by the fact that the Washington Monument was off center from the axis of the Mall. (Today almost no one realizes that the new axis of the Mall is not parallel with Constitution Avenue.) Details of implementation softened and, to most eyes, improved that axis, but its significance remains. The cross axis from the White House through the Washington Monument was also a preoccupation of the commission. The formidable plaza that was to be at the base of the monument was never built, and while many plans have been proposed, there has never been an agreement to build one.

placed south of the White House. The commission proposed a location west of the Capitol, near the Botanical Gardens in an area of fine trees.

The *Washington Evening Star,* an early supporter of the commission, led a furious attack on January 14, 1908:

> The placing of the monument upon this utterly unfit site in a swamp was furtherance of the scheme to get possession of the Botanic Garden, destroy all its trees and convert it into a bare asphalted street styled "Union Square." Their contention that only two or three trees would need to be disturbed . . . is an illustration of the false pretenses that have characterized every step of their progress . . . They knew also that the possession of the Botanic Garden was only the entering wedge for their plan for the destruction of all the noble shade trees in the People's Park from the Capitol to the river to make way for a sixteen-hundred-feet-wide track of desolation as bare and as hot as the Desert of Sahara.

A cartoon entitled "Group of Le Notre-McKim Tree Butchers and Nature Butchers" accompanied the article.

The loss of Andrew Downing's trees troubled many people at the time—and since. The Washington chapter of the American Institute of Architects published a resolution calling "attention to the fact that when adopted, the first step towards [the plan's] fulfillment shall be the planting of trees in their allotted places."

Even after the battle for the Senate Park Commission Plan had been won, skirmishes would continue. The new Union Station, one of the commission's most important recommendations, created few problems because the groundwork had been laid by Burnham, Alexander J. Cassatt, president of the Pennsylvania Railroad, and Senator McMillan. The location proposed at the old Baltimore & Ohio Station on New Jersey Avenue would have required that Massachusetts Avenue be sunk into a tunnel. The location north of Massachusetts Avenue was chosen when Congress agreed to condemn two blocks south of the avenue to provide a forecourt for the monumental station that Burnham would design.

It was more difficult to determine a location for the Lincoln Memorial. The planned Union Station Plaza, Meridian Hill, Arlington Cemetery, and the Soldiers' Home were among the proposed sites. A monumental avenue and tramway between Washington and Gettysburg apparently received serious, though brief, consideration. As an Illinois representative, Joseph Cannon considered his views on a memorial to President Lincoln to have special merit. He particularly opposed the commission's recommended location at the end of the extended Mall, in what Cannon called "that God damned swamp." The Commission of Fine Arts was in favor of the location near the Potomac, quoting statesman John Hay: "The place of honor is on the main axis of the plan. Lincoln, of all Americans next to Washington, deserves this place of honor. He was of the immortals. You must not approach too close to immortals. His monument should stand alone, remote from the common habitations of man . . . Of all sites, this one near the Potomac is most suited to the purpose."

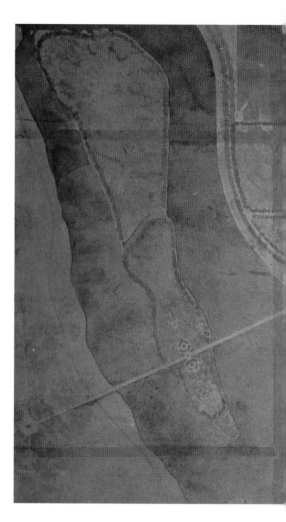

Layout of the Senate Park Commission Plan, 1902. *CFA*

Painting of aerial view of the Senate Park Commission Plan, 1902. *CFA*

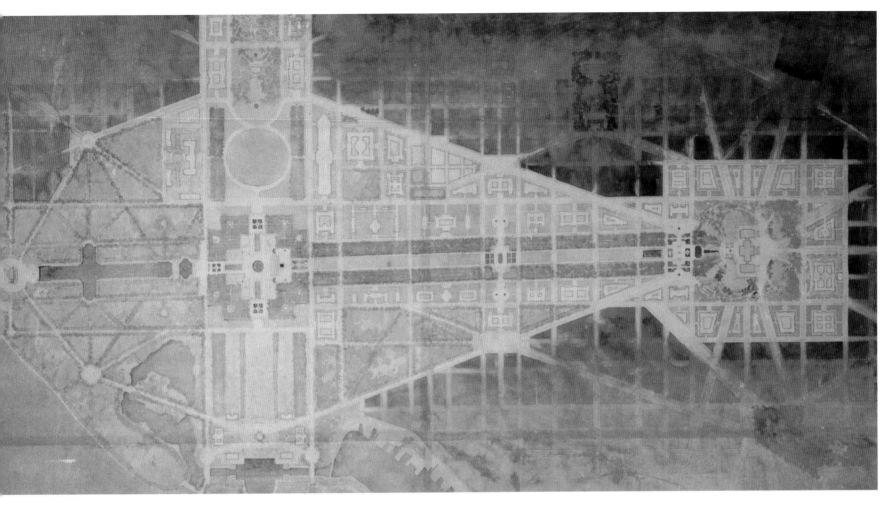

Federal Triangle viewed from the Washington Monument, 1914. *NA*

The Post Office building dominates this view of the area that became the Federal Triangle. One of L'Enfant's original major streets was Ohio Avenue, the diagonal street southwest of the Post Office. It would disappear and Ohio Avenue's mirror image—Indiana Avenue—which intersected Ohio at Eleventh Street, would be truncated. The light industry (in the foreground) around Ohio Avenue would move from the center of the city. This process of increasing commercial use in the center, the most accessible part of the capital, had existed since the city's earliest days and would be accelerated by the Senate Park Commission's recommendations.

The Mall viewed from the Washington Monument, 1915. *CFA*

This photograph shares a vantage point with an image from 1901 (see page 104). The original Department of Agriculture building, designed by Adolph Cluss, was demolished; the new buildings that replaced it (later joined together by a third addition) appear in the right foreground, four hundred feet from the center line of the Mall. The railroad station has disappeared from the Mall, replaced by the new Union Station, which can barely be seen in the distance at the extreme left. The new National Museum of Natural History of the Smithsonian Institution, classical in design, appears in the left foreground. After World War II, debates over appropriate style would enliven the possibilities for federal architecture.

"Group of Le Notre-McKim Tree Butchers and Nature Butchers."

Washington Evening Star, January 14, 1908. *LCND*

The cartoon, which illustrated an editorial protesting the location of the Grant Memorial, bore the caption: "The group of tree butchers and nature-butchers . . . are represented as on their way with axes to make a 'clean sweep,' as they proclaim, of all the grand old trees on the Mall. They are costumed in architectural straight lines. Architect McKim leads the party. He is blowing a big horn—his own. He also has a big head. Architect Donn will be recognized by the conceited upturned nose. In the rear are men bearing a great number of tubbed trees intended to replace the big trees destroyed."

The Lincoln Memorial Commission, appointed by Congress, accepted the Commission of Fine Arts' recommendation, as well as its choice of Henry Bacon as architect. Congress voted its approval in January 1913, and the memorial was finally dedicated in May 1922.

The triangular area between Pennsylvania Avenue and the Mall—"Murder Bay"—had frequently been proposed for public acquisition, and it was notable that the various government offices were poorly housed in buildings scattered about the capital. In 1916, Congress created a Public Buildings Commission. In 1925, in response to President Calvin Coolidge's request, Congress appropriated $50 million for public buildings, and in 1928, it authorized the acquisition of private lands in the triangle, not to exceed $25 million, as recommended by the Senate Park Commission. As proposed by the Commission of Fine Arts, consultants were hired to create an urban design plan that would flesh out the Senate Park Commission's recommendation. All of the buildings were completed between 1932 and 1937.

What became known as the Federal Triangle housed the Departments of Commerce, Labor, Post Office, Justice, and Internal Revenue,

The Mall viewed from above the Capitol, 1933. *ACIC*

Memorial Bridge, the Lincoln Memorial, and the Reflecting Basin were in place; the Department of Agriculture and other federal buildings had intruded into southwest Washington. The Mall east of Fourteenth Street remained unfinished.

The Mall viewed from the Capitol dome, 1940. *CFA*

Once the locations for the new Department of Agriculture and the Grant Memorial were settled, the implementation of the Senate Park Commission Plan was assured. The Mall would be a public open space, eight hundred feet wide between the buildings that lined each side, and the romantic landscape would be replaced by an open grass carpet bordered on each side by a "bosque," a formal arrangement of trees, stretching from Third to Fourteenth Street.

the Interstate Commerce Commission, and the Federal Trade Commission. The National Archives building, within the triangle, was located on the ceremonial Eighth Street axis. Various architects were employed for the different buildings, following an agreed-upon, neoclassical architectural palette. The late-nineteenth-century Romanesque Old Post Office remained, and later plans to demolish it were abandoned.

By 1940, the "Memorial Bridge" recommended by the Senate Park Commission had been completed. Spanning the Potomac River, it connected the Lincoln Memorial and Arlington Cemetery. In addition, the House and Senate office buildings framed the plaza east of the Capitol, and the Supreme Court Building faced the Library of Congress across East Capitol Street. The National Gallery of Art had been built, and the Jefferson Memorial was finally under construction, after acrimonious debate.

Also by this time, the circular park that Andrew Jackson Downing had envisioned between the White House and the Mall had been laid out as an ellipse. West of the Ellipse, and south of the Corcoran Gallery, the buildings of the American Red Cross, the Daughters of the American Revolution, and the Pan-American Union faced the Department of Commerce, which rose on the east of the Ellipse. Facing the Mall west of Seventeenth Street stood the buildings of the Pan-American Union Annex, Public Health Service, Federal Reserve, National Academy of Science, and American Institute of Pharmacy. Two very different views of urban design had been put in place—one east and one west of the Ellipse. East of the Ellipse, the uniform facades of the Federal Triangle frame and define the Mall and the avenues. West of the Ellipse, buildings are set on wide lawns, with little formal relationship to their surroundings.

The Departments of the Interior and State and various quasi-governmental functions were housed in new buildings on undeveloped land in the Foggy Bottom area. The Department of Agriculture and the Bureau of Engraving expanded south across Independence Avenue. These buildings developed independent of any urban design scheme. The 1902 Senate Park Commission's plan did include most of the land they occupied, but its proposal for south of the Mall never generated the level of interest that led to the creation of the Federal Triangle.

Julius Garfinkel & Company, 1930. Designed by Starrett and Van Vleck. *Allen Karchmer*

Interior of the Capitol Theater. Designed by C. W. and George C. Rapp. *LCPP*

Travel on F Street, 1923. *LCPP*

An impressive streetcar network focused on Downtown contributed to the area's prosperity. The automobile, a "jitney," indicates the future of transportation.

Neighborhoods

Commerce grew rapidly in the centers of American cities through the first three decades of the twentieth century. Washington's neighborhoods were affected by this growth in varying ways.

Downtown

By 1900, a cluster of multistory private office buildings had been built in Downtown east of the White House. During the first thirty years of the twentieth century, this area steadily attracted office development. Many of these early office buildings had impressive classical facades. A number have been demolished, but those remaining have been grouped into an Office Building Historic District along Fifteenth Street.

Fourteen department stores could be found in Downtown in 1900. Woodward and Lothrop added two hundred thousand square feet of space during the first two years of the new century. In 1902, the store concentrated its operations in a single building covering most of the block on the north side of F Street between Tenth and Eleventh Streets. Typically, department stores grew by accretion, cannibalizing adjacent structures. In 1930, however, architects Starrett and Van Vleck designed a handsome, neoclassical building for Julius Garfinkel & Company on the northwest corner of F and Fourteenth Streets.

The aesthetic appeal of Downtown increased with the growth of the motion picture industry. After World War I, movie houses moved from storefronts to elaborate, specially designed palaces. In 1927, the Fox Theater, later called the Capitol, opened with 3,500 seats occupying six floors. A Wurlitzer organ and a fifty-piece orchestra enabled audiences to enjoy vaudeville entertainment before films were shown.

During the Great Depression, commerce in Downtown continued to exist, if not prosper. Retail establishments persisted along the east-west streetcar lines on F and G Streets and the north-south streetcar line on Seventh Street. Centre Market was replaced by the National Archives; but Kann's on Eighth and Market Place, Lansburgh's on Seventh and E Streets, Hecht's on Seventh and F Streets, Woodward and Lothrop on F and Tenth Streets, and Julius Garfinkel & Company on F and Fourteenth Streets still competed for the department store market, as they had since early in the century.

In the 1920s, Russians, both Jews and Gentiles, were the largest immigrant group in northwest Washington, reflecting recent upheavals in their homeland. Eastern European Jews flocked to a flourishing Downtown residential community, where the predominantly Eastern European congregation Chai Adom purchased the Assembly Presbyterian Church at Fifth and I Streets. The congregation renamed the picturesque wooden church Ohev Sholom and replaced the steeple with a dome. Merchant Leon Shinberg noted that the Jewish community was bordered by K, Q, Fifth, and Ninth Streets, "with 8th and 9th Streets being predominantly the German-Jewish community, and 7th and east of 7th Street being the eastern Jewish community."

The number of Italian immigrants, only about 100 in 1880 in Downtown, surged to almost 1,500 in 1920 in the northwest section of the city alone. Italian laborers succeeded the Irish in "Swampoodle," northeast of Massachusetts Avenue, but they also worked as food and produce merchants throughout Washington. The first Roman Catholic church established for an Italian Congregation, Holy Rosary, was founded in 1914 in an existing building at First and H Streets. A few years later the church constructed its own building four blocks away at Third and F Streets, close to the Seventh Street retail corridor.

African-American residents made up approximately one third of the population of northwest Washington in 1910 and 1920, concentrated primarily east of Seventh Street and north of Massachusetts Avenue. Segregation prohibited black consumers from shopping in the major Downtown stores. Secondary retail areas frequented by African-Americans appeared on the periphery, including one on Seventh Street between Massachusetts and Florida Avenues. Here black- and white-owned businesses were intermingled, but the clientele was largely black. By 1923, only the trolleys and buses, Griffith Stadium, and Carnegie Library, which opened on Mount Vernon Square in 1903, were not segregated. As one of the few integrated places, the library served an important role for African-American residents.

Washington's Chinatown had been established on the north side of Pennsylvania Avenue east of 4½ Street in the 1880s. In 1890, there were ninety-one Chinese residents. While Chinese laundries and restaurants were scattered throughout the city, only Chinatown had Chinese stores. Although the population grew to several hundred by 1930, there were no more than fifteen women; the Chinese Exclusion Act of 1882 prevented wives from joining their emigrating husbands. Washington's Chinese community developed its own social structure, and by 1930, it was dominated by two "tongs," organizations that served as family associations, fraternal organizations, and benevolent societies for men who were deprived of their families and who faced overt racism.

The obliteration of this Pennsylvania Avenue neighborhood to make way for a proposed municipal center in 1931 created a crisis for the Chinese community. On Leong Tong, the larger of the two tongs, with about two hundred members, worked secretly through real estate agents to obtain space in the 600 block of H Street for all eleven member businesses. Hip Sing Tong, On Leong's fifty-member rival, first threatened to go elsewhere but eventually followed On Leong to the new Chinatown.

When the new location was announced, the reaction was immediate and negative. Area businessmen circulated a petition in opposition—to no avail. Besides bringing new and distinctive businesses to the Seventh and H Street area, Chinatown continued to serve a larger Chinese community. In 1936, there were about 800 Chinese in Washington, with 145 laundries and 42 restaurants dotting the city. Only Chinatown had a marked Chinese atmosphere, with its concentration of distinctively ornamented Chinese-owned businesses. On Leong Tong, renamed the On Leong Merchants Association at the time of the move, led the way. The association bought a double building at 618–620 H Street and added a balcony at the second level and a tile roof above the third floor. Other buildings were soon similarly remodeled with elements recalling Chinese architecture.

617 H Street, c. 1923. *CHS*

Well-maintained residences existed in Downtown during the first decades of the twentieth century and even into the late 1980s.

Outdoor market, part of Centre Market at Seventh Street and Pennsylvania Avenue, 1922. *LCPP*

A young merchant offers produce to Secretary of Agriculture Henry C. Wallace and his wife.

Carroll Row, c. 1800; razed 1887.
NGS

Built by Daniel Carroll, a friend of George Washington, Carroll Row was one of the first group of Capitol Hill houses to be sacrificed to federal expansion when it was razed to make way for the Library of Congress. The row had provided a fashionable boardinghouse for congressmen, including John Quincy Adams and Abraham Lincoln.

Caldwell House, 1809; razed 1933.
CFA

The Caldwell House was replaced by the Jefferson Annex to the Library of Congress. Elias Caldwell's parents were both shot by British soldiers during the American Revolution. Elias was adopted by Judge Elias Boudinot, who financed his education at the College of New Jersey (Princeton University). Caldwell went on to become clerk of the Supreme Court. As a cavalry captain in the War of 1812, during the retreat from the Battle of Bladensburg he moved the Supreme Court library to his own house; the Supreme Court building was soon burned.

Grant's Row, 1871; razed 1929.
LCPP

A speculative venture by Captain Albert Grant, an architect and Union veteran, Grant's Row was built on East Capitol Street. The two large houses in the center were priced at $75,000, which proved to be too expensive. Grant had assumed Capitol Hill would become the fashionable part of the city, but soon after the Civil War, Dupont Circle and the West End became the desirable residential neighborhoods. In the Washington Social Register, "The Elite List" reported that in 1889 only 128 out of 4,000 "elite" lived on Capitol Hill.

Purdy's Court in 1908.
IMP

Purdy's Court was a typical alley community, located just east of the Capitol. In response to similar conditions, Eleanor Roosevelt began her campaign in the 1930s for low-cost government-sponsored housing.

Capitol Hill

At the beginning of the twentieth century, the Navy Yard was the largest ordnance production and research center in the world, and it continued to be one of Washington's largest employers until after World War II. By providing work for unskilled labor, it helped successive waves of new immigrants to establish themselves in the new world. The crescent of older buildings between the Capitol and the Navy Yard offered affordable housing in the area.

After the depression of 1893 had ended, Capitol Hill developers concentrated on empty land north and east of the Capitol–Navy Yard corridor. Almost all dwellings were row houses, built on speculation. Red brick remained the material of choice, and facades often had projecting bays but little in the way of ornamentation. By World War I, fashion dictated flat fronts, often with a roofed porch jutting from the front of each house. New materials came with the new styles—rough-surfaced bricks in shades of yellow and gray, red-tiled roofs.

During the early part of the twentieth century, older structures, generally residential, were beginning to be demolished to make room for newer, usually commercial buildings. Because Capitol Hill was less fashionable than the old Downtown or Dupont Circle, however, it never suffered the devastation of the more desirable neighborhoods. The Hill's population grew steadily from the beginning of World War I until the end of World War II. Although the area gained a few new shops and apartments, many of the neighborhood's streets still retained their earliest buildings.

Changes took place near the Capitol because of federal expansion. Thomas Law's and Daniel Carroll's eighteenth-century houses were demolished to make room for congressional offices, the Folger Library, and the Library of Congress; and the Supreme Court replaced the old "Brick Capitol." One of Capitol Hill's oldest residences, the Maples, was altered in 1937 and became the headquarters of Friendship House, an agency that had originated in 1904 to provide social services to the Navy Yard area's working poor and to non-English-speaking immigrants.

Shaw

Until 1900, Shaw—south of P Street—was a preferred neighborhood for middle-class white residents. The area around Iowa Circle near Thirteenth Street at Vermont Avenue was particularly desirable. Fine Victorian row houses, some embellished with ornamental ironwork, were built in the 1870s and 1880s after street paving and other improvements by the territorial government, under Alexander "Boss" Shepherd, encouraged development of what was then pastureland. In the early twentieth century, Iowa Circle began to lose cachet as a prestigious address for whites when residential areas west and northwest of Shaw were developed, but there were still white residents in Shaw until the beginning of World War II.

North and east of Iowa Circle (renamed Logan Circle in 1930), the Shaw neighborhood had been home to many African-Americans since before the Civil War. Early in the twentieth century, Washington began to develop a black middle class, with a commercial and intellectual

Billy Erskine performing at the Lincoln Colonnade, U Street NW, in the mid-1930s. *SS*

Ku Klux Klan marching on Pennsylvania Avenue, 1926. *LCPP*

Shaw's U Street was the heart of the black community in Washington. It was here that African-Americans celebrated in 1938 when Joe Louis won the heavyweight championship, and here that Duke Ellington played the piano at Jack's Place and the Poodledog Cabaret. Fraternal groups met in the True Reformers Hall, as did the black D.C. National Guard, church groups, and other organizations.

elite concentrated in Shaw. This populace hoped for improved conditions during Woodrow Wilson's presidency, but although Wilson was an eloquent spokesman for the Progressive Movement, it soon became clear that neither the president nor the rest of the Progressives had any interest in improving the lives of black Americans. Wilson, who described himself as a "southern man," sanctioned the extension of racial segregation throughout the federal bureaucracy. With this official endorsement, discrimination increased nationally and locally.

Legislation proposed in Congress during the Wilson administration was specifically aimed at the civil rights of black Washingtonians. Laws were considered that would officially segregate the civil service—already segregated in practice—as well as those that would segregate streetcars and prohibit interracial marriages. Washington's African-Americans

Stoneleigh Court apartments, 1906. *LCPP*

The eight-story Stoneleigh Court was constructed in 1902 on the southeast corner of L Street and Connecticut Avenue. The Alexander Robey Shepherd mansion appears beyond the Stoneleigh, at K Street and Connecticut Avenue. The trees lining Connecticut were probably planted at "Boss" Shepherd's direction.

Mayflower Hotel, 1925. *LCPP*

In this view the Stoneleigh Court apartments can be seen on the right, just beyond the Mayflower on Connecticut Avenue at Desales Street. Traffic on Connecticut Avenue had changed since 1906, when the photograph at left was taken.

Longfellow Building, 1940.
Designed by William Lescaze.

The Longfellow Building, on the northeast corner of Connecticut and Rhode Island Avenues, was the forerunner of the typical modern Washington office building, built to the lot line on all sides. It is on the National Register of Historic Places.

responded with protest and public education and by establishing organizations fostering civic pride. The National Association for the Advancement of Colored People (NAACP) served all three purposes and was widely supported. Although the NAACP was not originally organized in the city, by 1916 its Washington branch was the largest in the country. African-American-owned businesses continued to flourish in Shaw, particularly along U Street.

During the summer of 1919, called "Red Summer" because of its bloodshed, twenty or more riots by whites against blacks occurred throughout the nation. A race riot broke out in Washington on July 19 and continued for five days. A white mob, mostly soldiers, sailors, and Marines, attacked black inhabitants in several locations. One of the areas supposedly targeted was "Colored Boulevard," or U Street, Shaw's principal commercial and entertainment street. It was estimated that two thousand armed black residents of Shaw, some veterans of the same war in which their white attackers had fought, assembled along U Street ready to fight to deter rioters. The Ku Klux Klan, revived during World War I, was strong enough by 1926 to march in full regalia on Pennsylvania Avenue, with no government intervention. Lynching of African-Americans went unchecked throughout the 1920s and beyond, but Washington was spared this most virulent expression of racism.

Dupont Circle

Dupont Circle remained a desirable address throughout the early twentieth century, although new suburban development was drawing well-to-do residents from other parts of the older city. The neighborhood also attracted a black middle class, concentrated in the northeast section above T Street. The 1700 block drew so many distinguished black professionals that it was known as "Strivers' Row." In Washington historian Mara Cherkasky's unpublished oral history, a resident, Inez Brown, recalls "the block as being very beautiful . . . people had their yards and their hedges and shrubbery and their trees and flowers, and it was just very attractive and very desirable." Poorer black residents lived in the area too, but they settled on the narrower streets such as Seaton Street, which had smaller row houses. While Dupont Circle always had both black and white inhabitants, Cherkasky's research indicates two very separate communities. The Dupont Circle Citizens Association, formed in 1922, was all white; the Midway Civic Association, formed in 1939, was all black. For outsiders, however, the neighborhood was characterized by the elaborate mansions of a wealthy white upper class.

In 1940, Dupont Circle was still a fashionable residential neighborhood; however, the area south of P Street included many commercial buildings as well as fine apartment houses. Approximately half of the establishments on Connecticut Avenue between Farragut Square and Dupont Circle were retail stores. The Mayflower Hotel on Connecticut Avenue and Desales Street, the Carleton Hotel on K and Sixteenth Streets, the Roger Smith Hotel on the north side of Pennsylvania Avenue at Eighteenth Street, and other hotels were constructed in what realtors called the West End in the 1920s. The Statler Hotel (which later became the Capital Hilton) was erected at Sixteenth and K Streets just before World War II. These hotels would become important gathering places for military personnel during the war.

Foggy Bottom

The character of Foggy Bottom began to change around the turn of the century. During the nineteenth century, it had been an industrial center because of its access to the Chesapeake & Ohio Canal and the Potomac River, but increased use of rail transport diminished the area's importance to local businesses. Without rail connections, Foggy Bottom could not compete with the area around the rail yards to the northeast, and a number of businesses moved or closed. Many Foggy Bottom residents followed their jobs. Breweries might have continued had it not been for another untimely blow—Prohibition. The Christian Heurich Brewery did reopen in 1933, but it never regained its pre–World War I success and closed permanently in 1960.

East of the industry along the Potomac, Foggy Bottom had always been a residential neighborhood. Most housing in the area was modest, however—typically two stories high with no basement. With their very wide blocks, the older, central Washington neighborhoods, particularly Foggy Bottom, commonly featured alley housing. This property began to be acquired from low-income, often black residents; many other alley dwellers, who rented their houses, were easily displaced. By 1940, the area west and south of the White House and Lafayette Square had become a favored location for public and private institutions. The National Institutes of Health occupied two buildings on the earlier Naval Observatory site. George Washington University filled a block and a half between G and H Streets, and American University occupied a half block south of G Street.

Southwest

The years between 1895 and 1930 were the golden age of residential Southwest. The area's population peaked at approximately thirty-five thousand in 1905. Community institutions reached their full development, with an array of churches, schools, voluntary associations, social agencies, and activities for young and old, black and white. Southwest's

Foggy Bottom, 1915. *LCPP*

This photograph shows a group on an Easter hike with an old canal boat in the right foreground and the abandoned Godey's Lime Kiln in the background.

Foggy Bottom, looking northwest from the Washington Monument in 1922. *NA*

The "temporary" World War I buildings are visible on the Mall. The buildings of the Pan-American Union and the Daughters of the American Revolution are visible on the right, and the new Department of the Interior building is at the far right. The State Department building, then under construction, is on the southwest side of Virginia Avenue.

Jewish population grew from 30 to 190 families and supported a host of institutions, including a synagogue, social service agencies, and the Hebrew Free Loan Association.

The city's first settlement house for white residents, the Barney Neighborhood House, opened in this area in 1900, followed by the Southwest Neighborhood House for black residents. Southwest began to resemble a self-contained small city, offering work and services for most of its inhabitants. In Kathryn Schneider Smith's *Washington at Home* (1988), a longtime resident recalled, "Southwest was a little

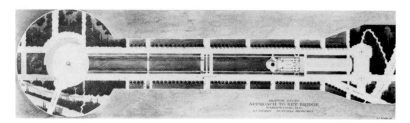

Southwest near First Street, 1934. *NA*

The Capitol is visible in
the background.

**Dumbarton "Buffalo" Bridge over
Rock Creek at Q Street, 1915.**

Designed by Glen Brown and his
son, Bedford, working with the
Commission of Fine Arts, the
Dumbarton Bridge over Rock Creek
was flanked at both ends by a pair of
American bison created by sculptor
A. Phimister Proctor. It is generally
known as "Buffalo Bridge."

**Proposed monumental avenue, Key
Bridge to Rock Creek, 1928.** *CFA*

In 1928, the municipal architect
of the District of Columbia devised
a plan that would make Georgetown
conform to the classicism of the
Senate Park Commission Plan for
the city's monumental core. The
plan attempted to improve traffic
by building a parkway 350 feet wide
from Key Bridge to Rock Creek,
removing all the buildings between
M and Prospect Streets and replacing them with Beaux-Arts facades.
The plan was not well received in
Georgetown and quietly vanished.

town in those days. The streets were paved with brick and lined with tall,
stately elms, like European towns. Everyone knew each other. Whether
there was good news or bad news, we all shared the joys and the sorrow."

Southwest's strong social ties concealed many problems, however.
Federal agencies competed with homeowners for scarce space. The
Bureau of Engraving, the Department of Agriculture, and other government agencies spread into residential areas, replacing blocks of
modest row houses with massive office buildings. Private commercial
interests also expanded, and warehouses, markets, and freight yards
spilled over into residential sections.

These changes increased noise, congestion, and dirt, making the
area less desirable for residents who could afford to move elsewhere.
Absentee landlords, especially the owners of alley houses, reduced
maintenance, diminishing the quality of low-income housing. The
population of Southwest fell to thirty-two thousand in 1920 and to
twenty-four thousand in 1930. As commerce and poverty increased, so
did the ratio of poorer black to wealthier white residents, and Southwest gained a reputation as rundown, crime-ridden, and "blighted."

Southwest residents complained of neglect from the city. Harry
Wender, an activist member of the Southwest Civic Association in the
1930s, for years called for better city services in his area. He wrote, "Truly
an orphan among communities, its problems have never seemed to concern anyone with sufficient interest to attempt their solution." Wender
recalled the battle both the white and the black civic associations waged
to have "obnoxious 4½ Street" repaired and renamed Fourth Street:
"We got the cobblestones removed and the street paved. We got the
street widened and lights put up. Then we put up the biggest celebra-
tion in the history of the city . . . It was the first time that Negroes and
whites paraded together in the history of Washington."

Georgetown

Until World War II, Georgetown still supported a complete cross section of commercial activities, residential communities, and social classes.
Although the capital prospered during and after World War I, and the
population of the District of Columbia grew by almost one third from
1910 to 1920, the population of Georgetown declined by almost one
fifth. Those who lived in Georgetown in the 1920s and 1930s remem-
ber it as a somewhat unfashionable, run-down community with a
small-town character.

In 1915, the city replaced a low-level bridge over Rock Creek at Q
Street with the handsome Dumbarton Bridge. Houses, including the Dumbarton mansion, were moved so that Q Street could be cut through to the
bridge. The streetcar maintenance yards on P Street were eliminated, and
an apartment building took their place. Eventually, five large, walk-up
apartment buildings occupied P and Q Streets adjacent to Rock Creek.

While residents may have approved of the bridge, many
objected—strenuously—to the apartment construction it helped to
trigger by providing new frontage on Q Street and better access to P
Street. John Bilder, a housing reformer, and Bernard Wyckoff, a new
Georgetown resident in 1922, became active in the fight against con-

Children on Georgetown street, late 1930s. *LCPP*

Even though the proportion of single men and women increased, Georgetown continued to be an attractive place for families after

World War I. The narrow streets somewhat inhibited through traffic, and citizens paid attention to the quality of parks and playgrounds. The Progressive Citizens Association actively supported Georgetown's schools, churches, and library.

Cissell Alley, 1908. Photographed by Lewis Hines, from Charles Weller's *Neglected Neighbors in the Alleys, Shacks and Tenements of the National Capital. MLKL*

This photograph of Cissell Alley appeared with the caption: "Their only playground: 'Cissell

Alley' with its ancient cobble stones and its little houses crowded with white people." Historian Kathryn Schneider Smith interviewed former residents of Grace Street, around the corner from Cissell Alley, who remembered a large empty lot across the street from the alley with a fine view down the Potomac.

struction. Backed by incensed citizens, in 1924 they obtained a zoning regulation from Congress to limit new construction in Georgetown to forty feet in height. The law also restricted the construction of new apartment houses, flats, and hotels and the enlargement of existing buildings for such uses. Two years later, the Progressive Citizens Association of Georgetown was formed to represent homeowners' interests and to compete with the Georgetown Citizens Association, a business organization of white men.

Georgetown had always had an unusual number of clubs and social groups devoted to music, sports, bicycling, and almost every kind of personal betterment. Creating the zoning regulations, however, was the most ambitious public action that residents had tackled. In 1928, the District proposed another Georgetown "improvement" that they had little trouble defeating—a monumental avenue cleaving the heart of commercial Georgetown from Key Bridge to Rock Creek.

Many of the older Georgetown families moved out of the area during the early twentieth century. Almost half of the 219 Georgetown families listed in the Social Register in 1903 had left by 1916, replaced by less prominent families. After World War I, this pattern changed. Dennis Gale, in a doctoral thesis for George Washington University that examines demographic changes in Georgetown, reports that beginning in the 1920s, professionals replaced blue-collar workers, both white and black. In the 1930s, the trend accelerated.

Following the stock market crash of 1929, Washington suffered less than most of the country. Accompanying President Franklin D.

Roosevelt's inauguration, young "brain trusters" brought a new luster to Washington. Thousands of new government workers came to run the Works Progress Administration, the Public Works Administration, the National Resettlement Administration, and other recently created agencies. There were about seventy thousand government employees in Washington in 1933; that number more than doubled by 1940 and quadrupled by 1943. It was said that Eleanor Roosevelt suggested that the young people flooding into the capital investigate Georgetown as a convenient and relatively inexpensive neighborhood.

Typical population movements during this period in most of the United States saw skilled and unskilled workers replacing middle- and upper-class families in cities; the transformation of Georgetown, however, was an unusual phenomenon. Conspicuously, the newcomers were recent college graduates. State Department officials, along with a handful of prominent wealthy people, brought attention to Georgetown. Among them were Dean Acheson, later secretary of state under President Harry S. Truman; Newton Baker, secretary of war under President Woodrow Wilson; Robert Bliss, diplomat and civil servant; and F. Lamont Belin, ambassador to Poland.

During the Roosevelt administration, the newcomers to Georgetown had families or were soon to begin them. In the 1930s, the Progressive Citizens Association accordingly focused its attention on neighborhood quality and social reform, addressing issues such as alley dwellings. The Georgetown Citizens Association deplored the lack of parking and the traffic jams on M Street.

Georgetown waterfront west of the Aqueduct Bridge, about 1920. *NA*

Shown in the photograph is the staging area for Key Bridge, constructed from 1917 to 1923 to replace the Aqueduct Bridge. The docks and trestles of 1890 have disappeared, replaced by low sheds associated with shipments of gravel, coal, and ice.

Under New Deal funding, Allied Architects Inc. was established to provide sketches of the original appearance of buildings in Georgetown and to show how removal of later architectural additions would improve them. Thus, the earliest signs of a formalized, conscious movement to restore Georgetown to its nineteenth-century appearance began in 1938 and 1939. During World War II, attention was diverted from preservation, but the Progressive Citizens Association of Georgetown succeeded in planting the idea that the residents—politically and legally—might impose architectural standards on construction and remodeling in Georgetown.

The Georgetown waterfront was one of the neighborhoods of the capital that particularly concerned early-twentieth-century social reformers. In his book *Neglected Neighbors in the Alleys, Shacks and Tenements of the National Capital* (1908), Charles Weller described overcrowding in poorly constructed housing, lack of running water and sanitary facilities, and what he saw as a breakdown of family structure and a decline in health and morality attendant on destructive physical surroundings. In *Port Town to Urban Neighborhood* (1989), Kathryn Schneider Smith recognized the problems Weller identified but concentrated on another, more benign aspect of life on the waterfront—the sense of community.

While the waterfront continued to be a location for light industry, mixed with small clusters of row houses, its composition gradually changed. Southwest Harbor became the District's major port; the railroad yards on Delaware Avenue north of the new Union Station handled valuable goods that once had been shipped through Georgetown. The city built an incinerator on K Street between Wisconsin Avenue and Thirty-first Street, and the General Services Administration erected a heating plant with coal yards and coal-handling facilities between the C & O Canal and K Street next to Rock Creek. In the city's 1920 zoning ordinance, the Georgetown waterfront was labeled "industrial."

The L'Enfant Neighborhoods in 1940

In 1940, dense, mixed-use neighborhoods were clustered around the center of Washington, all within walking distance of Downtown. There were more than one hundred multistory apartment buildings in the Dupont Circle and Foggy Bottom neighborhoods between Sixteenth Street and Rock Creek, south of Q Street, mostly built before 1930. Sixty were notable enough to be recorded by name in the Sanborne Insurance Atlases and the Baist Real Estate Atlases. While the sections of Shaw east of Sixteenth Street were less fashionable, one hundred multistory apartments also stood in this area; more than thirty were worthy of record in the atlases.

All these neighborhoods were largely populated by families with children. There were eleven public and two Catholic secondary schools west of Sixteenth Street, an equal number of churches, and two orphanages; hospitals, libraries, and fire stations could be found throughout the central area of L'Enfant's original city. In addition, the area was sprinkled with "colored" churches and schools. There was institutional but not geographic segregation. Geographic segregation would develop late, abetted by widely affordable private transportation.

By 1900, the city was expanding beyond its Florida Avenue boundary; between 1900 and 1940, most of Washington County was incorporated, platted, developed, made accessible to the center, and included as part of Washington City. The Highway Act, which Congress passed in 1893, and which was clarified in 1898, extended the L'Enfant street pattern to the District of Columbia line. Streetcar lines, many privately financed by suburban developers, were built beyond the center, into and eventually beyond the surrounding District.

Beyond L'Enfant's City

The settlement of the District of Columbia beyond the city center laid out by L'Enfant occurred primarily between 1900 and 1940. Anacostia, across the river from the Navy Yard, was platted soon after the Civil War, and Chevy Chase was begun at the District line in the 1890s. Adams Morgan, Kalorama, and LeDroit Park were natural extensions of Washington's city center. The remainder of the District developed—less systematically—as the avenues were extended and eventually paved and streetcar lines were added.

Cleveland Park grew along Connecticut Avenue, Mount Pleasant and Brightwood along Sixteenth Street and Georgia Avenue, Tenleytown along Wisconsin Avenue, and Brookland along Rhode Island Avenue. Takoma Park, which covered an area within and just beyond the District line, was Washington's first commuter-rail suburb, built around a Baltimore & Ohio station.

Chevy Chase

Chevy Chase, the most ambitious and one of the most attractive and architecturally successful of the suburbs, was founded by the Chevy Chase Land Company, incorporated in 1890. It was the creation of two wealthy westerners, Nevada Senators Francis G. Newlands and William M. Stewart, and retired Army Colonel George A. Ames. Newlands is credited with being the force behind the venture, but Stewart was probably equally important. He bought $300,000 worth of the first stock option, and the Senate backed the creation of Rock Creek Park and the charter of the Rock Creek Railway Company. The company privately financed the extension of Connecticut Avenue to the District of Columbia line and constructed the electric railway at a cost of $1.5 million. In 1903, the *Washington Post* reported that streetcars made the six-mile trip from Pennsylvania Avenue to Chevy Chase in thirty-five minutes, every fifteen minutes.

The Land Company also built an amusement park with a small lake two miles beyond the District line. There, prospective buyers and city pleasure-seekers listened to concerts at the giant blue seashell-shaped bandstand, rowed in the lake for five cents per half hour, bowled, rode the carousel or the ponies, shot in the shooting gallery, or danced at the dance pavilion.

Development was controlled by building regulations and covenants. Houses on Connecticut Avenue were to cost no less than $5,000, and on other streets, no less than $3,000. On Connecticut Avenue, a setback of thirty-five feet was required, and on other streets, twenty-five feet. Alleys, apartments, row houses, and business establishments were forbidden.

The Chevy Chase Land Company provided amenities not found in other subdivisions. Land was given to the public school, All Saints Episcopal Church, post office/library, and hook-and-ladder company. Newlands was the first president of the Chevy Chase Club, which was devoted to riding. When golf became popular in the early twentieth century, it became a golfing club. A 1916 promotional brochure trumpeted: "Chevy Chase for Homes . . . each earmarked by the individuality of its owner . . . [a town] planned to meet the requirements of discriminating people." The varied architecture is described in *Washington at Home* as "Shingle, Colonial Revival, Tudor, French Eclectic, Spanish Eclectic, Mission, Neoclassical, Italian Renaissance, Prairie and Craftsman styles."

Because retail stores were limited and controlled, the Land Company arranged for goods to be delivered. In November 1920, the *Chevy Chase News* described this system: "Coal was ordered through the Land Company, and during summer months a wagon was sent to the city for ice several times a week. If medicine were needed it could be telephoned for and delivered to a car conductor at Fifteenth Street and New York Avenue, or anywhere along the route . . . The conductor would get off the car at Connecticut Avenue and Irving Street and put the medicine in a small box erected for that purpose."

Despite the effort that the Land Company put into amenities, Chevy Chase developed slowly. In 1903, there were apparently only forty-nine families living in the area. Disbursements exceeded income for years, and the Land Company did not pay its first dividend until 1922.

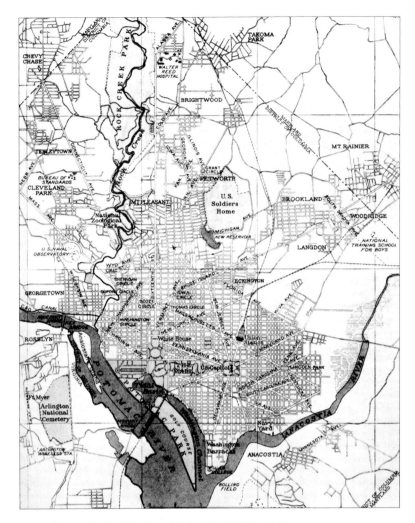

Map of streets in the District of Columbia, 1923. *LCGM*

A Chevy Chase car of the Rock Creek Railway Company. *CCHS*

Chevy Chase, looking east along Rosemary Street to Connecticut Avenue, early 1920s. *RAT*

This photograph was taken around the time Chevy Chase began to be profitable. The settlement pattern of detached houses on fifty-foot-wide lots differed from the nineteenth-century row-house arrangement of the L'Enfant city neighborhoods. Empty lots and young trees indicate that the neighborhood was still new. Front lawns and side yards were dictated by the Land Company.

"Henderson's Castle," enlarged and remodeled 1902, looking north from Florida Avenue. *ES*

Senator John Brooks Henderson built the Richardson Romanesque "Henderson's Castle" in 1888 on Sixteenth and Boundary Streets. The extension to the west (left) of the house is the servants' quarters.

Adams Morgan

Adams Morgan combines several late-nineteenth-century neighborhoods —Meridian Hill, Lanier Hill, and Washington Heights. An area of fine row houses west of Eighteenth Street, Washington Heights developed early in the twentieth century. Prestigious apartment buildings, such as the Wyoming on Columbia Road and the Ontario on Ontario Place, were also built in Adams Morgan in the early twentieth century. By the 1920s, the area entered what Jeffrey Henig, Adams Morgan historian, calls its "white-glove era." The Knickerbocker Theater opened in 1917, and the caterer Avignon Frères arrived in 1918, followed by Ridgewell Caterers and Gartenhouse Furs. In the years following World War I, Adams Morgan was home to prosperous middle- and upper-middle-class Washingtonians.

Kalorama

Kalorama was part of a six-hundred-acre land grant from Charles II to John Langworth. The property passed through several hands and was purchased in 1807 by the poet Joel Barlow, apparently at the urging of Thomas Jefferson. Barlow named his estate Kalorama after the Greek word for "fine view," because of its site on hills overlooking the Potomac River.

In 1887, Kalorama was platted into a number of subdivisions. An article in a June 1882 issue of the *National Republic* addressed "Suburban Residences": "The city has extended so far to the north and west that the heights of the Holmead estate [Kalorama] are now becoming the most attractive portion of the city for residences. The summer temperature is at least five degrees lower than in the city, and refreshing breezes sweep over from the valley of Rock Creek. No other city in the country . . . has been so lavishly supplied by nature with locations for rural homes."

**George Goode house,
north of Columbia Road
in Kalorama, c. 1890.** *SIA*

Ambiguities in the Highway Act of 1893 stopped development until an amended act in 1898 exempted pre-1893 subdivisions from being replatted. In 1887, the District commissioners extended Massachusetts Avenue through Kalorama and built a circle to be named in honor of Stephen Decatur. In 1890, the circle was rededicated to General Philip Sheridan. Mrs. Sheridan built a house at 2211 Massachusetts Avenue from which she could see Gutzon Borglum's statue of the general. During the next two decades, Massachusetts Avenue was lined with the grand Beaux-Arts mansions that still make it one of the most elegant avenues in Washington. Many of these imposing early-twentieth-century houses function today as embassies.

Cleveland Park

In its history and development, Cleveland Park followed somewhat the same pattern as Kalorama. Acquired by George Bell as part of a large land grant patented in 1723, it encompassed an area adjacent to the road to Frederick Town, an old Indian trail used by Maryland farmers delivering tobacco to the port of Georgetown. In the early 1790s, land was purchased by General Uriah Forrest, former mayor of Georgetown and aide-de-camp to George Washington. Forrest and his partners,

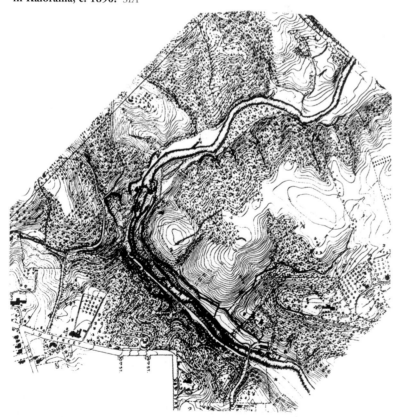

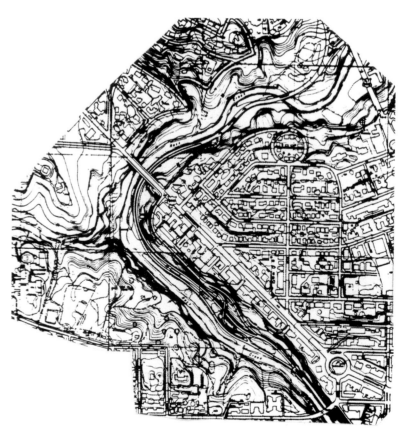

Map of Kalorama, 1884. *ACE*

The Army Corps of Engineers surveyed Washington County beyond its developed areas and published the results in 1884. Among the seventy-five plates, which were sold for ten cents each, was this contour map of Kalorama.

**Map of present-day
Kalorama.** *DCDPW*

successful tobacco merchants, assembled about 1,280 acres, which they patented in 1794 as "Pretty Prospects."

During the early nineteenth century, Pretty Prospects was gradually divided into parcels for country estates. Philip Barton Key built Woodley (now the Maret School) in 1800; Major Charles Nourse built the Highlands (now the Sidwell Friends School) in the 1820s; and H. H. Dent built Springland (still a private residence) in the 1840s. Frances Trollope described Pretty Prospects in 1830: "The country rises in a beautiful line of hills behind Washington which form a sort of undulating terrace on to Georgetown; this terrace is almost entirely occupied by a succession of Gentlemen's Seats."

In 1865, Uriah Forrest's daughter, Ann, gave 23½ acres to her son, George Forrest Greene, who constructed Forrest Hill, a "roomy stone dwelling, built of native stone found on an adjacent field. It was a quiet home for a gentleman of moderate means and refined taste . . . on a hill commanding an extensive prospect, looking on nothing but beauty and breathing nothing but health." The house was purchased by President Grover Cleveland before his wedding to his young ward, Frances Folsom. Transformed into a Victorian summerhouse with a turret overlooking Washington, "Oak View" was the summer White House during Cleveland's first term in office. Another summer resident was Gardiner Greene Hubbard, founder of the National Geographic Society, who hired Boston architect Francis R. Allen to design "Twin Oaks," a frame Colonial Revival summerhouse. Today it is the only nineteenth-century summerhouse surviving in Cleveland Park.

Cleveland Park billed itself as a rural location, close to the city. In 1903, the *Washington Star* called it "Queen of Washington Suburbs," describing it in terms familiar to home buyers: "The park is a cool and pleasant resort. The breeze from the hills makes life one grand sweet song, and the music of the birds stirs the soul."

Construction of Connecticut Avenue, with bridges over Rock Creek and Klingle Valley, by the Chevy Chase Land Company had created development potential all along the avenue. In 1894–95, John Sherman and Thomas Waggaman formed the Cleveland Park Company. Sherman, who was responsible for the design, construction, and sale of houses, followed many of the practices of the Chevy Chase Land Company. He built a stone-lodge community center, provided a stable for residents' horses and carriages, and created a fire and police station.

Sherman employed distinguished local architects to design one-of-a-kind houses. Between 1895 and 1901, he retained Paul Pelz, one of the architects of the Library of Congress, Centre Market, and other important buildings; Waddy Wood, who later designed the Woodrow Wilson house; Frederick Bennet Pyle; and Robert Thompson Head. A 1904 advertising brochure emphasized the community's architectural quality: "Among the sixty houses of the Park, with a single exception there is no repetition of design . . . They are recognized as the most beautiful and artistic homes in the District. In fact, they are known and spoken of far beyond the limits of the District for their beauty and originality."

Cleveland Park differed from Chevy Chase in its access to nearby places of employment. The National Bureau of Standards, which pro-

"Oak View," Grover Cleveland's summer White House, 1868. *LCPP*

"Twin Oaks," Gardiner Greene Hubbard's summerhouse, 1888. *LCPP*

Cover of sales brochure celebrating the benefits of life in Richmond Park, part of Cleveland Park. *MLKL*

Art Deco Uptown Theater on Connecticut Avenue, 1936. *HSW*

"Park and Shop" on Connecticut Avenue, 1930. *HSW*

The Broadmore Apartments are in the background.

center was encouraged on Connecticut Avenue. In 1920, the city's first zoning law controlled development on the avenue, providing for four commercial centers and allowing the remaining abutting property to contain high-rise apartments. The Monterey Pharmacy opened in 1923 on the ground floor of the Monterey Apartments, followed in 1925 by the Great A & P Tea Company and Piggly Wiggly Groceries. One of the country's first shopping centers with off-street parking opened on Connecticut Avenue at Broad Street in 1930, and in 1936, the Uptown Theater opened just down the avenue (both were still in operation in 2000). By 1940, Cleveland Park was fully developed and, with the exception of the clogged automobile traffic that would arrive later, looked much as it appears in the twenty-first century.

Anacostia

Uniontown, which became "Old Anacostia," was Washington's first suburb. In contrast to the streetcar-dependent, middle-class post–Civil War suburbs, it was laid out to attract a working-class population that could walk across the Anacostia River bridge to jobs in the Navy Yard. It did, however, share with the other suburbs close connections to the center, combined with claims of easy access to the countryside.

The site was first identified on a 1612 map, drawn by Captain John Smith, as the Indian village of Nacochtanke. It later took its name from a latinized version of that Indian name, meaning "a town of traders." Thomas Jefferson suggested that Andrew Ellicott add to his Washington map the words "or Annokostia" to the name "Eastern Branch of the Potomac," but the river would continue to be called the Eastern Branch until early in the twentieth century.

In 1853, the federal government purchased land for the Government Hospital for the Insane. Later renamed St. Elizabeth's, the hospital became one of the country's most distinguished institutions of its kind. In 1854, the Union Land Association bought and platted one hundred acres near St. Elizabeth's. Advertised as "situated in the most beautiful and healthy neighborhood around Washington," the land also came with covenants that restricted residence to native-born whites and decreed that there could be no pigs or soap-boiling. Congressional legislation changed the name to Anacostia in 1886—the name Uniontown was extraordinarily popular throughout the country after the Civil War.

One of the developers of Anacostia, John Van Hook, built a large house on Cedar Hill overlooking the community. The Union Land Association failed in the panic of 1873, however, and Van Hook sold Cedar Hill. Despite the failure of his Freedman's Bank, the buyer was Washington's most distinguished black resident, Frederick Douglass, who received a loan from an abolitionist friend. The black and white communities both grew, with separate businesses and institutions. Between 1881 and 1910, six public elementary schools were built for white children and two for black. The area's first secondary school was built in 1935 for the white community; black students would travel across the river until Anacostia High School was integrated in 1955.

Anacostia lagged behind northwest Washington in public services. In 1891, the *Washington Evening Star* reported that "the streets of

vided three hundred jobs, the Geophysical Laboratory of the Carnegie Institute, and the U.S. Geological Survey were located just north of Cleveland Park in the 1900s. The Naval Observatory (today the residence of the vice president) moved from Foggy Bottom to a hilltop just south of Cleveland Park in the 1890s.

In one respect, the policies of the Cleveland Park Company diverged from those of the Chevy Chase Land Company. Despite the fact that the neighborhood was closer to Downtown, a commercial

Hillsdale [in Anacostia] have the appearance of being neglected by the authorities . . . the taxpayers are becoming restive under this neglect. Howard Avenue, for instance, is . . . not even provided with a sidewalk. Water lines are delayed because residents could not afford the costs of installing the pipes from the street."

South of Pennsylvania Avenue, Anacostia, which had contained only 2 percent of the District of Columbia's population in 1920, grew rapidly during the 1930s. Under pressure from the Anacostia Citizens' Association, the District government finally paid attention to the neighborhood—the swampy Anacostia River banks were turned into a park and playground, and a reservoir was added at Fort Stanton Park.

LeDroit Park

LeDroit Park began in 1873 when speculators Anzi Barber and Andrew Langdon bought a fifty-five-acre tract of farmland just beyond Boundary Street. Though outside the city limits, the subdivision was only one block from the end of a recently completed horsecar line, which was later electrified. The developers also emphasized that "walking time"—still the principal method of getting around the city—from this area to the center was comparable to that from Georgetown or Capitol Hill.

The neighborhood was quickly threatened by both the residential and commercial development spreading beyond Boundary Street. In 1867, Howard University was built just north of the area that would become LeDroit Park and was soon the country's leading black university. Howardtown, a black community, was platted in 1870 adjacent to Howard University.

Barber and Langdon built a cast-iron and wood fence around LeDroit Park, which contained gateways only on the side nearest to Downtown. Watchmen were hired to close the gates at night and to keep out intruders, and applicants were screened to permit white residents only. LeDroit historian John Proctor recalled in 1928 that the suburb was "as exclusive a settlement as one might want or imagine . . . its residents were of the very highest type."

James H. McGill had been hired to design and build forty-one detached and semidetached houses during the community's first four years, and over the next decade, he erected twenty-three additional houses. The picturesque houses McGill designed, along with perennials and evergreens to enrich the townscape, were favored by the professionals who bought in LeDroit Park. Former resident Charles Hamilton remembered that "LeDroit Park during that period was the 'flower garden' of Washington. Every resident took pride in cultivation of all kinds—roses and chrysanthemums."

As the city spread northward, newcomers began to fight against the neighborhood's exclusivity. Howardtown expanded, and its residents tore down LeDroit Park's fence. Replaced with barbed wire by LeDroit citizens, it was torn down again. A final effort to replace the fence failed, leaving traffic to flow through the neighborhood. Washington newspapers reported that after "the fence war . . . the park soon lost its former characteristics and became a part of the city with all its advantages and disadvantages."

Navy Yard Bridge across the Eastern Branch to Uniontown, shortly after the Civil War. *NA*

The bridge connecting the future Anacostia community with the Navy Yard was the escape route for John Wilkes Booth when he fled Washington after he had assassinated President Abraham Lincoln.

Birney Public School in Anacostia, 1899. *LCPP*

Birney was one of the two schools built for African-American children between the 1880s and 1910.

Anacostia marshes, c. 1882. *NA*

By the 1930s, these areas were dredged and filled.

Gothic cottage in LeDroit Park on Anne Cooper Circle at U Street, c. 1875. Designed by James H. McGill. *LCPP*

Civil War Medal of Honor winner Major Christian Fleetwood and his family next to their LeDroit Park house, c. 1900. *LCM*

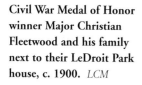

Griffith Stadium and public housing north of LeDroit Park, 1941. *MLKL*

In 1893, Octavius A. Williams, a barber, became the first African-American to own a house in LeDroit Park. His daughter recalled that "Just after we moved in and were having dinner one night, someone fired a bullet through the window . . . [her father] left the bullet in the wall for years so his grandchildren could see it." In her autobiography, *A Colored Woman in a White World*, Mary Church Terrell, a suffragette and civil rights worker with an international reputation, wrote of the problems of persuading real estate agents to even show her available houses: "Finally I selected one only one house removed from Howardtown . . . located in LeDroit Park." When the Terrells made a bid, the white owner refused to sell. A white real estate agent friend bought the house, then transferred the title to the Terrells. Four years later, in 1894, they moved to a large LeDroit house and lived there for fifteen years. By that time, a number of black homeowners lived in LeDroit Park.

The changing profile of LeDroit residents reflected a shifting racial pattern throughout the city. Once racially mixed, with residential

segregation limited to small areas, such as alleys or blocks on one side of a street, during the first part of the twentieth century the city's black and white inhabitants regrouped into larger racially homogeneous concentrations.

As it was in other city neighborhoods, U Street in LeDroit Park became the important center for Washington's black community, especially at Georgia Avenue, one block west of LeDroit Park. In this area, African-American-owned stores joined seven movie theaters, a YMCA, two newspapers and several publishing firms, and a number of Baptist and Methodist churches and elementary schools. By 1940, two distinguished black secondary schools, Armstrong Technical School and Dunbar High School, were located in LeDroit Park. Dunbar High School was named after the most famous resident of the neighborhood, Paul Lawrence Dunbar, who was described by William Dean Howells in *Harper's Weekly* as the best black poet in the country. Dunbar came from Ohio to LeDroit Park, where he found "a very congenial and delightful circle of friends." In 1899, Dunbar and his new wife, the writer Alice Moore, moved into an old McGill house at 321 Spruce Street. In his essay "Negro Society in Washington," published in the December 14, 1901, issue of the *Saturday Evening Post*, Dunbar wrote of the black middle-class experience in Washington: "Here exists a society which is sufficient unto itself—a society which is satisfied with its own condition, and which is not asking for social intercourse with whites. [In LeDroit Park are] homes finely, beautifully and tastefully furnished. Here comes together the flower of colored citizenship from all parts of the country."

LeDroit Park thrived as a socially elite, black middle-class neighborhood. When former resident Charles Hamilton returned to the neighborhood he found nothing changed except "the tint of the complexions of the inhabitants . . . the darker race . . . now made LeDroit Park the most orderly and attractive 'colored section' of Washington."

While LeDroit Park's physical setting changed little during the early decades of the twentieth century, its surroundings changed enormously, as more and more row houses and businesses crowded its edges. In 1919, Clark Griffith built his thirty-four-thousand-seat baseball park; its bleachers and center field wall abutted the backyards of houses on U Street. Later, during the Depression, the National Capital Housing Authority (NCHA) built public housing on the northern boundary of LeDroit Park using New Deal financing. When the Williston Apartments opened on W Street, all thirty units were immediately filled. The NCHA also opened the V Street Homes and Kelly Miller Dwellings, totaling 169 rental apartments. The V Street Homes building was constructed on the site of Bland's Court, an old alley community that had been frequented by Paul Dunbar.

Mount Pleasant

In the early nineteenth century, the area that became Mount Pleasant was home to the Washington Jockey Club's racetrack. Before the Civil War, the area was divided into estates. John Holmstead owned forty-six acres west of Fourteenth Street and north of Boundary Street. He called his home Meridian Hill; the name was later applied to the park on the east side of Sixteenth Street above Florida Avenue.

Immediately after the Civil War, lots had been platted in what became Mount Pleasant. Maine native Samuel P. Brown bought land, at bargain prices, from a southern sympathizer who had fled Washington. Brown attracted so many residents from New England that after the Civil War, this area had many of the physical and civic characteristics of a New England village, with a union hall and regular town meetings. Bordered by Rock Creek and situated on rolling land above the city north of Boundary Street, Mount Pleasant's location justified its name.

The neighborhood, however, was isolated from the center by the escarpment that formed the northern border of L'Enfant's city. Although there was a horsecar line on Fourteenth Street connecting the area to Centre Market, in 1890 Fourteenth Street was still an unpaved road. In an 1898 letter to Senate District Committee Chairman James McMillan (sponsor of the Senate Park Commission Plan), a Mount Pleasant resident complained that it took more time to commute downtown than to travel to Baltimore.

Most of the neighborhood did not develop until Sixteenth Street was improved early in the twentieth century. Missouri Senator John Henderson's wife, Mary, had lobbied to make Sixteenth Street an "avenue of the presidents," home to embassies, and Samuel Brown secured an electric streetcar line for the street and straightened and widened it. While Sixteenth Street never became Mary Henderson's embassy row, it was soon lined with imposing, generally classical houses. The Mount Pleasant Citizens Association, founded in 1910, campaigned for the construction of parks and community buildings, including a school and a branch library. By the 1930s and 1940s, large apartment buildings on Sixteenth Street brought traffic and short-term residents to the community.

Brightwood

Brightwood's first settler was James White, whose descendants lived in the area until after World War II. By 1772, White had built a log cabin on his 536 acres of land, acquired by royal patent. Before the Civil War, the area provided high-quality fruit and vegetables, and greenhouses supplied trees for Andrew Jackson Downing's "greening" of the Mall.

Brightwood, on the Seventh Street Toll Road (now Georgia Avenue), was the site of Fort Stevens, the only fort among the ring of defenses around Washington to become engaged in battle during the

Picnicking at a Rock Creek ford near Mount Pleasant, c. 1900. *NZP*

Civil War. When General Jubal Early's Confederate cavalry threatened the city, President Lincoln rode out to watch the skirmish in his famed top hat; he was ordered to take cover under penalty of arrest.

The toll gate near James White's homestead was the center of the community that became Brightwood in 1861, when the area acquired a new post office. That the area was attractive is suggested by "Boss" Shepherd's choice of it in the 1870s as the site of his country estate, later subdivided as Shepherd Park.

The Brightwood Railway Company was chartered in 1888. After it failed once, it was reorganized at the insistence of the Brightwood Avenue Citizens Association. By 1910, there were 459 households in Brightwood, three times as many as in 1880. The black population, almost half the community in 1880, declined to about 15 percent in 1910.

Between 1910 and 1940, Brightwood was absorbed into the expanding city of Washington. One of the most active participants in its development was Harry Wardman, described in his obituary by the *New York Times* as the "man who overbuilt Washington." According to Smith's *Washington at Home,* it was estimated that when he died in 1938, one-eighth to one-tenth of the city's population lived in buildings built by Wardman.

Tenleytown

In 1713, Thomas Addison and James Stoddert were awarded a patent of more than three thousand acres from Charles Calvert, Lord Baltimore. Their land, which they named "Friendship," stretched from today's American University to Bethesda, Maryland. Around 1790, John Tennally opened a tavern on an old Indian trail that became Braddock Road, the first military road in colonial America. Tennally Tavern set the tone, and the area had a raffish reputation throughout the nineteenth century.

During the Civil War, an army encampment supported Fort Pennsylvania, renamed Fort Reno after General Jesse Lee Reno. After the Civil War, Fort Reno became a largely black community, home to newly freed slaves, with three churches—Baptist, Methodist, and Episcopal—and a grammar school. By 1874, there were also four churches devoted to white congregations—Roman Catholic, Baptist, and two Episcopal. Because of its taverns, however, the village continued to have an unsavory reputation, for drunkenness and fights.

By the 1920s, Tenleytown was overtaken by the development spreading north from the center. The Friendship Citizens Association lobbied for civic improvements; the old houses around Fort Reno were demolished to make way for Fort Reno park, part of a plan to turn all the Civil War forts into a ring of park/recreation centers.

Land was acquired for a water reservoir, and for Alice Deal Junior High School in 1931 and Woodrow Wilson Senior High School in 1935. By the 1930s, Braddock Road had become Wisconsin Avenue, and it was paved and had a streetcar line. Responding to increasing travel by automobile, most major streets were paved. In 1939, chain-store shopping came to Tenleytown, and a People's Drug Store opened on Wisconsin Avenue. In 1940, Sears, Roebuck and Company built a department store at the intersection of Wisconsin and River Road; Giant Food Shopping Center opened across the street and included a rooftop garage.

Real estate agents apparently thought "Friendship" to be a tonier designation than Tenleytown, and by 1940, the name on the neighborhood post office had changed. The town's name soon reverted to Tenleytown, however.

Brookland

The area around what would become Brookland was farmland before the United States or the city of Washington had come into existence. Early in the nineteenth century, Nicholas Queen gave his daughter

Anne 150 acres from his 1,500-acre estate. In 1840, Jehiel and Anne Queen Brooks built a large house they called "Belair"; a reputation for clean, pure air persisted as the area developed.

In 1873, the Baltimore & Ohio Railroad built its western branch along the western edge of the Brooks farm. In 1885, the Catholic University of America established a suburban campus beyond the western edge of the farm. Colonel Brooks's heirs sold 140 acres to developers who platted a subdivision in 1887, which they called Brookland. A real estate brochure summed up Brookland's virtues in 1892: "Brookland... has an elevation of two hundred feet above the Potomac River at high tide...A charter has been granted the Suburban Street Railway Company to build an electric road from the Centre Market to Brookland...The District...[has] built a Brick Schoolhouse, erected Street Lights, and laid plank sidewalks on part of the streets."

Catholic University had begun to influence the area as early as 1889, when the Brooks mansion was converted to a Catholic school to be operated by St. Anthony's Church. The erection of the Franciscan Monastery and the Shrine of the Immaculate Conception added to the area's Catholic architectural presence. Over time, many Brookland houses were rented or bought by Catholic orders. In the years between the world wars, more than fifty orders were represented, and their members, walking from home to church or university in their habits, helped Brookland earn its nickname, "Little Rome."

Takoma Park

Takoma Park was a commuter-railroad suburb that originally developed around the Metropolitan Branch of the Baltimore & Ohio Railroad. The Metropolitan Branch, completed in 1873, ran from the downtown station on New Jersey Avenue to Point of Rocks, Maryland, and is still an active commuter line.

The community began in 1883, when Benjamin Franklin Gilbert invested $6,500 in a ninety-acre parcel that lay partly in the northeastern corner of the District of Columbia and partly in Maryland. Gilbert took the name Takoma from an Indian word meaning "high up, near heaven"; he changed the c to a k to avoid confusion with Tacoma, Washington.

In his 1886 real estate brochure, "The Villa Lots of Takoma Park: A Suburb of Washington City," Gilbert advertised lots ranging from fifteen cents to five cents per square foot, lower than the eighteen cents per square foot offered in Washington City. He pointed out to government workers that "all you need is a moderate income. Many Department clerks are paying sums as monthly rentals that would buy a home in Takoma Park if applied to purchase money...[and taking account of] the keeping of a cow, the raising of chickens, and a garden spot," the cost of living could be further reduced.

Gilbert continued to assemble land and lay out subdivisions, and by 1888, he had space for a thousand-acre community. He built the 140-room North Takoma Hotel in 1892, with its own railroad depot; and he persuaded Boston physician R. C. Flowers, after whom Flower Avenue is named, to buy land above Sligo Creek at the northeastern corner of the suburb for a sanitarium (although the doctor's plans were never realized). Gilbert was warned by his friends in the real estate business that the hotel was a risky venture, but he went ahead nonetheless. He built it as the panic of 1893 swept the country; afterward, he never recovered financially and finally lost control of Takoma Park.

The town preserved the lovely woods within which it was built, but early residents had little else to cheer about. In the beginning, this cluster of houses, seven miles from Downtown, had no electricity, no piped-in water, no paved roads or sidewalks. Residents tutored their children in their houses until 1887, when Montgomery County, in Maryland, built a four-room frame schoolhouse on Tulip Avenue. The Takoma Park Citizens Association persuaded the District of Columbia to build the classical-style Takoma Park Elementary School in 1901, which functioned until the 1950s.

In 1903, Gilbert persuaded Elder Ellen G. White and other Seventh Day Adventist Church leaders to relocate the church's headquarters from Battle Creek, Michigan, to Takoma Park. The Adventists bought land near the town center for a general conference headquarters building and for a structure that would house the operations of the church's Review and Herald Publishing Association. They also bought fifty acres of Dr. Flowers's undeveloped land for the Washington Training College and Washington Sanitarium, now called the Washington Adventist Hospital. In 1907, electric power lines were brought in to serve the hospital, and gas mains and telephone lines followed. Soon the residents of Takoma Park shared these modern conveniences.

Demolition in the City Center

As residential neighborhoods beyond the city center proliferated, the center began to empty out. The fine residential area around F Street near the Treasury had been engulfed by commercial expansion before 1900. By World War II, two other residential neighborhoods in today's Downtown—one centered on Judiciary Square and the other on Lafayette Square—had been replaced by commerce. East of Seventeenth Street and south of K Street, older buildings gave way to commercial and government office buildings. In the western part of the center, older buildings were replaced by multistory apartments, hotels, and retail stores. A number of public and private institutions opened in Foggy Bottom. A new building type appeared throughout the city center, particularly in the row house neighborhoods west of Connecticut Avenue: the multistory parking garage for private automobiles.

Neighborhoods in central Washington became more dense. Vacant lots were filled in; low buildings were replaced by tall ones. In addition to changes in neighborhood scale, there were changes in quality. Some of the city's most distinguished buildings were destroyed by 1940; many are described in James M. Goode's *Capital Losses: A Cultural History of Washington's Destroyed Buildings* (1979).

Buildings demolished between 1900 and 1940. *JRP*

The areas shaded in black on this map of Washington's center in 1900 indicate buildings that were razed by 1940. The extensive demolition that occurred between Pennsylvania Avenue and the Mall, and on the Mall itself, was the work of the Senate Park Commission.

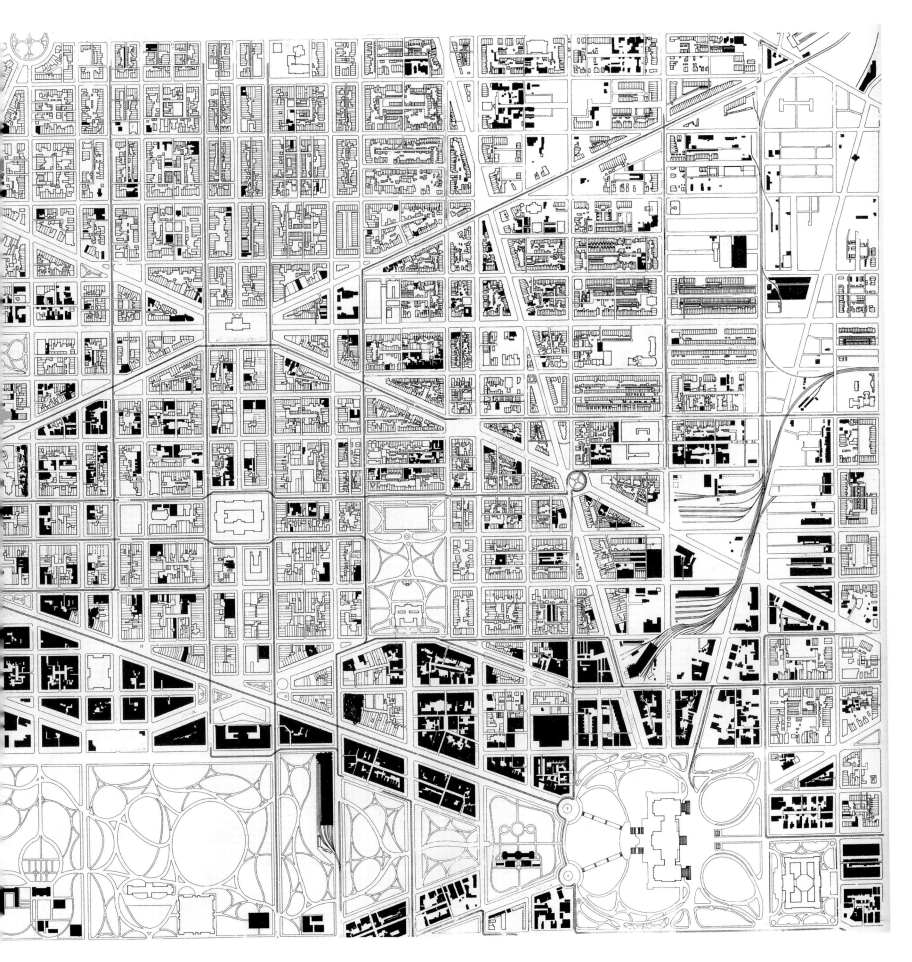

143

McLean House, 1860; razed 1939. *LCPP*

One of Washington's most opulent mansions, the McLean House was rebuilt by architect John Russell Pope in 1907, on I Street, south of McPherson Square in Downtown. Evalyn Walsh McLean was famous as the owner of the Hope Diamond and as a hostess of wildly extravagant parties.

Franklin Terrace, c. 1875; razed 1934. *RAT*

This 1880 photograph of K Street in Downtown shows the elegant row houses just west of Franklin Square, typical of the opulent houses and rows in Downtown that were demolished in the first half of the twentieth century. The wide (147-foot) right-of-way permitted the setback of these residences, which boasted front lawns behind cast-iron fences. The east row was designed by Adolph Cluss. The last house was razed to make room for the Little Tavern Sandwich Shop and the Otts Service Station.

Palmer House, 1884; razed 1926. *RAT*

In *Capital Losses,* James Goode observes: "What a refreshing interlude the Palmer House would be today had it survived among the rows of repetitious and mediocre commercial construction of K Street. If this house had been in a residential section of London, Paris or Vienna that had become commercial in the twentieth century it would have stood a far better chance of survival . . . preserving a charming ambience while still providing the necessities of modern day life."

Bancroft House, 1851; razed 1922.
MLKL

The preeminent nineteenth-century American historian George Bancroft served Presidents Jackson, Polk, and Lincoln. His last post was as American minister to Berlin under Presidents Johnson and Grant, after which he returned home to finish his ten-volume *History of the United States* and its six-volume revision. When he was not writing, he spent his time entertaining Washington intelligentsia in his house on Lafayette Square.

Hay-Adams House, 1884; razed 1927. Designed by H. H. Richardson. *CFA*

This Lafayette Square double house on the corner of Sixteenth Street in Downtown was demolished to make room for the Hay-Adams Hotel. John Hay and Henry Adams were leaders in late-nineteenth-century Washington intellectual circles. Hay, secretary to President Lincoln, later negotiated the Hay-Poncefort Treaty, which led to the creation of the Panama Canal. Adams wrote *Mont-Saint-Michel and Chartres* and *The Education of Henry Adams,* both classics.

Baltimore & Potomac Station, 1873; razed 1907. *GWU*

During the nineteenth century, all southern rail traffic used the Baltimore & Potomac Station (also known as the Pennsylvania Station, after the holding company). The station and its 130-foot train shed, along with piles of coal, were removed from the Mall by the Senate Park Commission, as were other historically important Victorian buildings. On July 2, 1881, President James A. Garfield was assassinated at the station by Charles Guiteau, a mentally deranged office seeker. In 1903, engineer Joseph Brady left the station and headed south on his ill-fated journey, to be immortalized in the ballad "The Wreck of Old 97."

Richmond Hotel, 1883; razed 1922.
Designed by Gray & Page. *GWU*

The Richmond, on the northwest corner of H and Seventeenth Streets, was originally designed as an apartment house, with a corner tower and roofscape patterned after Chambord, the Loire Valley chateau. Two Greek Revival mansions were demolished to provide space for the hotel. Bancroft House can be seen behind the hotel, on the right. Many post–Civil War hotels stood for only half a century.

Brown's Hotel, c. 1805; razed 1935. *ES*

Like many nineteenth-century buildings, this structure at Pennsylvania Avenue and Sixth Street was elaborately remodeled several times, but it served as a hotel continuously for 130 years. As the Indian Queen and then as Brown's Marble Hotel, it was (with the National Hotel across the street) the most fashionable hotel in Washington before and during the Civil War.

St. Charles Hotel, 1820; razed 1926. *LCPP*

The porch that was added circa 1860 gave this Federal-style building a southern flavor. Six pens for holding slaves were built in the basement—which extended beneath both Third Street and Pennsylvania Avenue—with grilles for light and ventilation. After the slave trade was outlawed in the District of Columbia as part of the Compromise of 1850, southern planters stayed at the St. Charles, which also housed their slaves.

**Shoreham Hotel, 1887;
razed 1929.** *LCPP*

The Shoreham, on the northeast corner of H and Fifteenth Streets, was a pre-Beaux-Arts mélange of styles. It was a fashionable apartment hotel for members of Congress from New York and New England. Woodrow Wilson and his family lived there when he was inaugurated as president; it was also a meeting place for Wilson's advisers—William McAdoo, Joseph Tumulty, and Bernard Baruch.

**Arlington Hotel, 1869;
razed 1912.** *HSW*

Built by William Corcoran in Washington's then fine residential area at Vermont Avenue and I Street, the Arlington was the most luxurious of the post–Civil War hotels, catering to kings and ambassadors. The financier J. P. Morgan stayed only at the Arlington, in his private suite of rooms. The Arlington and Ebbitt House were considered the best hotels in Washington until early in the twentieth century, when the new Willard and the Raleigh became more desirable.

**Ebbitt House, 1872;
razed 1926.** *CHS*

A favorite of generals and congressmen, the Ebbitt House, at F and Fourteenth Streets, was elaborately decorated on the interior as well as on the exterior. It had a twenty-five-foot-high marble-encrusted lobby and a famous, intricately paneled bar. The Old Ebbitt Grill, which initially moved east on F Street when the Ebbitt was demolished, today can be found on Fifteenth Street, half a block north of F Street.

Metropolitan Methodist Church, 1854; razed 1936. *HSW*

Methodists had worshiped in Washington since the early 1790s but had built no church of any consequence before the Civil War. In 1852, eight members of the old Wesley Methodist Church purchased the southwest corner of C Street and 4½ Street NW in Downtown, one of the most desirable residential neighborhoods in the capital. The General Conference of the Methodist Church voted to call for funds to erect a building that could seat two thousand people.

The Gothic Revival church had a spire 240 feet high, making it the tallest private structure in the city. The first 100 feet consisted of stone; the rest was made of wood. The wood tower swayed more than six feet in a windstorm in 1876, dropped into the masonry base, and was reinforced and rebuilt.

Pews were assigned to each state and territory, and to the president, vice president, and other dignitaries. In 1884, the building debt of $200,000 was finally paid off. The church was known as the "Westminster Abbey of American Methodism."

Trinity Episcopal Church, 1849; razed 1936. Designed by James Renwick Jr. *LCPP*

William Corcoran provided the lot on Third and C Streets and probably persuaded Renwick to use the Gothic Revival plan that had been rejected for the design of the Smithsonian. When the church was built, this was one of the most fashionable neighborhoods in the city, and the church was surrounded by hundreds of handsome Federal houses.

Foundry Methodist Church, 1864; razed 1902. Designed by Adolph Cluss and Joseph Wildrich von Kammerhueber. *LCPP*

The church was built during the last years of the Civil War. Constructed at costs double that of the original estimate, it was attractive when completed, but its Downtown location at G Street and Fourteenth Street NW was rapidly becoming commercialized. Noise from streetcar lines on both Fourteenth and G Streets made services unpleasant. The building was sold, and the congregation moved to Sixteenth and P Streets.

Freedman's Savings Bank, 1869; razed c. 1900. *SI*

The Freedman's Savings Bank originated when Civil War Union General N. P. Banks established banks for black soldiers and free blacks in Norfolk, Virginia; Beaufort, South Carolina; and New Orleans. In 1865, Congress established a permanent Freedman's Savings Bank, with branches throughout the East. In 1869, the bank moved into its new quarters on Lafayette Square, built at the then enormous cost of $200,000. By 1873, the Freedman's Savings Bank held $57 million for 72,000 depositors. However, many managers and cashiers, white and black, were corrupt or incompetent; there was little oversight; and loans were often made without collateral. After the

panic of 1873, the trustees fired the honest but incompetent Reverend John W. Alvord (a white chaplain in Sherman's army who had proposed the bank) and appointed Frederick Douglass as executive head. Three months later, the bank collapsed.

Corcoran Office Building, 1873; razed 1917. *LCPP*

This Renaissance Revival building occupied the entire block of Fifteenth Street from Pennsylvania Avenue to F Street. Local artists had studios here, and two generations of art students took lessons in painting and drawing from Washington's most important artists. This building, considered the best location for viewing inaugural parades, was replaced by the Washington Hotel.

Riggs Bank, 1824; razed 1904.
Designed by George Hadfield. *HSW*

Located on H and Fifteenth Streets in Downtown, this bank was a branch of the Second Bank of the United States, the nation's largest private bank. When President Andrew Jackson stopped depositing federal funds there, Second Bank sold many of its branches and soon closed. This particular branch was purchased by the newly formed Corcoran and Riggs Bank.

Shepherd Centennial Building, 1875; razed 1911. *AOC*

Alexander Shepherd's Centennial Building, named to honor the hundredth anniversary of the American Revolution, was erected on the corner of Twelfth Street and Pennsylvania Avenue. It was the most modern office building in Washington at the time. Shepherd was removed from office in 1874; he was forced to sell the Centennial and other properties when he moved to Mexico in 1880.

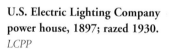

U.S. Electric Lighting Company power house, 1897; razed 1930. *LCPP*

Stilson Hutchins, founder of the *Washington Post,* visited Thomas Edison's laboratory to investigate the first practical electric light in 1879. Hutchins built Washington's first electric generator in his new building in 1880. Many electric companies were begun during the next decades; all of them, including the U.S. Electric Lighting Company, were eventually absorbed by the Potomac Electric Power Company. The site of U.S. Electric, on the northeast corner of Constitution Avenue and Fourteenth Street, was subsumed by the Federal Triangle.

Manassas Panorama Building, 1885; razed 1918. *LCPP*

Located on the present site of the Commerce Building, this structure, 125 feet in diameter, contained a huge mural of the Second Battle of Manassas, which was subsequently replaced by depictions of the Battle of Shiloh and then of the Battle of Gettysburg. In 1903, it became the Automobile Livery Building, the city's first automobile garage.

Harvey's Restaurant, c. 1830; razed 1932. *LCPP*

Remodeled with this cast-iron front in 1866, Harvey's was the city's most famous restaurant for almost a century. Located on the southeast corner of Pennsylvania Avenue and Eleventh Street, it was leveled to make way for the Federal Triangle. First known as Harvey's Ladies' and Gentlemen's Oyster Saloon, the restaurant was steaming five hundred wagon loads of oysters a week by 1863. Every president from Ulysses S. Grant to Franklin D. Roosevelt dined at Harvey's.

Department of Agriculture, 1868; razed 1930. Designed by Adolph Cluss. *NA*

Because of the rapid expansion of the frontier, the Department of Agriculture was created in 1863 and elevated to cabinet rank in 1869. The department collected and distributed seed stock for American farmers. Noted for its formal gardens, which extended to Constitution Avenue, it also included greenhouses and experimental gardens. Cluss's building was demolished because it extended into the Senate Park Commission's plan for the Mall.

Ringold House, 1812, 1872; razed 1914. *NA*

This early-nineteenth-century mansion, built on the northeast corner of L and Twenty-fifth Streets, was frequently rented to distinguished occupants. Two British ministers to the United States lived in the house: Sir Charles Bagot in 1816, and Sir Frederick Bruce in 1865. In 1872, it was purchased by the Columbia Hospital for Women, and the house was demolished in 1914 to make way for the present hospital building. Columbia was one of the first hospitals in America to establish a prenatal clinic and is one of the oldest American hospitals for women.

Van Ness Mansion, 1813–17; razed 1908. Designed by Benjamin Latrobe. *LCPP*

This Greek Revival mansion, on C Street and Seventeenth Street NW, was initially a social center for members of Congress. The elegant house was abandoned as a residence after the Civil War because of its location on the malaria-ridden Tiber Canal and was later demolished to make way for the Pan-American Union building.

British Legation, 1872; razed 1931. *MLKL*

Constructed on the northeast corner of Connecticut Avenue and N Street, the British Legation was the first significant structure to be erected near Dupont Circle. Its location influenced the development of the area in the late nineteenth century as the most elegant residential sector of Washington. Within ten years after the British minister occupied the legation, Phillips Row was built adjacent to it and Alexander Graham Bell soon built his house a few doors to the south.

Academy of the Visitation, 1877; razed 1923. Designed by Adolph Cluss. *LCPP*

The completed Catholic academy occupied a full block on Connecticut Avenue south of L Street. The nuns, who belonged to a poor convent, supported their school until 1919 by selling parts of the four-acre tract on which the building stood.

Streets and Other Public Open Spaces

Much of the most effective planning for public open space was accomplished in the twentieth century, supplementing the eighteenth-century work of L'Enfant. The National Capital Parks, a branch of the National Park Service, which manages the public parks of the capital, traces its lineage to the three original federal commissioners appointed by President George Washington in 1791. Under the agreement made by the president with the nineteen landowners on March 29, 1791, the commissioners consented to convey, without compensation, the portions of these proprietors' land needed for streets.

Because of the complex street intersections in the L'Enfant plan, many street fragments were scattered about the city. These parcels, plus L'Enfant's circles and squares, were labeled "reservations" and assigned numbers. Land was also needed for public buildings and public improvements. Soon after Andrew Ellicott had completed his official engraving of L'Enfant's plan, 541 acres were purchased for this purpose at $66.67 per acre, for a total of approximately $36,000.

This land was under the jurisdiction of the commissioners, who were replaced in 1802 by a superintendent appointed by the president. In 1816, the office of the superintendent was abolished and his duties assigned to a commissioner of public buildings. The act of March 3, 1849, establishing the Department of the Interior, provided in Section 7 "that the . . . powers now exercised by the President . . . over the Commissioner of Public Buildings shall be exercised by the Secretary of the Interior."

A congressional act in 1898 reassigned the commissioners' duties, noting that "the park system of the District of Columbia is hereby placed under the exclusive charge and control of the Chief of Engineers of the United States Army." After several more permutations, a 1933 executive order established the Office of National Parks, Buildings and Reservations of the National Park Service, a division of the Department of the Interior.

In 1866, Major Nathaniel Michler had reported to the Senate on the suitability of the valley of Rock Creek as a public park, and in 1890, Congress authorized the establishment of Rock Creek Park as a national park. A commission headed by the army chief of engineers acquired 1,606 acres in the Rock Creek watershed at a cost of $1,174,511.45. Later purchases brought the park area to 1,737 acres.

Two more parks were added after 1900, largely on land dredged from the Potomac River. West Potomac Park, between the Mall and Rock Creek, became part of the National Capital Parks in 1907. East Potomac Park, dredged from swampy land southwest of the Washington Monument, became part of the National Capital Parks in 1913. Parts of both parks were incorporated into the Senate Park Commission Plan. In 1913, the Rock Creek and Potomac Parkway Commission was established; Rock Creek Parkway and Potomac Parkway, completed in sections over a number of years, became among the most heavily traveled roads in the District of Columbia.

The recommendations of the Senate Park Commission had inspired successive reforms: the establishment of the Commission of Fine Arts in 1910, the Act to Regulate the Height of Buildings passed the same year, and the Washington Zoning Ordinance of 1920. Only the work of L'Enfant and the Senate Park Commission have exceeded the importance of the Act to Regulate the Height of Buildings in creating the physical character of the national capital. The act sets building heights as a function of street width. On residential streets, the maximum height is 90 feet; in commercial areas, it is street width plus 20 feet, with a maximum of 130 feet, except that 160 feet is permitted on the north side of Pennsylvania Avenue between First and Fifteenth Streets. Certain architectural embellishments, and mechanical spaces set back from the face of the building, are permitted above the cornice line.

These height limitations have been attacked in Congress, the courts, and the press. They have been defended with passion by the Commission of Fine Arts, the Committee of 100 on the Federal City, and private citizens. The private nonprofit Committee of 100 on the Federal City was founded in 1923 "to sustain and to safeguard the fundamental values—derived from the tradition of the L'Enfant plan and the McMillan Commission—that give the Nation's Capital so much of its distinction, its beauty, and its grace as a community," according to a description by Richard Striner in 1995.

In the early 1920s, many citizens feared that the achievements of the preceding two decades might prove to be tenuous without continued oversight and advocacy. In 1938, Frederic A. Delano, President Franklin D. Roosevelt's uncle, recalled that when he was asked to become chairman of the American Civic Association in 1923, he also was explicitly "asked to undertake the revival of the recommendations of the 1901 commission, and I began my work by asking 100 citizens to join me."

The Committee of 100 on the Federal City was divided into ten subcommittees, each consisting of ten individuals: architecture; forest and park preserves; school sites; playgrounds; housing and reservations for housing; zoning; streets, highways, and transit; extension of metropolitan Washington beyond the District lines; waterfront development; and industrial development and limitations. Based on recommendations of the subcommittees, the Committee of 100 issued its first report in January 1924, recommending "a major extension of Washington's park and forest preserves under the guidance of an overall planning agency that would focus on park planning as one of its major responsibilities."

For years, prominent Washingtonians had worried about the loss of open, scenic countryside around the capital. The Washington Board of Trade had drafted a bill to create a National Capital Park Commission authorized to acquire lands in the District, as well as in Virginia and Maryland, with the advice of the Commission of Fine Arts. With the support of the 1924 report of the Committee of 100, the Ball-Gibson Act, creating the National Capital Park Commission, was passed in June 1924. The April 1926 Capper-Gibson Act renamed the 1924 agency the National Capital Park and Planning Commission (NCPPC). Its mandate included preparing and maintaining a com-

Rock Creek watershed. *DH*

This detail is taken from the "Topographical Map of the District of Columbia and a Portion of Virginia" (excluding urbanized areas) compiled under the direction of the Army Corps of Engineers in 1884.

Senate Park Commission Plan, 1902, showing the proposed park system. *PC*

prehensive plan for the nation's capital and its environs, and encompassed transportation, subdivisions, public housing sites, sewerage, zoning, commerce and industry, and other elements of city and regional planning.

Frederic Delano was chairman of the Committee of 100 from 1923 to 1944 and concurrently chairman of the NCPPC during most of its formative years. Delano, who was active in implementing NCPPC plans, helped promote passage of the Capper-Cramton Act in May 1930, which authorized funds for parkland acquisition within the District and for the George Washington Memorial Parkway on both sides of the Potomac, and acquisition of land for the extension of the parks along Rock Creek and the Anacostia River into suburban Maryland.

During the Depression and the New Deal, the legacy of the Senate Park Commission continued to expand. In 1930, the Shipstead-Luce Act was passed, which permitted the Commission of Fine Arts to

New Hampshire Avenue, c. 1920. *CFA*

New Hampshire Avenue was typical of the tree-lined streets in central Washington during the early years of the twentieth century.

review new construction not only within but also adjacent to the city's monumental core as well as to the capital's national parks and other strategic sites and vistas. New Deal reforms created some problems, however. The influx of federal workers produced housing shortages and the capital's first major traffic problems. The programs conceived to address crises prompted shortcuts around the comprehensive planning process. Despite Delano's professional stature, and the fact that Franklin Delano Roosevelt was his nephew, the power of the NCPPC was diminished by short-term policy demands.

Soon after, in the 1940s, World War II preempted almost every long-term planning provision for the federal city in favor of the demands of war. In 1941, for example, the War Department built the Pentagon on the banks of the Potomac, over the objections of both the Commission of Fine Arts and the NCPPC. Secretary of the Interior Harold Ickes warned against "further encroachment on the parks and playgrounds of the National Capital" and commented sourly on the "grab bag method of putting a road or a building on any bit of vacant land that can be discovered."

Watching as the woods were demolished to make way for L'Enfant's avenues, Thomas Jefferson had expressed momentary disillusionment with democracy, wishing "that, in the possession of absolute power, I might enforce the preservation of these valuable groves." By planting sixty thousand trees of many species, Alexander "Boss" Shepherd reversed that process. Despite being labeled "tree butchers," the Senate Park Commission created on the Mall some of the loveliest groves in the world, choosing the American elm for the "architectural character of its columnar trunk and the delicate traceries formed by its wide-spreading branches." In 1912, flowering cherry trees, a gift to the United States from Japan, were planted along the edges of the newly formed Tidal Basin and the shores of East Potomac Park. In addition, in 1927, Congress authorized the creation of the National Arboretum.

By the end of the 1930s, however, the use of streets, particularly in the center of the city, began to change. Gradually but steadily, streets were transformed from public open spaces into arterial roadways for automobile traffic. Trees were cut down, street pavements widened, and sidewalks narrowed. All of this would alter the character of the center.

Travel to and within the National Capital

Between 1900 and 1940, citizens of Washington still traveled by streetcar, but motor buses were replacing the streetcars, and motorcars were beginning to replace both streetcars and buses. In 1900, seventeen streetcar lines entered Downtown along the Seventh Street and the F and G Street shopping area. They were still operating in 1940, with faster and more attractive, comfortable cars. Before World War II, Washington had one of the most effective urban transportation networks in America, with the wide, tree-lined L'Enfant avenues carrying streetcars, automobiles, trucks, and pedestrians. The livery stables that had existed in 1900 had been replaced by parking garages and gas stations.

In 1940, the new Union Station was at the heart of the Atlantic coast passenger-rail corridor; a cluster of modern warehouses lined the freight yards along Delaware Avenue. Intercity bus service arrived at and departed from the new Greyhound Bus Terminal in the heart of what was then Downtown. A rudimentary intercity air service was based at a terminal located a ten-minute taxicab ride from the city center. After World War II, changes in travel—and the structure of the city—would accelerate.

Fourteenth Street, looking north beyond F and G Streets, 1931. *PEC*

Fourteenth Street, 110 feet wide, supported a streetcar line and three automobile lanes in each direction, along with sidewalks and pedestrian islands.

Pennsylvania Avenue, looking east from the Treasury Building terrace, 1908. *LCPP*

In the early 1900s, only a few automobiles appeared on Washington streets. By 1940, more than a third of the commuters to Downtown were traveling in private automobiles.

Traffic officer talking with passengers in a Haynes Roadster, 1915. *HSW*

Initially, automobile travel was a sport for the upper classes; the working classes rode streetcars. Transit companies paid the salaries of traffic police from 1898 to 1933.

Pennsylvania Avenue, looking east from the Treasury Building terrace, 1928. *LCPP*

By the late 1920s, automobile congestion on Pennsylvania Avenue had already compromised the efficiency of car travel; it also hindered the performance of the more efficient public transit. In contrast, private automobile drivers in European cities were not allowed (and still are not allowed) to intrude into streetcar travelways.

Standard Oil Company Building, 1932. *CFA*

When it opened in 1932, the 350-foot-long Standard Oil Company Building replaced the Capital Garage as the world's largest parking structure. It also had three floors devoted to automobile servicing and gaso- line stations as well as space for corporate offices, including the offices of the Ford Motor Company. Located on Constitution Avenue near the Capitol, it featured a neo- classical design faced with limestone and marble. In 1968, it was razed to make way for the Center Leg Freeway.

Capital Garage, 1926. *CFA*

With 1,300 parking spaces, the eight-story Capital Garage, located on New York Avenue between Thirteenth and Fourteenth Streets, was the largest garage in the country when it was built in 1926. It was razed in 1974.

Greyhound Bus Terminal, 1940. *LCPP*

While it could not compete archi- tecturally with Union Station, the Greyhound Terminal, built on New York Avenue in 1940, was a hand- some Art Deco structure. It was extant in 2000, as the entrance to a modern office building.

Passenger terminal of the Washington-Hoover Airport in 1932. *NA*

In 1930, the Washington-Hoover Airport was opened at the Virginia end of the Fourteenth Street bridge over the Potomac River. The aerial view shows the passenger terminal in the center foreground, with a private club and swimming pool visible on the left. The George Washington Memorial Parkway was under construction along the Potomac.

During the pioneer days of commercial aviation, the terminal's waiting room had less than a dozen seats. While the location close to downtown Washington was convenient, there was only one 2,400-foot-long runway, and industrial obstructions made expansion impossible. Air service moved to National Airport in 1941.

Passengers boarding a Ford Tri-motor airplane in Washington, bound for New York, 1935. *LCPP*

In 1926, the Philadelphia Rapid Transit Air Service contracted with the U.S. Post Office to carry airmail to Philadelphia on two round trips daily. By 1935, there were hourly passenger flights to New York from Washington-Hoover Airport.

Washington in 1940

- By 1940, the population of the city was 663,000. Faster travel was spreading the city beyond the ten-mile square, and 245,000 Washingtonians lived outside the District of Columbia boundaries. Despite continued concentration in the center, average residential densities throughout the city, which had increased over the course of the nineteenth century, began to decline during the 1930s.
- Many new federal buildings were evidence of the expansion of the U.S. government resulting from Franklin Roosevelt's New Deal. At the same time, construction of private office buildings in the center increased, despite the long Depression of the 1930s.
- It was only after an internal political struggle that the House of Representatives accepted the Senate Park Commission Plan. By the beginning of World War II, however, the railroad station had been removed from the Mall and rebuilt as Union Station, and the Mall was replanted—much as L'Enfant had probably intended—and extended west to the Potomac. The Lincoln Memorial and Memorial Bridge were completed, and the Jefferson Memorial was under construction.
- Government office buildings in the Federal Triangle had replaced "Murder Bay," the red-light district around Ohio Avenue. "Temporary" World War I buildings still occupied the Mall and were soon to return to active duty.
- The first apartment buildings had been built in the late 1880s; by 1940, there were more than two hundred multistory apartments between P Street NW and the Mall, and between Georgetown and the Capitol.
- Most important institutions were within walking distance of the Mall. The National Institutes of Health at D and Twenty-first Streets, American University at F and Nineteenth Streets, and Sibley Memorial Hospital at M and North Capitol Streets were all only a few blocks north of Constitution Avenue. (By 1970, these and other major institutions would vanish from the center.)
- The National Capital Transit System was one of the most efficient in the country, and by 1940, streetcar lines laced Downtown. Within the city center, electric power was underground, as prescribed by Congress, to avoid unsightly overhead wires. The newest streetcars were elegant, comfortable, and fast, and specially designed for the national capital. Streetcar lines extended to Cabin John Bridge, along Wisconsin Avenue and Georgia Avenue to the District line, along Rhode Island Avenue to Beltsville, and along Benning Road to Kenilworth and Seat Pleasant.
- In 1940, thirty thousand private automobiles entered Downtown during rush hour, compared to the approximately twenty thousand that entered the Chicago Loop some sixty years later. Multistory automobile garages dotted the city, and there were more than sixty gasoline stations within the city center alone. There were still seventeen "horse fountains" within the Downtown rights-of-way.
- Private automobile congestion was beginning to slow down the streetcars, but in 1940, 48 percent of commuters still traveled by public transit, and 15 percent of those who commuted to Downtown walked to work from the fine late-nineteenth-century neighborhoods surrounding the area.

Key

- single-family residences
- walk-up residences
- elevator apartment
- hotel
- retail
- private offices
- federal offices
- federal institutions
- private & foreign institutions
- local institutions
- industrial
- warehouse
- transportation

0 100   500   1000 ft

1. **Memorial Bridge***
2. **Lincoln Memorial***
3. **Reflecting Basin***
4. **World War I "temporary" buildings**
5. **Museum of Natural History***
6. **National Gallery of Art***
7. **Freer Gallery of Asian Art***
8. **Interstate Commerce Commission**
9. **Supreme Court***
10. **Library of Congress Annex***
11. **Folger Shakespeare Library***
12. **Senate Office Building***
13. **Union Station***
14. **Federal Reserve Building***
15. **Federal Trade Commission***
16. **National Archives***
17. **Department of Justice***
18. **Internal Revenue Service***
19. **Post Office Department***
20. **Department of Labor***
21. **Department of the Interior***
22. **Department of Commerce***
23. **State Department***
24. **War and Navy Building***
25. **Civil Service Administration***
26. **General Accounting Office***
27. **Tariff Commission***
28. **Federal Home Loan Bank Board***
29. **Constitution Hall***
30. **Pan-American Union building***
31. **District Building***
32. **D.C. East Administration Building***
33. District Courts*
34. **D.C. Juvenile Court***
35. **D.C. Court of Appeals***
36. **D.C. Police Court***
37. **D.C. Municipal Court***
38. **D.C. Post Office***
39. **Willard Hotel***
40. Washington Hotel*
41. **Department of the Treasury***
42. **Mayflower Hotel***
43. **Carleton Hotel***
44. **Roger Smith Hotel**
45. **Greyhound Bus Terminal***
46. **Capital Garage**
47. **Dunbar High School**
48. **Sibley Memorial Hospital**
49. **Daughters of the American Revolution***
50. **American Red Cross***
51. **Public Health Service***
52. **National Academy of Science***
53. **National Institutes of Health**
54. **George Washington University***
55. **American University**

Buildings and public projects constructed or
completed after 1900 are listed in **bold** type.

Buildings and public projects existing in 2000
are identified with an asterisk.*

0 100   500   1000 ft

Chapter 5

1940
to
1970

Streetcars on Pennsylvania Avenue,
April 18, 1959. Detail.

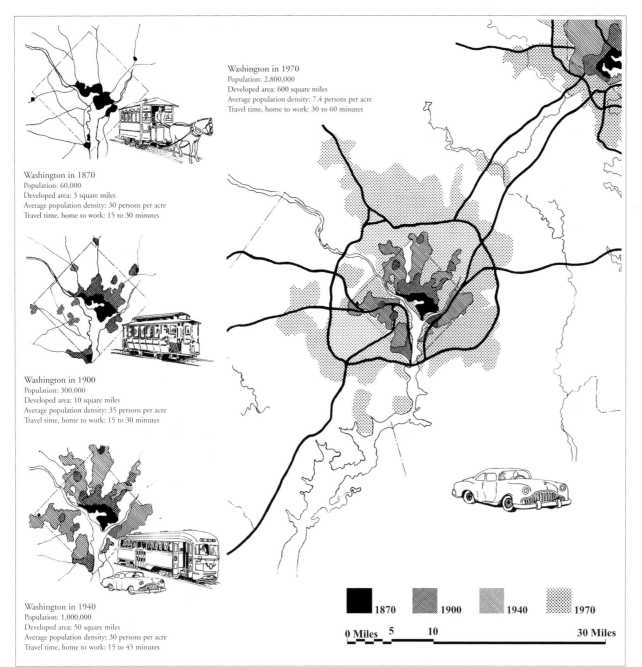

Washington in 1970
Population: 2,800,000
Developed area: 600 square miles
Average population density: 7.4 persons per acre
Travel time, home to work: 30 to 60 minutes

Washington in 1870
Population: 60,000
Developed area: 3 square miles
Average population density: 30 persons per acre
Travel time, home to work: 15 to 30 minutes

Washington in 1900
Population: 300,000
Developed area: 10 square miles
Average population density: 35 persons per acre
Travel time, home to work: 15 to 30 minutes

Washington in 1940
Population: 1,000,000
Developed area: 50 square miles
Average population density: 30 persons per acre
Travel time, home to work: 15 to 45 minutes

■ 1870   ▨ 1900   ▨ 1940   ▨ 1970

0 Miles   5   10   30 Miles

Transportation and population distribution in Washington and its surroundings, 1870–1970. *NCPC*

In 1870, trolleys were traveling on rails but were still powered by horses. People lived in row houses in a compact city. By 1900, the trolleys were powered electrically, and the city began to spread out. Many people, however, now lived in apartment buildings served by electric elevators, and the city center became even more compact. In 1940, travel was by streetcar and by private automobile, and many citizens lived in detached houses on fifty-foot lots. The city extended well beyond the District boundaries. By 1970, most people traveled by private automobile, with many living on one-acre lots at a distance from their workplaces. The city expanded in all directions at very low densities.

Changes between 1940 and 1970

The center of Washington grew steadily until the end of World War II. After the war, however, growth occurred primarily in the suburbs, at the expense of the older central city. The population of the District of Columbia, which was 663,000 in 1940, grew to 800,000 in 1950; by 1970, it was 756,000 and declining at a steady rate. In contrast, the population of the suburbs beyond the District line rose from a little more than 200,000 in 1940 to 1.7 million in 1970.

After World War II, increased private mobility was made possible by public investments in new streets and roads. In 1956, the National Interstate and Defense Highways Act created the process by which the federal government taxed gasoline and used the proceeds first for interstate highways, then for all types of urban and rural streets and roads. In the broadest sense, it became public policy to invest public money in the private land market. There were many consequences: the city expanded substantially beyond the District of Columbia boundaries as people chose to live on large lots far from where they worked; the new neighborhoods were racially segregated; and the commercial and residential center of the city was devastated.

In 1910, about 28 percent of the citizens of the national capital were African-American, concentrated in the old Downtown and Southwest neighborhoods. In every neighborhood, at least 20 percent of the residents were African-American.

In 1940, the racial composition of the capital was unchanged. At this time, the center of the city was still integrated racially; every neighborhood included many African-American residents. By this time, however, the new neighborhoods, beyond the older L'Enfant city, were racially segregated.

In 1970, almost three quarters of the population of the District was African-American; less than one tenth of the remainder of the region's inhabitants were African-American. Most of the upper-income white citizens of the District lived west of Rock Creek Park in neighborhoods that were, de facto, racially segregated.

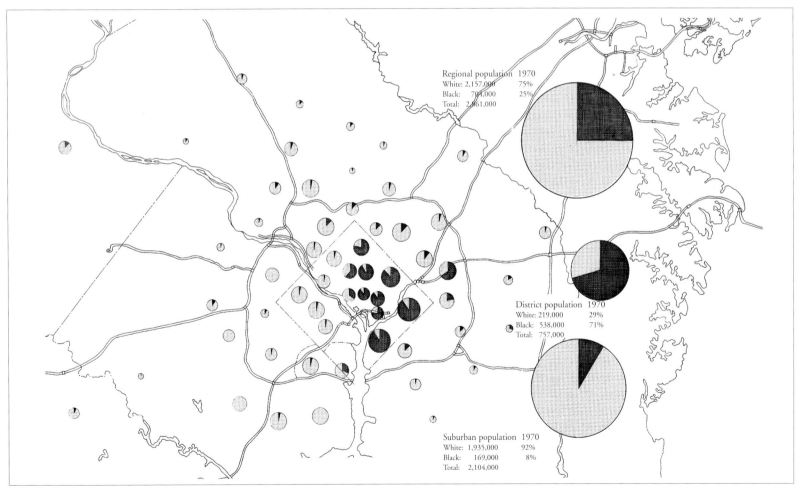

District population 1910
White: 237,100 72%
Black: 94,000 28%
Total: 331,000

District population 1940
White: 475,800 72%
Black: 187,300 28%
Total: 663,100

District population 1970
White: 219,000 29%
Black: 538,000 71%
Total: 757,000

Regional population 1970
White: 2,157,000 75%
Black: 704,000 25%
Total: 2,861,000

District population 1970
White: 219,000 29%
Black: 538,000 71%
Total: 757,000

Suburban population 1970
White: 1,935,000 92%
Black: 169,000 8%
Total: 2,104,000

Racial distribution in the national capital region in 1970. *JRP*

By 1970, about 25 percent of the region's citizens were African-American, only a slightly smaller percentage than in 1910. In 1970, the region's institutions were racially integrated, but outside the District of Columbia the geographic segregation of the races was, with a very few exceptions, complete. In the older towns, such as Vienna, Leesburg, and Manassas, about 15 percent, and in Alexandria about 30 percent, of the citizens were still African-American. Middle-class black citizens were moving from Anacostia to neighboring communities in Prince George's County.

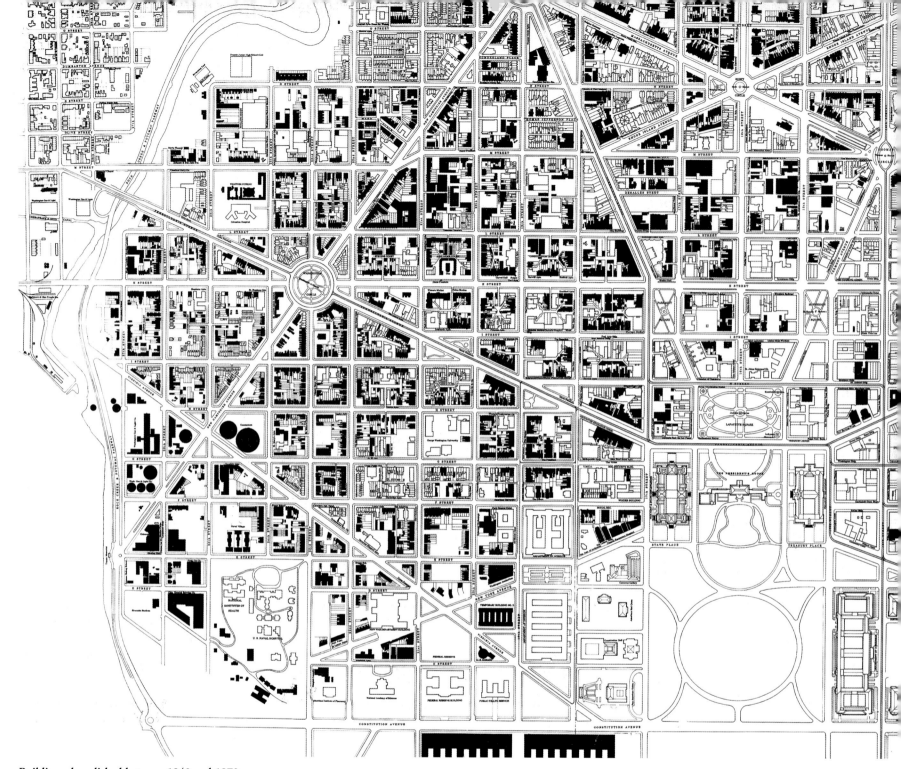

Buildings demolished between 1940 and 1970.
JRP

On this map of Washington's city center in 1940, areas shaded in black indicate buildings (largely private) that were razed by 1970. In the old Downtown, almost all of the elegant houses and a large number of the churches disappeared, along with many of the most architecturally distinguished nineteenth- and early-twentieth-century commercial buildings.

Federal Response to the Deterioration of the Center of the Capital

The private reaction to central Washington's difficulties was to pull up stakes and leave. The government did not have that option; any suggestion that the national capital should go west had long since faded away. After World War II, federal construction provided a stability to the center of Washington not available to other city centers, at least not at the

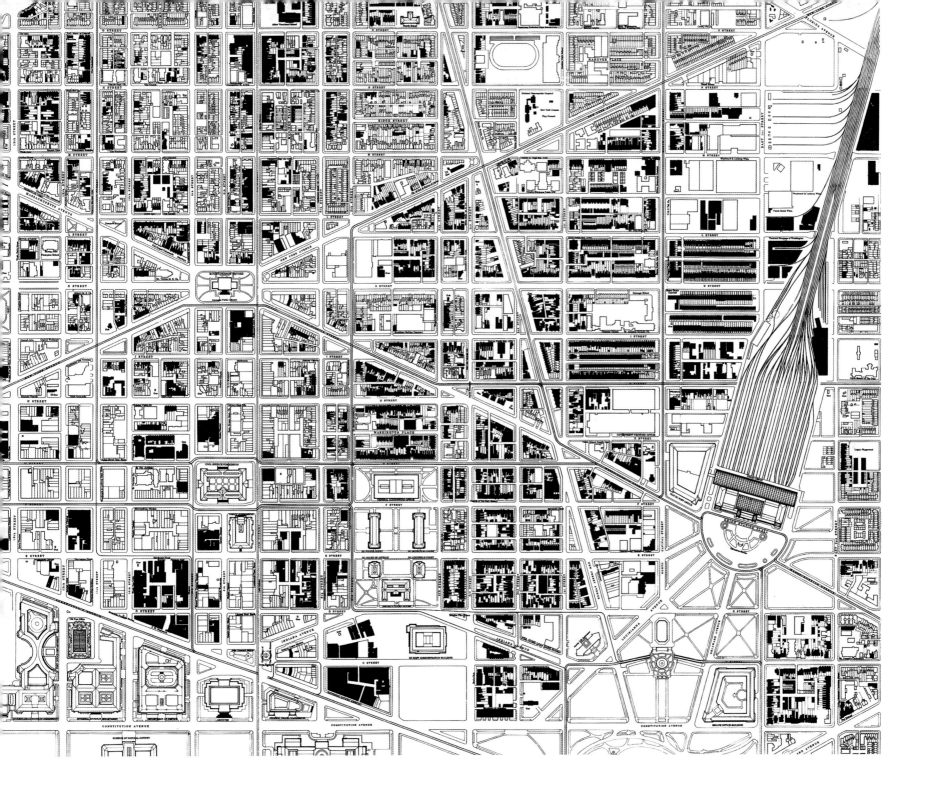

same scale. Congress initiated a number of programs aimed at shoring up urban neighborhoods, and many were applied first to the capital city.

The federal construction agency—the General Services Administration—built the massive Chester A. Arthur Federal Building in the Shaw neighborhood and, in the center on Pennsylvania Avenue, the even more massive J. Edgar Hoover Building for the Federal Bureau of Investigation (FBI). In Foggy Bottom, the government expanded the State Department building and erected a building for the Civil Service Commission. On Capitol Hill, new Senate offices were added in the

Everett M. Dirksen Building, and a new U.S. Courthouse was built on Constitution Avenue near the older courts buildings.

An almost entirely new federally developed area displaced older, smaller buildings in the Southwest neighborhood. The Sam Rayburn Building was constructed for the House of Representatives Office Buildings, and the James Forrestal Building for the Department of Energy. Buildings were completed for the National Aeronautics and Space Administration; the Departments of Education, Transportation, and Housing and Urban Development; and the Office of U.S. Currency.

J. Edgar Hoover Building for the Federal Bureau of Investigation. Designed by C. F. Murphy & Associates in the 1960s, completed 1974.

The FBI building was an example of the "new brutalism," the avant-garde architectural idiom of the moment.

New Executive Office Building, 1968. Designed by John Carl Warnecke & Associates.

Constructed of red brick, new office buildings behind the historic town houses on both sides of Lafayette Square did not entirely dominate the older, lower structures.

On the north side of Lafayette Square east of Sixteenth Street, St. John's Episcopal Church and Rectory and, west of Sixteenth Street, the Hay-Adams Hotel (a famous Washington scandal featuring Henry Adams and Clara Hay took place in the Hay-Adams House, on the site before the hotel) remained; but the Veterans Bureau was built beyond St. John's to the east, and the national Chamber of Commerce headquarters was built west of the Hay-Adams. Both were designed in the loosely neoclassical style considered appropriate for the national capital.

The remaining edges of Lafayette Square, the location of poorly maintained nineteenth-century buildings, seemed a logical place for new office construction. The federal government proposed demolishing the older public and private buildings surrounding the square and replacing them with standard government-issue office buildings. These proposals were at first supported by the Commission of Fine

Arts and the National Capital Planning Commission (NCPC), but that support was withdrawn. The most effective opponent of the demolition was the first lady Jacqueline Bouvier Kennedy, with help from her husband. Mrs. Kennedy wrote to the head of the General Services Administration, explaining how much the president hoped the historic buildings around the square could be saved. After a long battle, Mrs. Kennedy won; new space for federal offices was provided in tall, red brick buildings behind the older structures.

During the years following World War II, the federal government also took a direct hand in intervening in deteriorating urban areas. The Redevelopment Land Agency (RLA), an extension of the Department of Housing and Urban Development, supervised and financed the demolition and rebuilding of almost the entire Southwest neighborhood and invested in streets and redevelopment in the center and in the neighborhood of Shaw.

The Bureau of Public Roads, which became the Federal Highway Administration in the new Department of Transportation, financed and directed the planning—through the Maryland, Virginia, and District of Columbia Highway Departments—of a 450-mile urban expressway system for the national capital region. By 1968, a series of federal agencies had completed plans for a heavy-rail transit system (Metrorail) for the Washington region. Administration of Metrorail financing and construction was taken over by the Urban Mass Transit Authority when the Department of Transportation was created in 1968.

During his 1961 inaugural parade from the Capitol to the White House along Pennsylvania Avenue, John F. Kennedy is reputed to have commented on the shabby condition of the avenue's surroundings. He decided to do something about the problem. In 1962, the President's Advisory Council on Pennsylvania Avenue was formed, with Chicago architect Nathaniel Owings as its chairman and future Senator Daniel Patrick Moynihan as vice chairman. The council began work on a master plan for the area, reporting that Pennsylvania Avenue, the "nation's main street," was "a scene of desolation . . . [The area should be redeveloped to be] lively, friendly and inviting, as well as distinguished and impressive." The council's plan featured double rows of trees on the south side of the avenue and triple rows on the north side. The centerpiece was a grand plaza at the western terminus, with an imposing fountain on axis with Fourteenth Street, which was depressed under the plaza. The Federal Triangle was to be completed by demolishing the Old Post Office; and the Willard Hotel, the Washington Hotel, and the National Theater were all to be sacrificed to make room for the plaza.

To stem the deterioration in Washington's city center, both the federal and the local government acted indirectly, through historic preservation statutes. In 1950, the Old Georgetown Act was passed by Congress, establishing Georgetown as a federally protected historic enclave. Private initiatives, galvanized primarily by a group organized under the banner Don't Tear It Down, led to even more restrictive preservation measures enacted by the District of Columbia in the 1970s.

Model of the original President's Advisory Council on Pennsylvania Avenue plan, 1964.
PCPA

When the Pennsylvania Avenue Development Corporation replaced the President's Advisory Council in 1972, this ambitious plan was significantly modified.

Heart of Downtown, looking south, c. 1970.

Aerial view of downtown Washington, with
New York Avenue in the foreground,
Constitution Avenue in the background, and
Fifteenth Street on the right. The tall building
on the south side of New York Avenue, between
Thirteenth and Fourteenth Streets, is the Capital
Garage, which was no longer in use. The low
building visible on the south side of New York
Avenue, between Twelfth and Eleventh Streets,
is the soon to be abandoned Greyhound Bus
Terminal. Since early in the century, the only
large surface parking area was the unfinished
block of the Federal Triangle at the end of
Thirteenth Street. This changed rapidly as
commercial buildings were replaced by parking
lots. In 1970, many of the buildings shown here
stood empty.

Neighborhoods

Some of Washington's most historically important buildings disappeared early on. The Old State Department building, which stood east
of the White House in 1820, was razed immediately after the Civil War,
and "Duddington," the house that Daniel Carroll built after L'Enfant
demolished his earlier construction, was razed by 1900. After World
War I, however, the scale of demolition in the city's center increased,
and after World War II, whole blocks were destroyed. In the
Southwest neighborhood, the impact of almost entirely publicly sponsored "urban renewal" was enormous. The image of these sweeping
changes resonated in the minds of the residents of Capitol Hill, Shaw,
and Foggy Bottom, and the total demolition experienced in Southwest
was not to be repeated in other Washington neighborhoods.

Looking south from Mount Vernon Square, c. 1970.

An aerial view from above Mount Vernon Square, with the old Patent Office building visible at the top of the photograph, shows a particularly devastated part of Downtown. Seventh Street, once the major retail street, is lined with empty buildings.

Downtown

After World War II, Downtown businesses became desegregated, first voluntarily and through public pressure, and then by law. Hecht's opened its lunchroom to all, regardless of race, in November 1951, and other department stores as well as drugstores followed suit. At the same time, desegregation in the public schools caused many white residents to move out. Downtown became an increasingly black neighborhood and shopping district; three synagogues became African-American Baptist and Episcopal churches. The riots of 1968 that followed the assassination of Martin Luther King Jr. provided the final blow for faltering businesses. Once prominent stores such as Lansburgh's and Kann's closed, as white Washingtonians declined to shop in Downtown.

**Tuckerman House, 1886;
razed 1967.** *HABS*

Located at Sixteenth and I Streets,
the Tuckerman House was the last
of the fine Romanesque houses left
standing in the city in 1967. One of
the few remaining great houses near
Lafayette Square, a fashionable residential neighborhood before and
after the Civil War, it was demolished to make way for the Motion
Picture Association office building.

**Hale House, 1881;
razed 1941.** *CFA*

Hale House was a gift from Senator
Zachariah Chandler of Michigan to
his daughter, Mary, when she married
Senator Eugene Hale of Maine.
Located on the northeast corner of
Sixteenth and K Streets, it was one of
the social centers of political
Washington for more than fifty years.
It was demolished to make way for
the Statler Hotel, a stripped-down
moderne-style building.

**Mount Vernon Row, 1873;
razed 1969.** *MLKL*

Built on K Street west of Mount
Vernon Square, this was one of the
many Victorian rows erected after
the Civil War and the last to be
demolished. The style of the nine
Second Empire houses that made up
the row was popular in Washington
and Georgetown after the Civil War
as more people built grand, high-
ceilinged residences.

Judiciary Square row houses, 1857; razed, 1965, 1969. *WEB*

Residential development on Judiciary Square was triggered by the construction of George Hadfield's City Hall in 1820. By 1860, the square was surrounded by then very fashionable Federal-style row houses. In the 1960s, this block of seven row houses, on the east side of the square north of E Street, remained in good condition, but they were demolished to make way for a parking lot, despite protests by their owners.

First Congregational Church, 1866; razed 1959. Designed by Henry Searle. *LCPP*

Before the Civil War, two attempts by an abolitionist congregation to establish a Congregational church in Washington, essentially a southern city, failed. In 1865, the city's Congregationalists petitioned the National Council in Boston for aid; the request was granted. The architect described his creation, on the northeast corner of Tenth and G Streets NW, as "Byzantine."

Columbia Armory, 1855; razed 1964. *LCPP*

In 1798, Washington citizens organized their first militia to prevent slave insurrections and generally to patrol the city. This group served until the Civil War when the city finally organized a police force. The armory on the Mall was the first permanent home for the city's many volunteer militia. Like the Army Medical Museum, it was demolished because it did not fit the Senate Park Commission Plan.

Army Medical Museum, 1887; razed 1969. *AFIP*

The Army Medical Museum was razed to make way for the Hirshhorn Museum on the condition that its contents somehow remain on the Mall. The fourth curator, Dr. John Shaw Billings, had amassed the world's largest collection of antique microscopes by 1893. The museum contained some of the most popular, bizarre exhibits in Washington— for instance, bullet, probe, and bone fragments from President Abraham Lincoln's skull wound.

Security Storage warehouse, 1890; razed 1965. *SSC*

This Romanesque Revival, fortresslike building, one of many nineteenth- and early-twentieth-century structures in Downtown to be demolished between 1940 and 1970, had granite walls on the first floor, with brick above. It was one of the largest and most technically advanced storage warehouses in the country. After World War II, paintings valued at $250,000 were moved here from a German salt mine.

Belasco Theater, 1895; razed 1964. *ES*

The Belasco, on the east side of Downtown's Lafayette Square, was purchased by David Belasco and the Shubert brothers in 1906. From then until the Great Depression, the 1,800-seat auditorium with its baroque gilt decorations, three tiers of balconies, and thirty-two boxes was a center for plays, opera, and ballet.

Raleigh Hotel, 1898, 1905, 1911; razed 1964. *WEB*

One of the great early-twentieth-century hotels, the Raleigh was built on the southeast corner of Thirteenth and E Streets. When the Centennial Building was demolished in 1911, the Raleigh was expanded into the corner of Twelfth Street and Pennsylvania Avenue. In 1936, $300,000 was spent redecorating the Raleigh to compete with the Mayflower.

Home Savings Bank, 1902; razed 1968. *WEB*

Constructed on Seventh Street between K Street and Massachusetts Avenue, this was a mixed-use building of a kind common in Europe: it had commerce on the lower floors and luxury apartments above.

Washington Loan and Trust Company, 1924; razed 1974. *WEB*

Located in the heart of the financial district, on the southwest corner of Seventeenth and G Streets NW, the bank won an architectural award from the Washington Board of Trade in 1927. Yet despite a court injunction against demolition, the General Services Administration authorized a wrecking company to destroy the structure early on a Sunday morning.

Shubert Theater, 1907; razed 1960. *LEG*

The Shubert, on the east side of Ninth Street north of E Street in Downtown, featured vaudeville and also showed films. In 1950, when the National Theater was temporarily closed because of the racial integration of its audiences, the Shubert became the city's only legitimate stage.

Fox Theater, 1926; gutted 1963. *LCPP*

James M. Goode in *Capital Losses* says the Fox, on F Street between Thirteenth and Fourteenth Streets in Downtown, was "not only the largest movie theater ever built in Washington but its interior was by far the most palatial . . . Located in the east end of the National Press Building (on F Street), the 3,500 seat theater occupied six floors . . . the patron entered the building directly from F Street, walking through the vestibule, small lobby, and then the elliptically shaped grand lobby before descending the monumental bronze and marble stairway to the auditorium below. The interiors were as sumptuous as opera sets. Twenty-four marble columns supported the lobby dome, richly ornamented in both relief and mural paintings. The main auditorium was decorated in a Hollywood sort of Louis XVI. with gold and red draperies 'copied' from Versailles and Fontainebleau." Efforts to save the theater, still the city's center for opera, proved futile. It was eventually replaced by the John F. Kennedy Center for the Performing Arts, located on the Potomac River, distant from the center.

Capitol Hill

After World War II, Capitol Hill's nineteenth-century houses attracted the early preservation movement. Justice William O. Douglas, for instance, bought one of the Hill's historic houses in 1949. Preservation of the neighborhood started in the blocks east of the Capitol, coinciding with major demographic changes in Capitol Hill. Its middle class, both black and white, began to move away, lured by the suburbs and Veterans Administration loans. Newer housing in neighborhoods farther from the center was opened to African-Americans by the 1948 Supreme Court ruling declaring housing covenants unconstitutional. Many middle-class blacks had held blue-collar jobs with good wages at the Navy Yard, but the number of these jobs diminished when the yard stopped manufacturing weapons after World War II.

At the same time, low-income, mostly black families, displaced by the Southwest Urban Renewal project, moved into Capitol Hill's older rundown houses or into public housing. Adding to the mix were young families and single residents, predominantly white and upwardly mobile, who began to invest in and restore the houses between the Capitol and Lincoln Park. By 1960, the economic and racial mix changed from middle-class white and black to a combination of low-income black and middle- and upper-income white inhabitants.

The post–World War II history of Capitol Hill is unique. A haven for poor citizens displaced by public projects in other neighborhoods, it retained its nineteenth-century architectural qualities and was never subjected to large-scale private or public demolition.

Shaw

By the beginning of World War II, when many of the white residents had moved away from Shaw, blacks were still barred from most other parts of Washington by restrictive covenants. Continued racism after the Supreme Court's 1948 ruling overturning such covenants still limited their residential opportunities, but new options began to exist, and middle-class black residents started to leave Shaw for less crowded neighborhoods. Many single-family residences were then converted to multifamily use—often by renters. As poverty in Shaw increased, social problems multiplied. By the early 1960s, Shaw was clearly economically depressed, and the city began plans for massive redevelopment. After the 1968 riots, the need for help became even more pressing.

The Redevelopment Land Agency designated Shaw an Urban Renewal Area, according to criteria established by the Department of Housing and Urban Development. Thus the neighborhood became eligible for federal redevelopment funds in 1968. The Shaw community, however, led by local minister and activist Walter E. Fauntroy, presented government city planners with an organized community position: the "Model Inner City Community Organization." Remembering what they viewed as the debacle of redevelopment in Southwest, members of the organization were determined to shape city efforts in Shaw and prevent the wholesale destruction of the existing fabric of the community. As a result, Shaw retains most of its late-nineteenth-century structures. New condominiums and apartment buildings exist next to single-family row houses.

Aerial view of Shaw, looking north, c. 1970.

Rhode Island and Florida Avenues intersect in the eastern part of the Shaw neighborhood. Howard University, near the McMillan Reservoir, is visible in the upper left corner of the photograph. While Shaw was spared the wholesale demolition that occurred in Downtown and the West End, the neighborhood nevertheless lost a number of significant buildings.

One part of the old Shaw neighborhood disappeared with little notice, however. By 1970, more than one third of the area in the triangle between Massachusetts and New York Avenues and the railroad yards was either vacant or served as parking for automobiles. A large portion of this area had contained what was assuredly the worst housing in Washington. On the block bounded by L, K, North Capitol, and East First Streets, for example, in the section that had been known as "Swampoodle," former inhabitants lived in stacked "shotgun" flats at densities of over eighty families per acre, without indoor plumbing.

Meigs House, 1869; razed 1972. *CFA*

Besides designing his own house on the southeast corner of Vermont Avenue and N Street NW in Shaw, Montgomery C. Meigs designed and managed construction of the Pension Building and the Cabin John Bridge. He also oversaw construction of the Washington Aqueduct and the pre-fabricated iron dome for the Capitol.

Wylie House, 1843; razed 1947. *NGS*

Built on Thomas Circle in Shaw, the Wylie House (right) was the center of a fashionable residential neighborhood that came into being before the Civil War and lasted until World War II.

Dunbar High School, 1916; razed 1977. *CFA*

Located on the west side of First Street NW, between N and O Streets in Shaw, the school is described by Goode in *Capital Losses* as "one of the nation's most remarkable success stories in black education as the leading academically elite, all-black public high school in Washington from its founding in 1870 until it was integrated in 1955 . . . Having an almost spiritual interest in building individual and racial pride, the school was high in academic standards, resisting attempts by the School Board to change its status to vocational, commercial, or general."

Dupont Circle, looking south, 1924. *NA*

Built by a wealthy Chicago department store and real estate magnate in 1891, the three-story, fifty-five-room, white-brick Leiter Mansion (far right) dominated Dupont Circle for fifty-six years. At the beginning of World War II, the Leiter family rented the house to the federal government for office space. The mansion was sold in 1947 and demolished that same year; it was replaced by the Hotel Dupont Plaza. Within a few years, most of the grand Dupont Circle mansions had vanished.

Dupont Circle

The parties that would battle over the future of the Dupont Circle neighborhood—the older mansion dwellers, what would become the "counterculture," and the city's highway department—converged at the circle itself. L'Enfant had not designed his neighborhood centers as future automobile traffic circles, and by the beginning of World War II, traffic congestion around Dupont Circle had become a problem. The congestion worsened after the war, and an underpass was proposed, projected at a cost of $500,000. At first, there was little citizen opposition, but in 1947, when work began, residents protested, citing the price tag (which had escalated to $3 million) and neighborhood disruption. Their fears were confirmed. Construction left the park in the center of the circle a sea of mud, filled with construction equipment and littered with building materials, for more than three years. The trees were destroyed and the Dupont Circle fountain relocated.

Eleanor "Cissy" Patterson, owner and publisher of the *Washington Times Herald* and owner of one of the mansions on the circle, at first supported the tunnel, then called it a "blunder pass," writing that "if it is ever

Aerial view of the west end of the Dupont Circle neighborhood, looking east from above Georgetown, c. 1970.

By this time, many of the area's larger buildings had been demolished and replaced by parking lots.

finished, it will be the worst white elephant of them all." She was right. In 1961, the streetcars were replaced by buses, and the semicircular trolley tunnel was closed. The automobile and truck underpass remained, and the surface travelways widened at the expense of the park.

The park in the middle of Dupont Circle, which had been a quiet neighborhood green, changed in other ways as well. In the mid-1960s, it was the gathering place for hippies, cultists, black power advocates, and other members of the era's counterculture. It was also one of the staging areas for demonstrations against the Vietnam War. In the surrounding neighborhood, students and other young people moved into row houses converted to rooming houses, tiny apartments, or group homes; businesses disappeared or changed to meet a different market.

The Dupont Circle Citizens Association called on the Department of the Interior, which owned and managed the park, to oust "misfits, hoodlums, vagrants and perverts which . . . gather in large numbers" in the park. Some called for the park to be fenced and closed at night; however, it remained open and the neighborhood survived.

**Louise Home, 1871;
razed 1949.** *LCPP*

William Wilson Corcoran, the
city's great nineteenth-century philanthropist, established the Louise
Home in Dupont Circle in memory of his wife and his daughter,
both named Louise. The home,
"for the comfortable maintenance
and support (not including the fur-
nishing of wearing apparel)
of…destitute but refined and educated gentlewomen" occupied a
full city block on Massachusetts
Avenue between Fifteenth and
Sixteenth Streets.

**Shepherd's Row, 1873;
razed 1952.** Designed by Adolph
Cluss. *LCPP*

The house on the northeast corner
of Connecticut Avenue and
K Street was owned by Alexander
Robey Shepherd. The house next
door was owned by the architect
of the row, and the third house,
by Hallet Kilbourn. All three men
had made fortunes in real estate
speculation.

**Portland Flats, 1879;
razed 1962.** *KC*

The Portland Flats, on Thomas
Circle in the Dupont Circle
neighborhood, were the city's first
luxury apartments. Seven-room
apartments with twelve-foot
ceilings rented for $150 per month
at the time the building was razed.

Church of the Covenant, 1887; razed 1966. *LCPP*

According to James M. Goode in *Capital Losses,* the demolition of this church on the northeast corner of Eighteenth and N Streets NW was "the greatest recent loss to Washington's collection of outstanding Victorian churches . . . Inspired by Henry Hobson Richardson's personal interpretation of the Romanesque style, New York architect J. Cleveland Cady designed a dignified masterpiece in grey granite. Its great soaring tower was conceptually similar, in fact, to the Allegheny County Court House in Pittsburgh, considered one of Richardson's greatest works."

First Baptist Church, 1889; razed 1953. *LCPP*

The 140-foot Romanesque Revival tower was for years a landmark on Sixteenth and M Streets. Founded in 1802, the congregation occupied three previous Downtown sites before moving to Sixteenth Street near Dupont Circle. The church's second building, on Tenth Street, was sold in 1861 to John T. Ford, who converted it to a theater—the site of President Lincoln's assassination. The congregation founded Columbian College on Meridian Hill in 1819. In 1904, the church relinquished control, and Columbian became George Washington University.

Rochambeau apartments, 1902; razed 1962. *LCPP*

Goode considers this building at the southeast corner of Connecticut Avenue and I Street "probably the most exuberant example of early twentieth century Beaux-Arts in Washington."

Guggenheim House, 1906; razed 1956. *NEA*

The house was built by Simon Guggenheim, a Colorado miner and senator, on the northeast corner of Sixteenth and M Streets NW in Dupont Circle. Three historic landmarks, the Guggenheim House, the Williams House, and the Hotel Martinique, were torn down to make way for the National Education Association expansion.

John F. Kennedy Center for the Performing Arts, 1970. Designed by Edward Durell Stone Associates.

Edward Durell Stone achieved widespread recognition with the design of the American Embassy in New Delhi, India. He repeated the design numerous times over the course of his career—applying it to universities, hospitals, and the Kennedy Center (foreground). Beyond is the Watergate complex (1964–72), designed by Luigi Moretti and Mario di Valmarana, with Corning, Moore, Elmore & Fischer as associate architects.

Foggy Bottom

At the end of World War II, Foggy Bottom was still a low-income residential area, but it had changed since 1900. Industry was failing or moving away, and housing was officially substandard. A 1944 survey by the Washington Housing Association indicated that of 186 dwelling units in the blocks bounded by Virginia and New Hampshire Avenues and Twenty-third Street, one fourth had no water and one fifth had no electricity. Many were alley dwellings. Almost 90 percent of these units were rental properties. As elsewhere, this substandard housing was occupied by people with few housing options; the neighborhood was now predominantly inhabited by African-Americans.

Small-scale redevelopment started in Foggy Bottom after the war, however, as individuals bought small brick row houses, including many houses in the alleys, and renovated them. Renovation of this kind had been going on in Georgetown since the 1930s. "Gentrification" had a price; as property was improved, poor residents were forced to move because of rising rents, remaking Foggy Bottom from a mostly black neighborhood in 1950 into a largely white middle-income area by 1960.

In 1940, George Washington University was for the most part contained within the single block bounded by H and G Streets and Twentieth and Twenty-first Streets. By 1970, the university occupied ten blocks and owned all or parts of a number of the surrounding blocks. It was not university policy to provide dormitories, and students occupied many surrounding apartments.

In 1947, the Department of State moved to a new building at Twenty-third and D Streets, making the area attractive to department employees. Also in 1947, the Washington Gas Light Company dismantled its gas manufacturing plant. The last tanks were demolished in 1954, along with many other physical disincentives.

Soon after the demolition of the final two tanks, Potomac Plaza, an eight-story group of offices and apartments, was erected on the newly vacant site on the west side of Twenty-third Street between E Street and

Mills Building, 1902; razed 1964. *NA*

General Anson Mills, known as an expert at Indian fighting, surveyed and named El Paso, Texas. He also invented the cartridge belt in 1866 and made a fortune selling it. The belt was still in service during World War II.

Christian Heurich Brewery, 1894; razed 1962–66. *LCPP*

This was Washington's most famous brewery, and one of its most successful industries. Heurich, who was born in Germany, was orphaned, and worked in breweries, came to Baltimore and from his salary of $35 per week saved enough to buy Washington's Schnell Brewery. When the brewery burned down, he built this handsome brick building on Water and D Streets in Foggy Bottom. He worked until a few days before he died at age 102, the country's oldest active brewer.

Lemon Building, 1890; razed 1971. *WEB*

In 1902, the American Institute of Architects bought Tayloe's Octagon House on New York Avenue and Eighteenth Street in Foggy Bottom for $30,000. In 1971, the AIA razed the adjacent Lemon Building, despite protests from preservationists, to make room for the organization's glass and masonry administration building.

Virginia Avenue NW. An even more elaborate office-apartment complex was built south of Virginia Avenue. New multistory construction included the Howard Johnson Hotel that would be the home of President Richard M. Nixon's "plumbers" and the Watergate hotel-office-retail complex housing the Democratic National Committee's offices—the object of the plumbers' curiosity. A few dozen small row houses and the Christian Heurich Brewery, along with the remains of the Washington Gas Light properties, a Marine Corps carpenter shop, the Potomac Riding Stables, the Hygia Ice Company, a skating rink, and an arena, were sacrificed during the late 1960s to make way for the John F. Kennedy Center for the Performing Arts.

By 1955, the D.C. Department of Highways had planned four interstate expressways to meet at an interchange in the west end of Foggy Bottom. One eliminated the Georgetown waterfront, one went north through Dupont Circle, one went east into a tunnel under K Street, and one crossed the Mall. The Foggy Bottom Restoration Association, the Georgetown Citizens Association, and civic organizations led by the Committee of 100 on the Federal City fought a bitter and finally successful battle to prevent these interstate freeways from being built. By that time, however, the highway building agencies had gouged close to ten blocks out of Foggy Bottom, including the Montgomery Public School, and almost two hundred row house and apartment units, to complete the interchange for these nonexistent inner-city expressways.

In 1940, south of Pennsylvania Avenue and west of Nineteenth Street, there were more than 1,800 row houses and 40 apartment buildings. In 1970, fewer than 200 row houses were left in the area, most of them in the small enclave between Twenty-fourth Street, Pennsylvania Avenue, and the interstate remnant. During the post–World War II decades, Foggy Bottom was transformed from a working-class residential and mixed-use neighborhood to a home for some of Washington's largest public and private institutions.

Old Southwest, N and Union Streets, 1942. *LCPP*

Had the Elbert Peets plan been implemented, much of the old Southwest neighborhood might still look like this view.

Southwest

Local Southwest activist Harry Wender had complained that the city was ignoring his neighborhood, and in the 1930s, federal authorities agreed with him, labeling Southwest a neglected slum, a disease-ridden, crime-infested eyesore in the shadow of the Capitol. In 1946, Congress chartered the Redevelopment Land Agency with this mandate (from the new D.C. Redevelopment Act): "To provide for the replanning and rebuilding of slum, blighted, and other areas of the District of Columbia and the assembly, by purchase or condemnation, of real property in such areas and the sale or lease thereof for the redevelopment of such area in accordance with said plans; and to provide for the organization of, procedure for, and financing of such planning, acquisition, and sale or lease; and for other purposes." The act ensured that private enterprise would be given pref-

erence in the leasing or purchase of land for redevelopment, that proof of adequate off-site housing to accommodate displaced families be a precondition for approval by the District commissioners, and that displaced families be given preference in District or federal housing.

Also in 1946, the National Capital Park and Planning Commission completed a general plan for Washington, anticipating redevelopment areas in the southeast, southwest, and northwest. The National Housing Act of 1949 offered federal subsidies to cities for slum clearance, redevelopment, and low-rent public housing.

After several false starts, the Southwest Washington Urban Renewal area was approved in 1951, bounded by the railroad on Maryland and Virginia Avenues on the north, the Washington Channel (excluding Fort McNair) on the west, South Capital Street on the east,

Stores on Fourth Street SW awaiting demolition by the Redevelopment Land Agency, 1975. *HSW*

These were the last stores to remain open on Fourth Street.

and P Street on the south. The NCPPC prepared a Southwest neighborhood plan under the direction of Washington landscape architect and urban designer Elbert Peets. The aim of the plan was to maintain the neighborhood as an area for low-income residents, preserve the street pattern and architecture, and rehabilitate existing structures.

Not everyone agreed with the plan. A federal commission wrote that "The character of the buildings is so bad that partial rehabilitation is not justifiable economically." The *Washington Post* published a series of articles entitled "Progress or Decay? Washington Must Choose!" and called for a "bold approach" in reconstructing blighted areas such as Southwest to reverse "white flight" to the suburbs and rebuild the city's tax base. A review of what newspapers called "The Peets Plan" by the RLA and the Housing and Home Finance Agency (HHFA) concluded that extensive rehabilitation in Southwest was not economically feasible.

In January 1952, the RLA contracted with the firm of Harland Bartholomew, the chairman of the National Capital Planning Commission, and two local architects, Louis Justement and Chloethiel Woodard Smith, to prepare planning concepts for Southwest that would change its character completely. At the same time, the D.C. Department of Highways was planning an interstate freeway through the Southwest neighborhood. In searching for a suitable location for the highway, the architects recommended that it be close to the railroads, providing the largest possible residential area. The District Highway Department proposed a straight line along F Street, which was accepted by the commissioners, the RLA, and the NCPPC.

After HHFA financing was approved and appraising begun, in 1953 the RLA began to make the largest single land acquisition, in terms of both cost and number of parcels, ever undertaken by the federal government. In December 1952, two commercial property owners had challenged the constitutionality of the powers granted to the RLA by the federal government. In November 1954, a unanimous decision by the Supreme Court ruled that: "The power of Congress over the District of Columbia includes all the legislative powers which a state may exercise over its affairs . . . the concept of the public welfare is broad and inclusive . . . The values it represents are spiritual as well as physical, aesthetic as well as monetary. It is within the powers of the legislature to determine that the community should be beautiful as well as healthy, spacious as well as clean, well-balanced as well as carefully patrolled."

In the spring of 1954, the RLA began demolition, knocking down a group of alley houses, "a sore spot of crime, illegitimacy, refuse and disordered lives," according to the *Washington Post*. In this way, between 1954 and 1960 most of the old Southwest neighborhood disappeared.

Plans for the new neighborhood had been revised, reviewed, reviewed again, and occasionally reversed. The most difficult problem the agencies faced, however, was the rehousing of fifteen thousand poor black citizens. In 1966, sociologist Daniel Thursz found "a substantial amount of dissatisfaction" among African-American residents of Southwest. Families suffered social loss. He noted "the fact that they had friends and felt a part of a community which had been theirs for many years . . . it was home . . . they resent more than ever before the forced disintegration of the social milieu which was theirs in the old Southwest."

In *Washington at Home,* edited by Kathryn Schneider Smith, historian and neighborhood activist Keith Melder reflects:

> The new Southwest has undeniably handsome features. Still, the absence of variety found in other areas, where buildings were constructed at different times, makes Southwest look like a suburb. A reporter in 1973 found residents commenting "on the sterility of the renewal area, on its lack of soul."

In the larger context of recent history, the story of Southwest is not unique. Since 1950 the affluent have displaced the poor throughout inner-city Washington—but without wholesale, traumatic removal and rebuilding. Instead, on Capitol Hill, in Georgetown, and in parts of near Northwest, a process of restoration and gentrification occurred. Yet poor blacks, forced out of these sections by rent increases and real estate developers, moved just as surely as they had to when removed by urban renewal. Whether desirable or not, these practices diminished the values and practices of intimate, face to face community life, as remembered in Old Southwest.

The Southwest story illustrates the peculiar story of Washington as a federal laboratory for urban experimentation. Just as the 1901–1902 McMillan Plan to rebuild, beautify, and create a planned model city on the Mall served as a model for later federal planning in the 1920s and 1930s, Southwest's urban renewal—its old-new, lost-found neighborhood—taught Americans the advantages and disadvantages of dramatic urban change.

Buildings demolished in Southwest between 1940 and 1970. *JRP*

On this 1940 map of the area south of Independence Avenue, the buildings shaded in black are those that disappeared by 1970. The railroad came into the city on Virginia and Maryland Avenues soon after the Civil War. The curving line at the upper right of the map is the passenger line tunneled under East First Street, as planned by the Senate Park Commission. Most of the old Southwest neighborhood south of F Street, the present location of the Southwest Freeway, was taken by eminent domain and demolished between 1954 and 1960.

Axonometric map of Southwest, c. 1970. *JRP*

Crossing the Potomac River (on the left on the map) is Interstate 395, which connects with the Capital Beltway. At the point where it enters the Southwest neighborhood, it becomes known as the Southwest Freeway; where it enters the Capitol Hill neighborhood (on the right on the map), it is called the Southeast Freeway. With only a few exceptions, the structures north of the freeway are federal office buildings. The Southwest Washington Urban Renewal area is located south of the freeway.

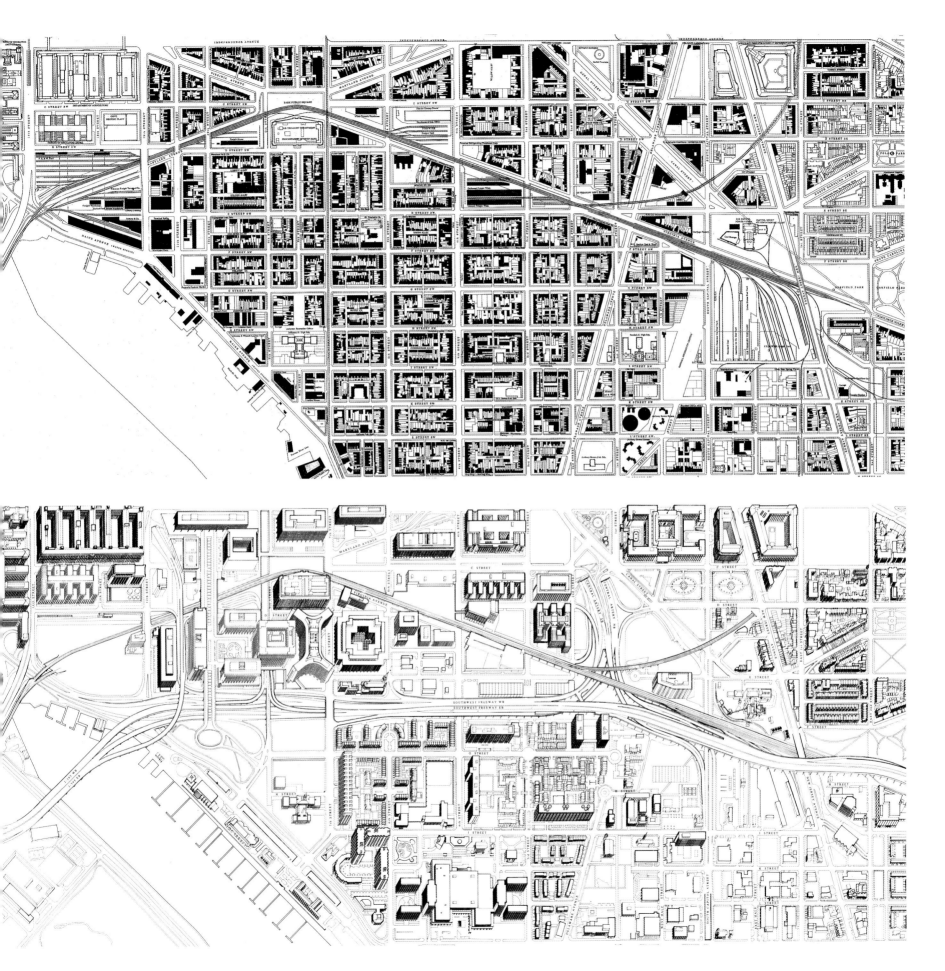

187

Georgetown

After World War II, residential patterns in Georgetown changed, but unlike the other residential neighborhoods around the center, Georgetown continued to transform in ways that had begun before the war. The population became wealthier, better educated, and even more professional. Despite some construction, the number of residents declined; family size became smaller and rooming houses were converted to single-family dwellings. While African-American ownership increased in the rest of the District of Columbia, it decreased in Georgetown: in 1940, black tenants occupied about 25 percent of all rental units; in 1960, black tenants occupied about 3 percent of rental units.

Renovation of residential properties by their owners rose sharply, particularly east of Wisconsin Avenue. The Progressive Citizens Association of Georgetown (PCAG) asked for rezoning, to residential use, of areas both east and west of Wisconsin Avenue. The rezoning was also supported by the Georgetown Citizens Association (GCA), a business group, which recognized that the future of Georgetown lay in the enhancement of its architectural and historic background. The alley dwellings at first were attacked as unfit places to live. By the early 1950s, however, the ban on alley dwellings was repealed as developers found it profitable to convert them into "coach houses," the gentrified term for alley houses.

The National Trust for Historic Preservation was established in Washington in 1949, and during the same year, a bill was drafted to make Georgetown a historic district. Two of the country's early preservation statutes, the Old Georgetown Act and the Old Stone House Act, were passed by Congress and signed by President Harry Truman in September 1950. The Old Georgetown Act was clarified in 1956, establishing Georgetown as a historic district. The act prohibited significant alterations to the exterior or any changes in visual appearance of buildings except as approved by a review board appointed by the government. This shifted preservation from a private act of property owners to

Buildings at Thirtieth and M Streets, constructed 1794; renovated 1955.

Original owner and builder Thomas Sim Lee was a friend of George Washington and a member of the Continental Congress. Once part of two-story town houses, the basements of these structures became lower floors when Alexander "Boss" Shepherd had M Street regraded in the 1870s. The buildings were renovated for commercial use by Howe, Foster and Snyder in 1955.

Lee House, constructed c. 1890; addition 1959. Designed by Hugh Newell Jacobsen.

Located at 2813 Q Street, the original, western (left) side of the house was too small for its new owners. Although objections were raised to the proposed addition—a mirror image of the existing building— it was approved by the Historic Preservation Review Board.

Trentman House, 1968. Renovation with addition Hugh Newell Jacobsen.

This modern row house at 1350 Twenty-seventh Street fits into its historic surroundings because of the attention to detail, proportion, and materials.

Georgetown waterfront and Whitehurst Freeway, early 1950s.
DCDT

Constructed in 1950 through the Georgetown waterfront, the Whitehurst Freeway could not be built today because of its impact on the Georgetown Historic District. To make way for the freeway, the historic Francis Scott Key house was demolished.

an action by a public authority, subjecting alterations to the judgments of designated architects and "qualified" citizens.

The Old Georgetown Act was opposed by Reverend Fox, the pastor of the Mount Zion United Methodist Church on Twenty-ninth Street, who argued that it would limit housing choices for African-Americans. He proved to be correct. Increasing house values in Georgetown made it attractive for low-income homeowners to sell and move to less expensive neighborhoods, while making Georgetown unattractive to low-income buyers. Although the restoration move-

ment did not cause the migration of African-American residents out of Georgetown, it clearly accelerated it.

The Progressive Citizens Association and the Georgetown Citizens Association disagreed on some matters. The GCA, for example, endorsed the eight-lane Three Sisters Bridge and Expressway through the Georgetown waterfront as well as the highway through Glover Archbold Park. The PCAG opposed both, vigorously and successfully. Eventually, in 1963, the PCAG and GCA merged to become the Citizens Association of Georgetown (CAG).

Georgetown in 1970

During the twentieth century, the primary change in residential Georgetown was the addition of five large, low-rise apartment buildings along Q Street near Rock Creek and the construction of a number of smaller apartment buildings north of Q Street, all built before World War II. Zoning restricting apartment building in residential Georgetown had been in effect since 1940, although the Dodge Mansion was converted into condominiums. Georgetown University had grown after World War II. The streetcar tracks had disappeared (except where residents rebelled against their removal) and were replaced by arteries for automobiles: Key Bridge, Rock Creek Parkway, and the elevated Whitehurst Freeway.

1. Dumbarton Oaks*: Harvard University Research Center.
2. **Georgetown University Library***
3. Office building*: Former Union Station terminal for streetcars.
4. **General Services Administration heating plant and coal yards***
5. **Whitehurst Freeway***
6. **I-66 interchange***: Remnant of abandoned Inner Loop freeways.
7. Key Bridge*
8. Dumbarton "Buffalo" Bridge*
9. Rock Creek Parkway*

Buildings and public projects constructed after 1940 are listed in **bold** type.
Buildings and public projects existing in 2000 are identified with an asterisk.*

Key

- single-family residences
- walk-up residences
- elevator apartment
- hotel
- retail
- private offices
- federal offices
- federal institutions
- private & foreign institutions
- local institutions
- industrial
- warehouse
- transportation

0 100   500   1000 ft

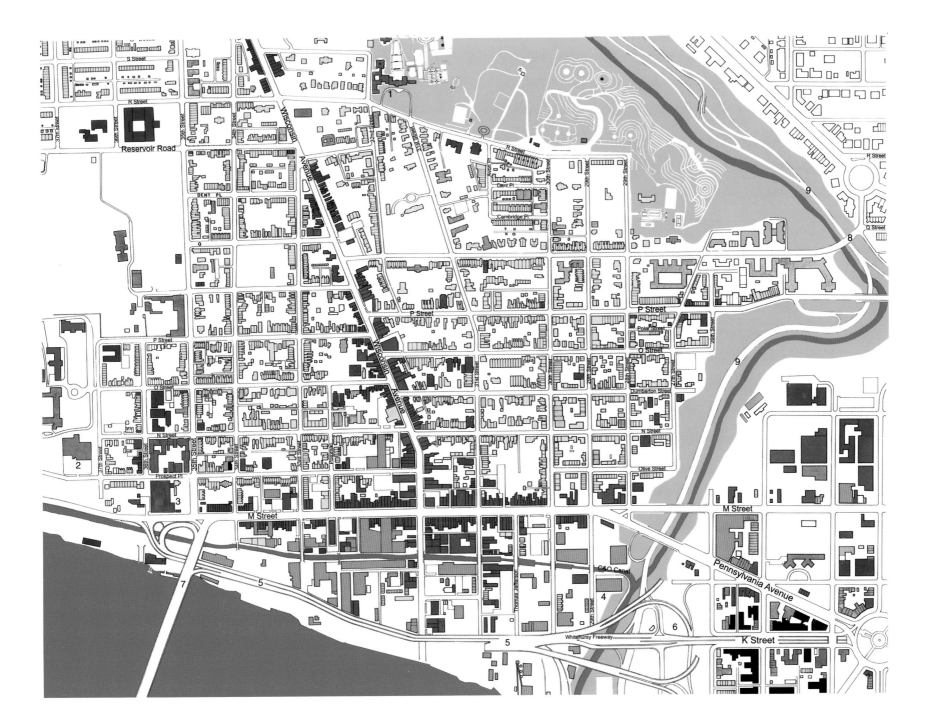

S Street

R Street

Reservoir Road

DENT PL

Wisconsin Avenue

R Street

Dent Pl

Cambridge Pl

P Street

P Street

P Street

Pomander Street

O Street

Wisconsin Avenue

Dumbarton Street

O Street

N Street

N Street

Olive Street

Prospect Pl

M Street

M Street

C&O Canal

Thomas Jefferson

Pennsylvania Avenue

Whitehurst Freeway

K Street

1

2

3

4

5

5

6

7

8

9

9

191

Changes in commercial Georgetown reflected the changes in residential Georgetown. In the 1940s, Georgetown retained most of the goods and services of the nineteenth and early twentieth centuries. After the war, these were gradually supplemented by antiques stores and dress and specialty shops, appealing to an increasingly upper-income clientele; restaurants began to appear in the late 1940s.

During the last quarter of the nineteenth century, riverfronts and harbors had been preempted by railroads and industry. After World War II, a number of cities—Boston, New York, Philadelphia, and San Francisco—had built freeways through these industrial waterfronts, and in 1950, the Whitehurst Freeway was built through the Georgetown waterfront.

The waterfront area was the last to be "restored." Many businesses were located in this area, and the houses were smaller and less elegant. The presence of the General Services Administration heating plant and coal-handling facility, a rendering plant, and the city incinerator did not add to the charm of the area south of M Street. Before World War II, the population had consisted of blue-collar workers, mostly white, but also including a number of African-Americans. Many of the waterfront area houses were renovated by new middle-class owners, and some by real estate investors.

A Georgetown Canal and Riverside Council was formed in 1961 to convert the area, 90 percent of which was zoned for commercial and industrial use, to residential use. A federal urban-renewal program was rejected, citing what citizens saw as the dismal Southwest Washington Urban Renewal project. The council and the Georgetown Business Property Owners Association compromised on a plan to permit some high-density construction. Both favored the continuation of the elevated Whitehurst Freeway, which constituted a barrier between Georgetown and the riverfront, because they felt it would encourage commuters to avoid driving through Georgetown.

Travel to and within the National Capital

A 1944 "Transportation Survey and Plan for the Central Area of Washington," prepared as part of a pre–World War II subway study, described commuter travel to the downtown: 48 percent of all commuters took public transit, 37 percent traveled in private automobiles, and 15 percent walked. The survey pointed out the importance to transportation efficiency of residential buildings close to places of employment:

> One of the most significant factors [regarding the home-work-home trip] is the number of people walking to work. Washington is unique in this respect... This is very fortunate. The pedestrian is the most economic user of street space, using approximately $1/13$ as much room as a transit passenger, and $1/200$ as much room as the average driver or passenger in a private automobile.
>
> He requires no parking facility and no capital investment for a transit vehicle to carry him. The number of people walking should be maintained, increased if possible, by protecting the attractiveness of

the area immediately surrounding the business district as a first class residential neighborhood.

In 1940, Washington had one of the most complete surface transit systems in the country, and its downtown was laced by a streetcar network. By the beginning of World War II, most streetcars were manufactured according to a design created primarily for the national capital. On New York Avenue west of Mount Vernon Square and on Pennsylvania Avenue between the Capitol and the Anacostia River, streetcars traveled on rights-of-way reserved exclusively for public transit. Providing streetcars with their own travelways meant that increasing automobile traffic would not slow the streetcars.

As a result of growing automobile congestion in the center, however, the prewar District of Columbia government had planned a downtown subway system, similar to the Boston system, in which the streetcars traveled in tunnels. With the intervention of the war, the system was never built, because the planned spacing between stations was too close to serve the expanding postwar urban region. This was unfortunate, since the earlier system would have served travel around the downtown with an efficiency that the future regional Metrorail system, with its deep, widely spaced stations, would not provide. The two in combination had the potential to save the center from the wrenching problems that dependence on the private automobile would create.

In 1952, Congress authorized a mass-transportation plan for the Washington region, and three years later, a mass-transportation survey was initiated through a supplemental appropriation to the budget of the National Capital Planning Commission. The work was managed by the chairman of the NCPC, Harland Bartholomew. Under Bartholomew, the NCPC approved the entire expressway system proposed by Maryland, Virginia, and the District of Columbia highway departments. In 1959, the NCPC also planned a thirty-three-mile rail transit system, less than one tenth the length of the proposed expressways. Half the rail system was to be above ground, in the median strips of the anticipated highways; half was to be underground, within the downtown area.

In 1960, Congress created the National Capital Transportation Agency, and in 1961, President John F. Kennedy replaced NCPC Chairman Bartholomew with Elizabeth "Libby" Rowe, a District citizen long active in the Committee of 100 and other civic organizations. Unlike Bartholomew, who argued for dispersal of jobs to the suburbs, Rowe believed that attention should be focused on the center; under her leadership, NCPC support shifted from freeways toward public transit. Led by C. Darwin Stolzenbach, appointed by President Kennedy to administer the National Capital Transportation Agency, attempts were made to suppress the expressway plan and to suggest an eighty-nine-mile rail transit system. The American Automobile Association called the scheme "the worst example of transportation planning in the country," a sentiment echoed by the American Road Builders Association. The controversies that the agency's proposals generated led the House of Representatives, in 1963, to reject a version of the thirty-three-mile transit system.

Streetcars on Pennsylvania Avenue, April 18, 1959. *Ara Mesrobian*

The last streetcar would travel on Pennsylvania Avenue on January 27, 1962— less than three years after this photograph was taken. The next day, buses would replace all streetcars in the District of Columbia.

Exclusive public transitway on New York Avenue, 1948. *LCPP*

In Washington, the wide L'Enfant avenues provided room for pedestrians and for public transit, with plenty of space remaining for automobiles and trucks. The arrangement became standard practice in the large, dense cities of Western Europe, where public transit was not sacrificed to automobile travel.

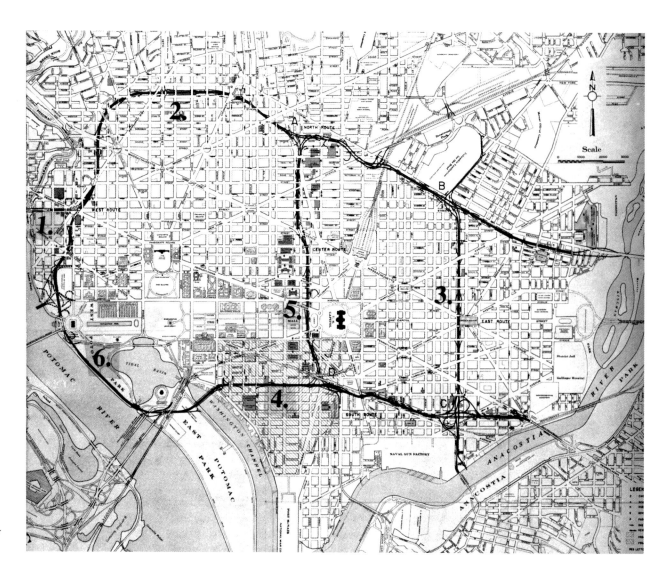

Proposed Inner Loop Freeway System, 1955. *FCC*

In the fall of 1966, Congress established the Washington Metropolitan Area Transit Authority (WMATA) to replace the National Capital Transportation Agency. This later agency was directly responsible to the governments of Maryland, Virginia, and the District of Columbia. Although District support for a rail transit system was never in doubt, such a system could not exist in the center without also extending into the suburbs beyond the District, and the support of Maryland and Virginia was at first uncertain. Construction of any WMATA system would depend primarily on bonds, rather than on congressional appropriation. Because bonding approval would rest on approval by voters in each jurisdiction, transit planning became political in a new way.

The system proposed by the WMATA was mostly underground within the District and, to save on cost, mostly aboveground beyond the District. While the transit system was almost entirely within the Capital Beltway, four short lines extended into Prince George's County, two long lines into Montgomery County, and two lines into northern Virginia. The projected cost (in 1968) was almost $2 billion, more than

twice the cost of the system defeated by Congress in 1963, primarily because of its expense. In 1968, Maryland and Virginia citizens voted overwhelmingly in support of the bond issues that would create the Washington Metropolitan Area Metrorail system.

The Highway Crisis

Less than a decade after World War II, more than twice as many commuters to downtown Washington traveled in private automobiles as by transit and walking combined. The percentage of automobile commuters was rising in cities all over America. In 1956, Congress passed the National Interstate and Defense Highways Act. The act laid the groundwork for a seventy-thousand-mile interstate highway system, with provisions for extensions of the system into cities that had the foresight to plan an urban highway network. By almost any criteria one of the most ambitious public works projects in history, the act changed the way people and goods move around the United States and helped to alter the character of American cities.

Interstate highway construction costs were financed from a Highway Trust Fund, replenished continuously by a dedicated tax on gasoline and other automotive products. Since 90 percent of the interstate highway construction costs were paid from the trust fund, the program was attractive to state and local transportation agencies. Disbursement of these monies was controlled by the Bureau of Public Roads, an agency of the Commerce Department, which in 1968 became the Federal Highway Administration (FHWA) within the new Department of Transportation. Control of the Highway Trust Fund made this federal agency extraordinarily powerful in setting transportation policy at all levels of American government.

The first expressway plan for Washington included a circumferential highway, the Capital Beltway, with nine radials extending beyond the beltway into the suburbs, eight radials extending inside the beltway into the center, and five expressways circling or crossing the downtown. Two more outer beltways, proposed but not mapped, would have created in the Washington region 450 miles of grade-separated, limited-access expressways.

The system was developed under the aegis of the federal Bureau of Public Roads and was designed and implemented by the Highway Departments of Maryland, Virginia, and the District of Columbia. The need seemed greatest in the center, and very early on the D.C. Highway Department conceived an elaborate Inner Loop Freeway System surrounding and penetrating the commercial and monumental center.

The system was supported by every local government and every local and regional planning agency, by the federal promise that 90 percent of the capital costs would be paid from the Highway Trust Fund, and originally, by most of the region's citizens. A decade after the passage of the Interstate Act, the Capital Beltway Interstate, Highway 395 (I-395), connecting the beltway to the Inner Loop, and the south leg of the Inner Loop (the Southwest and Southeast Freeways) were completed. The reaction of many citizens, particularly within the District, was negative, and the response to the Southeast Freeway through Capitol Hill—to its appearance, its performance, and the process by which it had been created—became violent and sustained. Plans to complete the system were challenged to a degree that made the rail transit battles seem mild. Pitted against one another were highway interests, federal agencies, planning agencies, neighborhoods, civic associations, the business community, and the District government.

In May 1968, under the title "A Layman's Who's Who on the Freeway Donnybrook" in the *Washingtonian,* Judith Hennessee summarized the battles, and the battlers, in the fight over the Inner Loop freeways:

> After twenty years and twenty million dollars worth of reports, studies, plans, a large part of the District highway program is sitting behind barricades somewhere in limbo . . . Through the years the squiggles on the maps have moved around with such startling rapidity that it became difficult to know where the freeway would strike

Rush-hour traffic on the Southeast Freeway, July 1974. *WP*

The Southeast Freeway, running through the Capitol Hill neighborhood, triggered the battle against subsequent freeway construction in the District of Columbia and, eventually, in the national capital region.

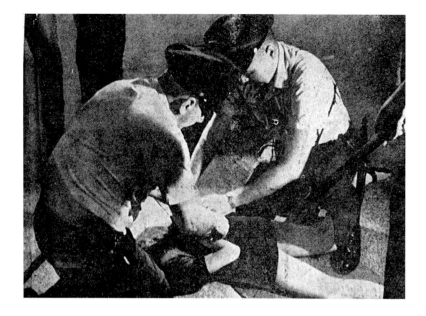

Police tie hands of struggling protester before City Council meeting, August 1969. *WP*

Sammy Abbott, mayor of Takoma Park, Maryland, speaking against the Inner Loop Freeway System before the City Council, August 1969. *WP*

An article in the August 10, 1969, *Washington Post* entitled "Fists Fly at Voting on Roads" reported that "A fist-swinging, chair-throwing melee erupted at Washington's city hall yesterday forcing the City Council to barricade its doors before voting approval of the Three Sisters Bridge."

next . . . With each successive change the sides have become more polarized . . .

At one end of the field are ranged the mighty highway lobby, a national Goliath made up of tire, gas, oil and automotive interests, the A.A.A., the Automobile Manufacturers Association, the Greater Washington Food Wholesalers Association, the American Trucking Association, the construction unions and the cement and construction industries into whose pockets most of the 90-10 money flows. With them are their captive Congressmen, as well as those who believe in freeways as a way of life. Locally, the downtown interests see the freeways as a boon to the city in general and business in particular . . .

"Freeways no! Subways yes!" is one of the rallying cries of the Emergency Committee on the Transportation Crisis. "A white man's road through a black man's home" is another. At the opposite end of the street from the Highway Lobby stands the Committee, a loosely knit but militant cross section of civic organizations and ministers, as adamantly opposed to freeways as the builders, planners and business men are for them. Marion Barry belongs, as does Julius Hobson; so does the D.C. Federation of Civic Associations and Neighborhoods, Inc.; Reginald Booker, of Niggers Incorporated, is Chairman.

The Emergency Committee had its genesis three years ago when Sam Abbott came home to dinner one night and was told by his wife that an 8-lane freeway was scheduled to run through their living room . . .

Peter Craig, presently with the [U.S.] Department of Transportation, spent six years disestablishing the Highway Department's origin-and-destination studies and data . . . and came to the conclusion that the Highway Department's statistics were full of helium . . .

But nothing moves like the ten cent dollar. The biggest public works program of all time, it has inflamed a good many Congressional imaginations; the very idea of halting the program is inconceivable, a shocking waste. This don't-look-a-gift-horse-in-the-mouth philosophy, rather than actual need, is at the root of the freeway fever.

Construction of a bridge across the Three Sisters, a legendary string of rocks between Rosslyn, Virginia, and Georgetown, was a preoccupation of Congress. In August 1969, the D. C. City Council (created in 1967 by an executive order that abolished the District of Columbia's three-commissioner government) voted "to comply" with the 1968 Highway Act approving the Three Sisters Bridge, a condition imposed by Congress if the city was to obtain appropriations for Metrorail.

In August 1970, Judge John Sirica, of Watergate fame, issued an injunction stopping work on the Three Sisters Bridge. In 1973, a new Federal Highway Act would enable urban areas to drop controversial proposals for interstate highways and transfer the highway money to rapid transit. The District of Columbia was specifically exempted from the act; Congress continued to insist that the Three Sisters Bridge connect to I-66 in Virginia, that the Inner Loop System be completed, and that a radial freeway connect the Inner Loop to the Capital Beltway in Maryland.

Residents of the District of Columbia would approve the Home Rule Act in May 1974. In 1976, new Mayor Walter Washington would propose to the City Council that an additional $493 million in federal highway funds be made available for Metrorail, saying "most of this money would come from elimination, once and for all, of plans to build the Three Sisters Bridge and the K Street Tunnel."

Finally, in 1976, Kentucky Congressman William Natcher would give up his fight to force the Three Sisters Bridge onto the District. Congress relented and permitted the District of Columbia to join with the rest of America's cities in transferring unused urban interstate funds to public transit. By winning the battle against the Highway Department's freeways, the citizens also provided funds to construct the financially hobbled Metrorail system.

After World War II, it was not unreasonable for Downtown merchants and city officials to believe that the loss of retail trade was caused, at least in part, by inadequate private automobile access. Given the destitution of the residential neighborhoods around Downtown, it may not have seemed foolish to substitute highways for row houses. In 1970, however, seventy thousand cars entered the center during rush hour each morning, as many (or more) rush-hour cars as entered central and lower Manhattan combined. The problems of Downtown were not ones of accessibility.

In an address to the Washington Board of Trade in 1968, Secretary of Transportation Alan S. Boyd repeated Lewis Mumford's warning: "Washington has proved a classic testing station for the question of whether a city dedicated wholeheartedly to traffic could survive for other purposes. The assumed right of the private motor car to go any place and park anywhere is nothing less than a license to destroy the city."

The Inner Loop would have demolished the Georgetown waterfront, cut a swath through Dupont Circle, Shaw, and the northern edge of Capitol Hill, slashed through the center of Capitol Hill at Lincoln Park and through the western edge of the Mall, and gone under K Street to a highway interchange in the neighborhood of Farragut Square. One connection to the Capital Beltway would have been constructed through Cleveland Park, Tenleytown, and Friendship Heights, one through Glover Archbold Park, one through the vicinity of Howard University, one through Takoma Park, and one through Rosslyn, Ballston, and Falls Church in northern Virginia. The northern Virginia connections were the only links ever constructed, built according to environmental regulations. Only the L'Enfant plan, the Senate Park Commission Plan, and the Act to Regulate the Height of Buildings have been more significant than the defeat of the Inner Loop in securing the quality and efficiency of the L'Enfant center of the nation's capital.

In the short term, winning the freeway battles could not stop the hemorrhaging of residents, businesses, and institutions from the center of the city. By 1970, more than half the people living within walking or short public transit distance of the center had moved to the Maryland and northern Virginia suburbs; the streetcar tracks had been dug up and the streetcars sent to Sarajevo; and the avenues had been abandoned to private automobile travel.

K Street, looking east toward Sixteenth Street, c. 1917. *NGS*

K Street, looking east toward Sixteenth Street, c. 1970.

Until 1937, K Street appeared much as it did in 1917. In 1937, however, the trees between Connecticut Avenue and Twelfth Street were cut down and replaced by frontage roads. The remaining trees, west of the avenue, were removed after World War II, along with most of the rest of the trees on Downtown streets.

Reflecting Pool, Lincoln Memorial, and "temporary" buildings on the Mall, 1943. *NCPC*

The buildings on the right were built during World War I. Those on the left were added during World War II.

The Mall

Almost since its inception, the Mall has been a place for national assembly, for commemoration and catharsis. In 1892, it served as the encampment for the Grand Army of the Republic; after World War I, "bonus marchers" (World War I veterans lobbying for their unpaid bonuses) argued their case for compensation from the Mall before they were driven across the Anacostia River. In wartime, the Mall has regularly been called to active service. During the Civil War, it was a marshaling ground for Union troops; during World War I, the War Department built "temporary" buildings at both the east and west ends of the Mall (those on the west end were still in use during World War II).

In 1965, the architectural firm of Skidmore, Owings & Merrill, under the direction of the Commission of Fine Arts, began a master plan for the Mall. The most important part of the plan proposed Constitution Gardens to replace the temporary buildings still remaining from World War I. In describing the genesis of the gardens, J. Carter Brown, chairman of the commission, related:

> Legend has it that the idea originated with President Richard Nixon's remark to John Ehrlichman, while on the presidential helicopter, that the site's temporary buildings, in which he had worked during World War II, ought to go. Supposedly, every time he flew over them Nixon would fire off memos asking why they had not been demolished. The Navy Department, rather accustomed to being three blocks from the White House, saw no reason to move. Luckily, the President of the

Marian Anderson at the memorial service for Harold Ickes held at the Lincoln Memorial, 1952.
LCPP

In one of the most moving gatherings on the Mall, people assembled, and the country gathered (over the radio), to listen to Marian Anderson sing from the steps of the Lincoln Memorial. In 1939, the great African-American contralto had been denied permission to sing in Constitution Hall, home of the Daughters of the American Revolution. Secretary of the Interior Harold Ickes—the Mall is managed by the National Park Service, under the Department of the Interior— with support from Eleanor Roosevelt, had arranged for Anderson to sing the national anthem on the Lincoln Memorial steps.

Civil Rights March on Washington, 1963. *LCPP*

The Reverend Martin Luther King Jr. stood on the steps of the Lincoln Memorial and told the audience, and the country, "I have a dream."

United States, as Commander-in-Chief, was able to realize his objective, an accomplishment of great consequence. However, Nixon's idea was to replace the "tempos" with what he called Tivoli Gardens, an amusement park, with two levels of parking underneath and a high density of excitement above.

The only post–World War II addition to the Mall to be built by 1970 was the National Museum of American History, designed by Steinman, Cain and White and finished in 1964. The temporary buildings erected during World War I were finally removed, however, and plans for the additions that would almost fully realize the work of L'Enfant and the Senate Park Commission were completed.

**Proposal for Constitution Gardens
(rejected), 1965.** Designed by
Skidmore, Owings & Merrill. *SOM*

The Commission of Fine Arts considered this initial scheme, which
responded to President Nixon's view
of the Mall, much too complex.
Architect Kevin Roche, then a member of the commission, worked with
David Childs of Skidmore, Owings
& Merrill to revise the scheme.

Master plan for the Mall, 1965–66.
Designed by Skidmore, Owings &
Merrill. *SOM*

The relationship between
Constitution Gardens and the
Lincoln Memorial Reflecting Basin
is shown in this model of the master
plan for the Mall. The model
includes the proposed extra row of

elms, rejected by the Commission of
Fine Arts. The Skidmore, Owings &
Merrill plan also depressed
Fourteenth Street under the Mall,
as both Major Nathaniel Michler
after the Civil War and Frederick
Law Olmsted Jr. in 1932 had
recommended. This idea was
rejected, but perhaps will reappear
in the twenty-first century.

Washington in 1970

- In 1950, more than 800,000 people lived in the city, but by 1970, the population had decreased to 756,500 and was still declining.
- By 1970, the city's activities had been rearranged again. Goods moved by truck instead of rail; consequently, warehouse and light industry moved to and beyond the Capital Beltway, the new interstate freeway encircling the city. Because people could travel in all directions by private automobile, their residences spread far into the surrounding farmland. Neighborhood institutions and retail stores followed their residential markets.
- By 1970, the late-nineteenth-century residential neighborhoods surrounding the center had been partially abandoned. The neighborhoods north of Downtown lost two hundred thousand of their three hundred thousand inhabitants. Many of the large, upscale houses in the Dupont Circle neighborhood became rooming houses, and the area was rife with drug trafficking.
- F Street lost stores to the suburban malls. Major department stores familiar to generations of Washington's citizens—Kann's, Lansburgh's, Garfinkel's—had closed or were about to close. Many stores at the east end of Downtown were closed. The Willard Hotel and other landmarks stood empty.
- Only the office industry continued to grow in the center. As blue-collar workers left the center, they were replaced in part by a white-collar labor force.
- The loss of vitality in the city center was reflected in the loss of many late-nineteenth-century and early-twentieth-century commercial buildings. When these were replaced at all, the substitutions were generally massive, architecturally undistinguished office buildings. Abandoned commercial and residential buildings were more frequently replaced by parking lots, the mark in post–World War II downtowns of a decaying commercial edge.
- The Whitehurst Freeway (west of the area shown in the map) and the Southwest Freeway (south of Independence Avenue) were built in the hope of providing access to the languishing downtown Washington retail sector. The urge to build freeways was understandable, but the problems of Downtown were not caused by inadequate automobile access. In 1970, more than seventy thousand private automobiles entered the center every morning rush hour. These automobiles traveled mainly on a transportation network that had been laid out by a French architect in 1791.
- Because the Capitol Hill and Shaw neighborhoods continued to provide houses for low-income citizens of all colors, they were spared either demolition (except for the oldest section of Shaw, which was obliterated) or large-scale rebuilding. However, the old Southwest area was razed and rebuilt by public agencies, and most of residential Foggy Bottom was eradicated and rebuilt as a combination of public and private institutions.
- After World War II, the Mall continued to host the nation's most important events and was ready for the additions that would largely complete the work of L'Enfant and the Senate Park Commission.

Key

- single-family residences
- walk-up residences
- elevator apartment
- hotel
- retail
- private offices
- federal offices
- federal institutions
- private & foreign institutions
- local institutions
- industrial
- warehouse
- transportation

0 100   500   1000 ft

1. State Department*: Expanded by 1970.

2. **General Accounting Office***: Moved from temporary earlier quarters.

3. **Employment Securities Building***

4. **Civil Service Commission***: Moved from temporary earlier quarters.

5. **U.S. Information Agency**

6. **Federal Deposit Insurance Commission***

7. **Museum of Science and Industry***

8. **John F. Kennedy Center for the Performing Arts***

9. **Lafayette Square office buildings***

10. Executive Office Building*: Formerly the State, War and Navy Building.

11. **Federal Bureau of Investigation***

12. **U.S. Courthouse***

13. **World Bank***

14. **International Monetary Fund Building***

15. **Watergate complex***

16. **Howard Johnson Hotel***: Infamous as the home of the "plumbers" of the Committee to Re-elect the President for the 1974 election.

17. National Portrait Gallery*: Former Patent Office.

18. National Museum of American Art*: Former Patent Office.

19. **The Longfellow***: An early modern office building of 1940, air-conditioned and built to the property line.

20. **George Washington Hospital***

21. **New Army Navy Club***

22. Sulgrave Club*: Former private mansion.

23. **Metropolitan Club***

24. **YMCA***

25. **YWCA***

26. **American Institute of Architects headquarters***: The group of buildings includes Tayloe's Octagon House.

27. **National Geographic Society***

28. **National Theater***

29. **Interstate 66 interchange***: Designed to connect four interstate freeways that were never constructed.

30. **Theodore Roosevelt Bridge***: Replacement for the abandoned Three Sisters Bridge project and interstate route through the Georgetown waterfront.

Buildings and public projects constructed or completed after 1940 are listed in **bold** type.

Buildings and public projects existing in 2000 are identified with an asterisk.*

0 100   500   1000 ft

Chapter 6

1970
to
2000

Aerial view of the Mall, looking west past the Capitol, 1985. *Dennis Brack, NGA*

Changes between 1970 and 2000

The year 1970 was a low point in the fortunes of American city centers, including the L'Enfant center of the national capital. In the three decades since that time, however, Washington's city center was again transformed. All American cities were damaged in the decades after World War II, as citizens and resources left the center. Two "industries" nevertheless did grow in this area throughout the twentieth century—the private office industry and the tourist industry. During the early 1970s, total employment in central Washington increased despite the loss in retail trade. The decrease in retail and blue-collar jobs began to be more than offset by the increase in white-collar office jobs and those service industries that support office work. In 1860, sixty law offices clustered around the city's Patent Office. By 2000, the Patent Office had moved, but the legal profession was thriving in the center of the nation's capital.

It was the private office industry, with considerable help from the tourist industry and supported by the continuing presence of the federal government, that was primarily responsible for reshaping Washington's center from an urban backwater in 1970 into the most dynamic location in the national capital region in 2000. *Washington Post* writer Joel Garreau's phrase "edge cities," coined in his 1991 book, *Edge City: Life on the New Frontier*, represented a significant insight as to the impact of urban development beyond city centers. At the end of the twentieth century, however, the center of Washington had about five times the employment of Tysons Corner, the quintessential edge city. With approximately 450,000 jobs in the central city and another 100,000 just across the Potomac River in Rosslyn and Crystal City (in only a midsized urban region), downtown Washington was in the year 2000 the second-largest employment center in America, roughly tied with Chicago. In terms of concentration of employment, downtown Washington and Chicago were exceeded only by "downtown" New York (central and lower Manhattan).

Three public initiatives, each nurtured, often painfully, during the postwar decades, also contributed to the economic success of the center of the capital. The first was historic preservation, which began in Georgetown with federal support in the 1950s. Still controversial in the view of a few, preservation took root in the center in the early 1970s. Impressive buildings that would have disappeared had it not been for District of Columbia preservation statutes continued to grace the downtown area at the end of the twentieth century. The most important contribution of the historic preservation movement, however, was the stabilization of the late-nineteenth-century residential neighborhoods at the edge of the downtown. The economic good health of the city center would not have existed, and could not have persisted, without the presence of high-quality residential neighborhoods within walking and short transit distance of the center.

The second initiative was the formation by Congress, in 1972, of the Pennsylvania Avenue Development Corporation (PADC), a public-private partnership. After several false starts, by the mid-1990s the PADC had completed its mission: Pennsylvania Avenue, described by Congress as a "scene of desolation," had become "distinguished and impressive." Private development along the avenue, sponsored by the PADC, had become profitable for its owners and for the city. An unusual institution in many ways, the PADC quietly closed its doors in 1995.

The third factor contributing to central Washington's turnaround was the creation of the Metrorail system. In March 1976, the first passengers rode the Metro Red Line. Ridership grew slowly, and Metro financing continued to be precarious at the end of the twentieth century. By 2000, however, it had become clear that Metrorail needed to expand its capacity to satisfy the growing demand for travel to and within the city center. Both the residential neighborhoods surrounding the center and the robust economy of the downtown area were dependent on Metrorail.

These transformations took place during a time of change in governance of the District of Columbia. In July 1996, the *New York Times* published a series of articles under the headline "Monument to Decay," opening with the statement: "In May 1974, residents of the District of Columbia approved the Home Rule Act in a referendum. For the first time in its history, the city was to be governed by a locally elected mayor and city council. Since then, the city has struggled with constraints placed on its independence by Congress, while grappling with persistent deficits and mismanagement by elected officials." The *Times* included a chronology of events, labeled "Steps on a Path of Steady Decline":

- In 1975, Walter E. Washington, the first Mayor elected under home rule, takes office along with the new city council.
- In 1980, an audit by the District's financial consultants turns up a $284 million debt, much of it from before home rule, and a $1.4 billion shortfall for city pension funds.
- In 1985, a constitutional amendment, proposed in 1978, to give the District full voting representation in Congress, dies after less than half of the states needed for ratification approve the amendment by the seven-year deadline.
- In 1990, Mayor Barry is sentenced to six months in prison, convicted of one misdemeanor charge of cocaine possession. A special commission finds the District facing an immediate fiscal crisis that is undermining the quality of life. Sharon Pratt Kelly is elected Mayor; during the campaign she vows to clean house with a shovel, not a broom.
- In 1994, Mr. Barry is reelected Mayor; the budget surpluses under Mayor Kelly are seen as the product of questionable accounting practices. The General Accounting Office reports that the District is insolvent and may run out of money by the summer. President Clinton signs legislation to create a financial control board for the District of Columbia.

Under the title "Home Rule: 'They Didn't Get a Good Deal,'" the *Times* described the District's financial difficulties in this way:

> For a hundred years before home rule, Washington had been governed by a Mayor and City Council appointed by the president, and

before that a three-member Board of Commissioners. Much of Washington's decline has come as a result of the deal made to allow the city to govern itself.

When public servants moved from the Federal payroll to the District's, Congress did not provide money for their retirement fund. The liability has ballooned to $5.1 billion... Medicaid costs have also expanded from $17 million in 1973 (to $844 million in 1996). In addition, the city inherited a set of books so poorly maintained that the $279 million deficit was not discovered for three years. Without a state government to funnel taxes of non-city residents back to Washington (and with the Congressional ban on a Washington commuter tax), the estimated $18.5 billion earned in the city by suburbanites is lost to the District. As a result, more than half the money in the District budget comes from local taxes. Other cities receive, on average, 75 percent of their budgets from state and Federal governments. In fact, other national capitals—like those of the United Kingdom, France, Italy, Japan—are generously subsidized by their governments.

Against this background of financial decay, the revitalization of the center in the three decades following 1970 was remarkable. (It is true, however, that by the time Mayor Marion Barry—who had begun his public career as a community activist—left office in 1998, private Washington fared better than when he became mayor in 1982.)

In 1995, the city's finances were still in disarray. In that year, a five-member District of Columbia Financial Responsibility and Management Assistance Authority, better known as the "Control Board," was created by Congress and appointed by President Bill Clinton to take control of the city's finances. The board was first chaired by Andrew Brimmer, then by Alice M. Rivlin, an economist with the Brookings Institution. Anthony A. Williams, an experienced public servant, became the city's chief financial officer. When the Control Board and Williams began their work, the District had an accumulated debt of $518 million; as the Control Board prepared to disband in 2000, the District had a surplus of $464 million. In 1998, the city budget was close to balanced, and Anthony Williams was elected mayor in a landslide.

Mayor Williams, with the support of the District Council and District Representative Eleanor Holmes Norton, made a number of changes in city agencies. The mayor spoke a number of times about the city's history and about the importance of planning for its future. Among the changes and additions to the city's responsibilities, he created a District Division (later Department) of Transportation within the Department of Public Works and appointed as director Dan Tangherlini, who had managerial experience in large transportation agencies. Williams also appointed a new director of the Office of Planning, Andrew Altman, who had an impressive record as planning director in West Coast cities. Despite the mayor's additions to the city's costs of doing business, in 2000 the budget of the District of Columbia had a surplus, one of the few times in its history.

National Permanent Building, 1977. Designed by Hartman-Cox Architects. This inventive contemporary office building makes exposed ductwork seem classical.

Rebuilding the Center

Post–World War II architecture in Washington represented a period of what the *AIA Guide* (3rd ed., 1994) called "ribbon wall horrors," buildings clad in plastic and aluminum. Of the almost two hundred buildings described in the *Guide* that were erected in the central business district and surrounding residential areas, only fourteen were designed and built in the thirty years between 1940 and 1970; forty were built in the twenty-five years between 1970 and 1995. Both government intervention and enlightened private development contributed to Washington's increasing architectural quality toward the end of the twentieth century.

In 1972, under President Richard M. Nixon, the Federal Design Improvement Program became an important initiative of the National Endowment for the Arts. The program aimed to improve the quality of federal and private architecture in the national capital and beyond by encouraging architectural competitions for building commissions. In 1990, the General Services Administration began an awards program and then a design excellence program in which peer-selection panels recommended designers for federal projects and reviewed their work. Today, architects from across America compete for work in the capital, and some of the most eminent firms from abroad are represented in the design of embassies for their respective countries. A notable example, completed in

800 North Capitol Street, 1990.
Designed by Hartman-Cox Architects.

In materials and detailing, this building complements, without directly copying, the nineteenth-century Government Printing Office on the opposite side of H Street.

Franklin Square, 1989–90.
Designed by Hartman-Cox Architects.

1994 on Massachusetts Avenue, is the Finnish Embassy by Heikkinen - Komonen. This distinguished building is a fitting example of work from a country whose currency is adorned with portraits of architects.

Architects working in the center of Washington have always been constrained, for better or for worse, by the fact that they are building within the national capital. Many late-twentieth-century structures exhibit an attention to dignity required of construction within the center, as well as a stylistic uncertainty typical of the period's architecture. Two characteristics of the L'Enfant plan have shaped buildings in Washington. As a result of the diagonal avenues, which create oddly warped building sites, many structures take tortured shapes. Examples include the East Wing of the National Gallery and the Inter-American

Courtyard of FBI Building, 1960–74. Designed by C. F. Murphy & Associates.

Many of Washington's government buildings hide lovely public open spaces.

Courtyard of the National Museum of American Art and National Portrait Gallery, renovated 1970. Renovation by Faulkner, Stenhouse, Fryer.

Shaded by several of the grandest American elms in the city, this quiet courtyard is one of the capital's most appealing outdoor lunchrooms.

Bank, at New York Avenue and Thirteenth Street, among others. In addition, because a great number of the L'Enfant streets are spaced far apart, many of the buildings are very large, some occupying entire city blocks. As a consequence, downtown Washington contains a building type unusual in America: low (because of height limitations) and doughnut-shaped, filling the building envelope, with a center open to the sky (the Treasury Building of 1839/1869) or with a glass-enclosed atrium (the State, War and Navy Building of 1871–88, now the Old Executive Office Building). Many of the massive government buildings constructed between 1900 and World War II without air-conditioning are filled with interior courtyards. Once mere light wells or storage bins, many have proved to be an urban design resource.

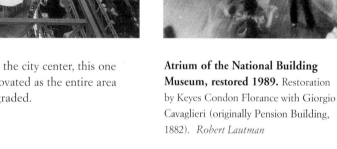

Interior of the Old Post Office, restored 1982. Restoration by Arthur Cotton Moore/Associates (originally built 1899). *James Oesch*

The soaring atrium, 100 feet wide by 190 feet long by 160 feet high, is surrounded by three retail stores and seven stories of offices. It will potentially become a hotel, continuing its adaptive reuse. Like many neglected nineteenth- and early-twentieth-century court-yards in the city center, this one was renovated as the entire area was upgraded.

Atrium of the National Building Museum, restored 1989. Restoration by Keyes Condon Florance with Giorgio Cavaglieri (originally Pension Building, 1882). *Robert Lautman*

The Pension Building, where Civil War veterans collected their pensions, became the traditional site of presidential inaugural balls. The building, designed by Montgomery C. Meigs and at one point almost abandoned, was given new life as the National Building Museum, created by an act of Congress in 1980 and first opened to the public in 1985. The museum, which houses the offices of the Commission of Fine Arts, mounts exhibitions and hosts lectures on architecture, engineering, urban design, and planning. Shortly after the building's renovation as a museum, the spectacular atrium was the site of the American Institute of Architects ball.

Interior of the Library of Congress, Jefferson Building, restored 1993.
Restoration by Arthur Cotton Moore/Associates (originally built 1886–92). *Robert Lautman*

The exterior of the Thomas Jefferson Building, based on the Paris Opéra, is a forbidding granite pile. The interior of the elaborate antechamber and central stair hall, the creation of Edward Pearce Casey with twenty-two sculptors and twenty-six painters, is dazzling. The octagonal main reading room, consisting of marble and wood beneath a 160-foot-high domed ceiling, forms a virtuosic finale; it reputedly left Henry James almost speechless. Before restoration, the stair hall had been subdivided into small offices. When the James Madison Building was completed across Independence Avenue, this beautiful, idiosyncratic space returned to its original use, as an antechamber to the main reading room.

Interior of International Square, 1985. Designed by Vlastimil Koubek. *VK*

This typical Washington office building covers almost an entire block around a central atrium (many structures of this era recalled the courtyards built in the nineteenth and early twentieth centuries), with retail shops on the ground floor and lower level and a garage below.

Interior of National Place, 1984.
Designed by Mitchell/Giurgola Architects and Frank Schlesinger Associates. *Harlan Hambright Associates, FSA*

An atrium around a shopping mall connects to a hotel and office building by Schlesinger, which also contains the National Press Club and the National Theater.

At the end of the twentieth century, downtown Washington, zoned primarily for commercial use, had become an enormously valuable cube of space, limited vertically by the Act to Regulate the Height of Buildings and horizontally by residential neighborhoods jealously guarded by politically sophisticated residents. Frenetic building activity during the last quarter of the century—including projects such as the Ronald Reagan Building (1998), the MCI Center (1998), and the Washington Convention Center (under construction), each with footprints larger than the Capitol—ensured that the space would soon be entirely occupied.

Competition for this rapidly vanishing space became most intense in the area north and east of Mount Vernon Square. When the District of Columbia was granted a limited form of home rule in 1974, Congress allowed the Office of Planning to prepare a comprehensive proposal for the area, subject to review by the National Capital Planning Commission (NCPC), which before the establishment of home rule had been responsible for the city's planning. A central objective of the downtown plan was the creation of a "living downtown," a mix of residential uses within the commercial city. Except for the work of the Pennsylvania Avenue Development Corporation, however, public agencies and the development community effectively paid only lip service to this objective, an objective increasingly difficult to attain as developable space continued to disappear.

In the 1970s, the University of the District of Columbia (UDC) prepared a campus plan for six blocks between Seventh and Ninth

MCI Center, 1998. Designed by Florance Eichbaum Esocoff King.

Civic groups opposed construction of the MCI Center because its large size required that H Street be closed between Sixth and Seventh Streets. Designed primarily for professional basketball and hockey, the center also hosts other civic events and has proved to be a good neighbor. Built over the Gallery Place Metrorail station, at the intersection of three subway lines, it requires no additional parking for private automobiles.

Streets and between M Street and Mount Vernon Square. After the land had been almost entirely cleared, the university abandoned the site and moved to Connecticut Avenue beyond Van Ness Street in northwest Washington. When, in 1998, it became obvious that the Washington Convention Center, built in 1983, was out of date, a convention center authority created plans for an enlarged facility within this residential sector of the Shaw neighborhood, on the original UDC site. Simultaneously, the Committee of 100 on the Federal City developed a plan for a residential neighborhood on the same site and argued in favor of locating the convention center north of Union Station, where it would not have a destructive effect on residential Shaw.

With a footprint five times the size of that of the Capitol, a truck dock extending into and forty feet below Ninth Street, and no provision for on-site parking (but with internal access to Metrorail), the proposed new convention center presented formidable problems for the Shaw neighborhood and for the city. One related proposal, to build a four-lane, one-billion-dollar expressway in a tunnel under New York Avenue, was abandoned. A proposal for an underground, five-thousand-car parking garage and truck-holding area east of Mount Vernon Square was vetoed by the District of Columbia Council in 1999; testimony suggested that downtown Washington already almost certainly contained more parking space than any other downtown in America, with the possible exception of central and lower Manhattan.

By rejecting the parking garage (and the baseball stadium planned above it), the council paved the way for a mixed-use residential community on the site proposed for the underground garage—in the triangle east of Mount Vernon Square between New York, New Jersey, and Massachusetts Avenues. Planning for this community is one of the initiatives of the new Office of Planning, with the support of a number of civic groups. If the planned residential densities develop, more people will walk to work from this new neighborhood during the morning rush hour than would have been carried by the abandoned billion-dollar underground expressway. The capital investment will be the cost of sidewalks.

The noted American urbanist Lewis Mumford believed that civilization was the product of city life, that when humans began collecting in villages and, later on, in cities, people who had encountered few other humans each year began to rub against hundreds of neighbors every week. Life became "political" in the sense that citizens were forced, constantly, to mediate between legitimate but conflicting interests. At the end of Washington's second century, competition for space within and around the commercial and monumental center had become unusually political. Three essential activities vied for space in and around the downtown: private and public offices, which provided the economic lifeblood of the city; Washington's public and private museums, which made the national capital unique; and the residential communities within and clustering around the center, without which central Washington would be sterile.

Demonstration in favor of preserving the Old Post Office, 1971. *DCPL*

Historic Preservation

Beginning in the 1970s, the historic preservation movement, a reaction to the architecturally destructive decades after World War II, became a force in shaping the city's downtown. The turning point in the movement was the battle to save the Old Post Office on Pennsylvania Avenue, a magnificent Richardson Romanesque building. The structure was first slated for destruction as part of the clearance for the Senate Park Commission's neoclassical Federal Triangle. The Old Post Office had been completed only a few years before the 1902 Senate Park Commission Plan, and the demolition of this relatively recent, imposing structure was delayed. In 1971, the Pennsylvania Avenue Advisory Council (soon to become the Pennsylvania Avenue Development Corporation) recommended razing the building, except for its tower.

Alison Owings, a news writer and producer for WRC radio, joined with Terry B. Morton of the National Trust for Historic Preservation to form a preservation advocacy group called Don't Tear It Down. The group focused on the Old Post Office and, on the first day of the second annual Earth Week, April 19, 1971, organized a march from the trust headquarters to the steps of the Old Post Office to publicize its cause.

In 1996, the Twenty-fifth Anniversary Program of the D.C. Preservation League, successor to Don't Tear It Down, reported that:

> Within two weeks Sen. Mike Gravel (D-Alaska) convened a previously scheduled hearing of the Senate Public Works Subcommittee on Public Buildings and Grounds to determine the federal government's overall preservation policy, as well as the fate of the Old Post Office. Among those testifying on preservation's behalf were James Biddle, Sen. Vance Hartke, Richard Howland, Charles Conrad, John W. Hill (of the National Endowment for the Arts), John Wiebenson (local architect active in preservation), and Arthur Cotton Moore, who later designed the renovation of the spared building. The force for preservation had become entrenched.

Old Post Office, restored 1982.
Restoration by Arthur Cotton Moore/Associates (originally built 1899).

The early successes of Don't Tear It Down were literally monumental. The Old Post Office, originally designed by Willoughby J. Edbrooke, was saved over a period of years with the help of many people, including Nancy Hanks, chairman of the National Endowment for the Arts from 1969 to 1977, for whom the building is now named.

215

Old Masonic Hall (Lansburgh's Furniture Store), 1868; restoration anticipated.

Franklin School, 1868; restored 1982. Designed by Adolph Cluss; restored by Hartman-Cox Architects with Navy Marshall Gordon and RTKL Associates Inc.

Willard Hotel, 1901; restored 1986. Conceptual restoration design by Vlastimil Koubek, with Hardy Holzman Pfeiffer Associates; restoration by Stuart Golding, Oliver Carr Company. *Carol M. Highsmith, PAAAP*

Washington's most famous hotel is the last in a succession of hotels that have occupied this site since 1816.

Renwick Gallery of the National Museum of American Art (Old Corcoran Gallery, later U.S. Court of Claims), 1859; renovated 1971. Exterior renovation by John Carl Warnecke & Associates; interior renovation by Hugh Newell Jacobsen. *Robert Lautman*

Old Executive Office Building (formerly State, War and Navy Building), 1871–88. Designed by Alfred B. Mullet.

Unlike other nineteenth-century buildings still in existence, Mullet's building has been preserved by not restoring it. The building was so reviled during its time that Mullet committed suicide two years after it was completed. President Harry S. Truman, an architecture buff, called it "the greatest monstrosity in America." Under President Herbert Hoover, Congress hired architect Waddy B. Wood "to bring it back to the sound classical lines of the Treasury," the 1839/1869 building with the same footprint located on the opposite side of the White House. Mullet's design was saved by the Depression, which also brought about the downfall of the president who tried to change the facade.

Riggs Bank Building, 1891; addition to west end, 1926. Renovated in 1998 as a Courtyard Marriott Hotel.

D.C. Public Library, 1902. Designed by Ackerman and Ross. Acquired in 1999 by the Washington Historical Society; in 2000, became the City Museum of Washington, D.C.

Established in 1894, the Historical Society of Washington, D.C., describes its role as having "served as an invaluable source for information about our nation's capital—its past, its neighborhoods, and most importantly, its people—for over a hundred years." In its mission to tell the city's many stories, the organization highlights Washington as a "vibrant community, where North and South, local and federal, urban and suburban, national and international, native and newcomer meet, with often surprising results." With new interest in preservation, which the society helped to create, its role is increasingly important.

Office building, 1991, using Greyhound Bus Terminal (1940). Restoration and design by Florance Eichbaum Esocoff King.

The office developers were granted zoning advantages in return for preservation of the bus station, one of many examples of adaptation of historic structures in Washington. Functionally, the Art Deco station is incorporated into the New York Avenue office building, but it retains its architectural integrity.

Mid-nineteenth-century "Red Lion Row" and new office building, 1985. Designed by Hellmuth, Obata + Kassabaum.

These historic buildings at 2000 Pennsylvania Avenue are still in use. They open to an arcade with one side formed by the old buildings and the other by a new office building, which has an undistinguished and unfortunately assertive facade.

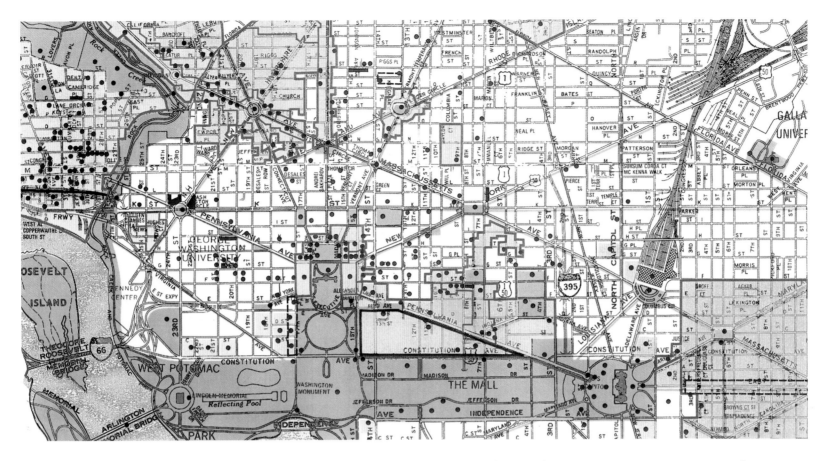

Historic buildings are indicated by dots. Georgetown, Foggy Bottom, Dupont Circle, and Capitol Hill are historic districts, protected by preservation statutes and astute residents. These historic districts, along with the Southwest neighborhood, form a stable residential ring around the central business district and monumental core that limits horizontal expansion of the commercial and governmental center.

A 1990s parking garage grafted onto facades of two of the "Six Buildings" (1792).

The original buildings on Pennsylvania Avenue between Nineteenth and Twenty-ninth Streets were among the earliest Federal-style buildings in the capital. Preservationists do not advocate this type of restoration, which they call "facadomy."

Many buildings that continued to exist solely because of the historic preservation statutes reverted comfortably to their original use. In 2000, the Willard Hotel still served as a hotel; the Renwick Gallery had changed its name, but not its function. A number of buildings, however, continued to be useful after their original purpose had disappeared. The Old Post Office became a retail space and office building; these functions were not successful and the building might become a hotel. As the National Building Museum, the Pension Building was given a more glorious second life than the Old Post Office; Riggs Bank at F and Ninth Streets NW became a successful hotel; and the Heurich Mansion, built in 1892 for the brewer Christian Heurich, was made the home of the Historical Society of Washington, D.C. Preservation at its best does not fossilize the city; adaptive reuse is its important objective.

Eventually, the District of Columbia passed a statute even more restrictive than the 1956 Georgetown Act. Preservation was to be managed by a Historic Preservation Agency and a Historic Preservation Review Board of citizens appointed by the mayor.

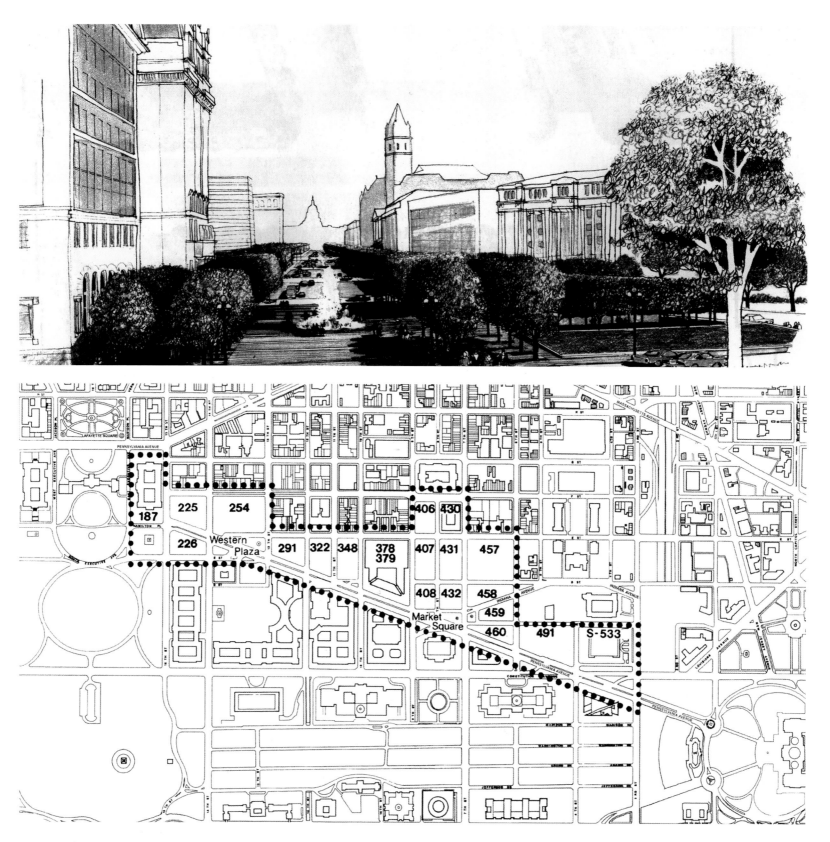

Drawing of Pennsylvania Avenue, proposed in the 1974 Pennsylvania Avenue Plan. *PAP*

Map of the "squares" for which the Pennsylvania Avenue Development Corporation was responsible. *PAP*

The dotted lines indicate the boundary of the PADC area. The squares were first numbered on the 1803 Nich King map, and the system continues to be used to identify locations in the District of Columbia.

An important section of the urban design plan was a set of axonometric drawings of each square in the area covered by the Pennsylvania Avenue Plan. The top diagram shows existing conditions; the bottom diagram illustrates the PADC requirements for development. The drawings specify that Hotel Washington (left) and the Willard Hotel are to be preserved, and that new retail shops and offices are to be constructed between them. Teams of developers and architects competed for the right to develop each square. The choice was based on the quality of the architecture and the previous performance and financial resources of the developer.

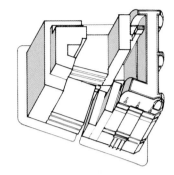

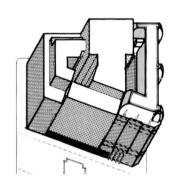

Square 225, 1995.

As mandated by the Urban Design Plan, retail and office infill occupies the sites between Hotel Washington and the Willard Hotel.

The Pennsylvania Avenue Development Corporation

The Pennsylvania Avenue Development Corporation transformed Pennsylvania Avenue—the nation's "main street"—into a boulevard in which L'Enfant and Jefferson would have taken pride. In passing the law that established the PADC on October 27, 1972:

> Congress determined that the national interest required that the area adjacent to Pennsylvania Avenue, between the Capitol and the White House, be developed and used in a manner suitable to its ceremonial, physical, and historic relationship to the legislative and executive branches of the Federal government . . . Congress considered not only the national significance of this great Avenue, but also the steady deterioration of its northern environs and the consequent economic and social liabilities imposed upon the District of Columbia.
>
> The Corporation's enabling act states that in order to insure proper development and use of the area and the elimination of blight, a comprehensive plan must be developed and implemented.

The Pennsylvania Avenue Plan, presented to and approved by Congress, included a land-use plan, an illustrated site (urban design) plan, landmarks and building preservation plans, and details such as a typical avenue landscaping plan and typical lighting section. The plan recommended that Pennsylvania Avenue be widened, with double rows of trees planted on the south side and triple rows on the north side; special brick paving was to be used for the sidewalks.

Between 1974, when its plan was approved, and 1995, when it completed its work, the PADC planted Pennsylvania Avenue with seven hundred willow oaks, added new paving, lights, and benches, and with the help of congressional appropriations and talented designers, created new and refurbished public open spaces: Pershing Park, Freedom Plaza, Market Square, the Navy Memorial, and John Marshall Park. The corporation also used $130 million in public investment to produce twenty-two private development projects, with $1.5 billion in private investment paying $69 million each year in taxes to the District of Columbia.

In 2000, Pennsylvania Avenue had become the street of L'Enfant's vision, two centuries after the architect described to President Washington "a direct and large avenue . . . with a middle way paved for heavy carriages and a walk each side planted with double rows of trees . . . a street laid out on a dimension proportioned to the greatness which . . . the Capital of a powerful Empire ought to manifest."

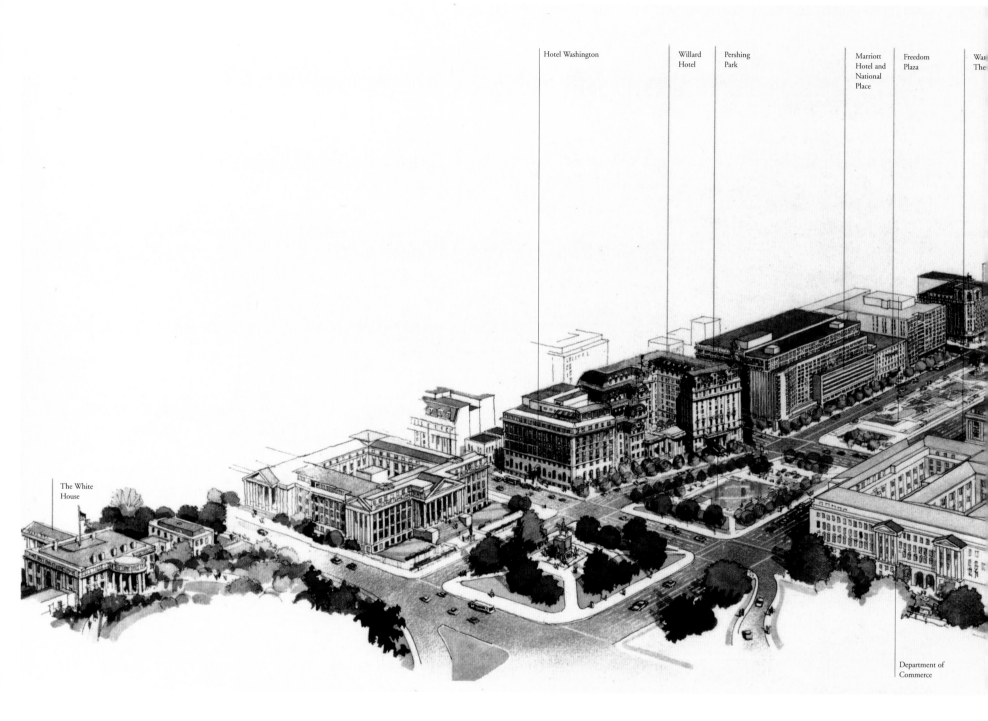

The White House

Hotel Washington

Willard Hotel

Pershing Park

Marriott Hotel and National Place

Freedom Plaza

War[ner] The[ater]

Department of Commerce

Projects of the Pennsylvania Avenue Development Corporation. Drawn by Frederick Schonbach for the American Enterprise Institute, 1982. *FS*

This early sketch of the PADC area shows work completed or planned in 1982: the Hotel Washington (Carrère & Hastings, 1917), renovated by the PADC with Mariani and Associates; the Willard Hotel (Henry Hardenberg, 1901),

renovated by Vlastimil Koubek with Hardy Holzman Pfeiffer Associates; Pershing Park by M. Paul Friedberg with Jerome Lindsay; Freedom Plaza by Venturi, Rauch and Scott Brown; and the Marriott Hotel and National Place by Mitchell/Giurgola Architects and Frank Schlesinger Associates, with the refurbished National Theater beyond. The renovated Warner Theater is just outside the PADC boundaries, on the north-

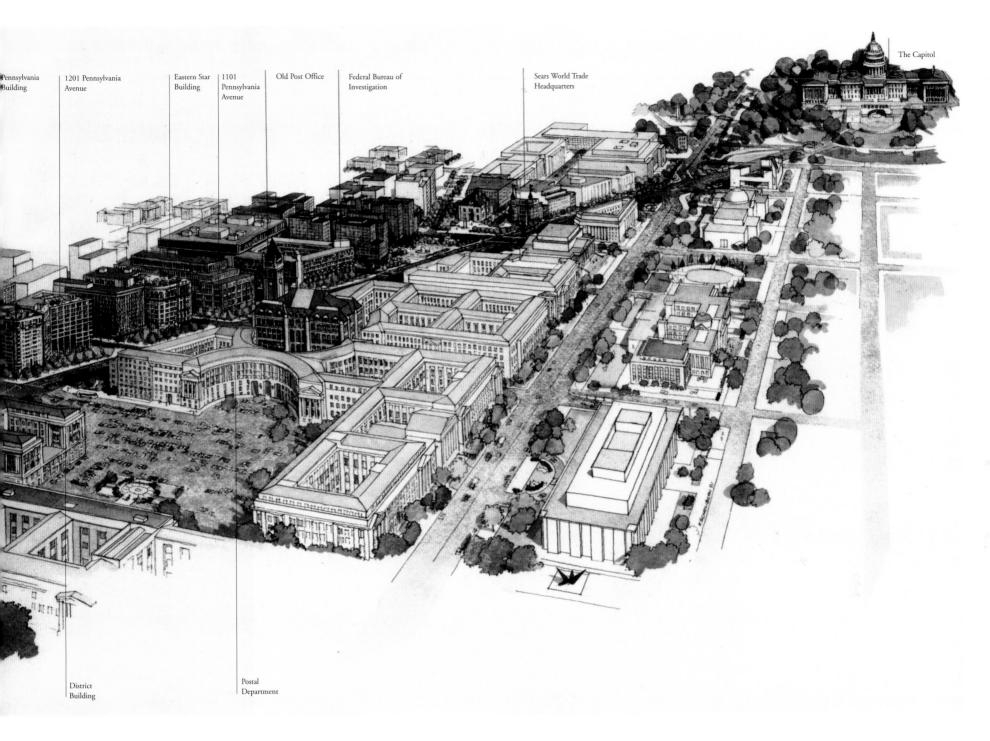

Pennsylvania Building

1201 Pennsylvania Avenue

Eastern Star Building

1101 Pennsylvania Avenue

Old Post Office

Federal Bureau of Investigation

Sears World Trade Headquarters

The Capitol

District Building

Postal Department

east corner of Thirteenth and E Streets. Along the avenue are the Pennsylvania Building by Segretti, Tepper, McMahon, Harned; 1201 Pennsylvania Avenue by Skidmore, Owings & Merrill (SOM); the Eastern Star Building (Marsh and Peter, 1898), renovated by SOM; 1101 Pennsylvania Avenue, which combines a number of historic buildings in a new composition by Hartman-Cox Architects with

Smith Segretti Tepper; and the Old Post Office (Willoughby J. Edbrooke, 1899), restored by Arthur Cotton Moore/Associates. Farther east on the avenue, the PADC would complete Market Square by Hartman-Cox Architects with Morris Architects, the Navy Memorial by Conklin Rossant with Stanley Bleifield, 601 Pennsylvania Avenue by Eisenman-Robertson/ Leo J. Daley, John Marshall Park

by Carroll R. Johnson, and the Canadian Embassy by Arthur Erickson. In the foreground, framed by the Department of Commerce, the District Building, and the Postal Department, is the parking lot that later would be occupied by the Ronald Reagan Building (1998).

Market Square, 1990. Designed by Hartman-Cox Architects with Morris Architects. *Carol M. Highsmith, PAP*

One of the most ambitious PADC developments was Market Square, at the intersection of Eighth Street and Pennsylvania Avenue. A private investment of $230 million, it includes 585,000 square feet of offices, 104,000 square feet of retail space, 720 basement parking spaces, and 210 housing units on the top four floors.

Pershing Park, 1981. Designed by M. Paul Friedberg with Jerome Lindsay. *Carol M. Highsmith, PAP*

The most popular public space on Pennsylvania Avenue is Pershing Park, between Fourteenth and Fifteenth Streets, featuring comfortable, shaded seating.

Ronald Reagan Building, 1988. Designed by Pei Cobb Freed & Partners. *PAP*

The last PADC project was the Ronald Reagan Building. Located on Fourteenth Street and Pennsylvania Avenue, it replaced a large open space that had been a parking lot. The building completed the Federal Triangle almost one hundred years after the triangle was conceived by the Senate Park Commission.

Neighborhoods

By the end of the twentieth century, residential Foggy Bottom had become only a fragment of what it once was; Shaw was under constant attack by commercial interests looking for cheap land; and a "living downtown" was to a certain extent only a slogan. In Capitol Hill, Dupont Circle, Southwest, and Georgetown, however, the center was surrounded by stable, racially integrated residential neighborhoods. These primarily late-nineteenth-century row house neighborhoods encircling Downtown had come to combine private amenity with public responsibility, minimizing the use of land and public utilities as well as vehicular travel.

The condition of neighborhoods in the District of Columbia beyond the center was varied. West of Rock Creek, the neighborhoods were composed of a middle- and upper-middle-class population, racially integrated but largely white. East of Rock Creek were middle-class, mainly African-American neighborhoods. There were still impoverished, largely African-American neighborhoods in northeast Washington and in Anacostia.

Downtown

The presence of about five hundred Chinese citizens living in Chinatown at the end of the twentieth century had preserved one residential neighborhood in the old Downtown. Chinatown was home to an elderly male population and also to recent immigrants, who traditionally began by working at unskilled restaurant and similar jobs. The area continued to serve as the hub of a much larger, primarily suburban Chinese community estimated at about thirty thousand people.

Another residential community in Downtown had begun in the 1990s. One objective of the Pennsylvania Avenue Development Corporation was to create a middle-class neighborhood centered on Seventh and Eighth Streets north of Pennsylvania Avenue. The twin Market Square buildings at the Navy Memorial contain apartments in their upper stories. The shells of several buildings, including Kresge's department store at Seventh and E Streets and the Bush Building at 710 E Street, were combined in a new building—the Lansburgh, which had apartments above the second floor and a theater and shops at street level. Even with a partial PADC construction subsidy, however, these apartments commanded upper-middle-income rents.

While some of the congregations had left the Downtown area, there were still many active churches. St. John's Church, across Lafayette Square from the White House, was almost two hundred years old in 2000 and still occupied its original building; the Church of the Epiphany, in the retail center on G Street between Fourteenth and Fifteenth Streets, and First Trinity Lutheran, on E Street at Judiciary Square, were only a few decades younger. On Tenth Street, First Congregational and St. Patrick's Roman Catholic Church faced each other across G Street; Asbury United Methodist was a few blocks north on K and Eleventh Street; and Mount Vernon Place Methodist stood on K Street, two blocks to the east. Turner Memorial Methodist

Gateway to Chinatown, Seventh and H Streets NW, 1986. Designed by Alfred Liu.

Built and ornamented by the Beijing Ancient Architectural Construction Corporation, this gateway was a gesture of friendship between the two sister capital cities. The arch is an authentic example of work that might have been done at the time of the Qing Dynasty. The seven roofs of the arch were crafted using the *dou-gong* system, which does not allow metal connectors.

The Lansburgh, 1991. Restoration and additions by Graham Gund Architects.

The primarily residential new building combines the shells of several older buildings around a courtyard. In addition to ground-floor retail shops, there is a 447-seat theater for the Shakespeare Theater group. The *New York Times* commented that "There is not a bad seat nor an uncomfortable one [in] the handsome oval auditorium."

Third Church of Christ, Scientist, and the Christian Science Monitor Building, 1971. Designed by I. M. Pei & Partners.

The octagonal church, tower, and office building face one another across a small plaza. Pei's exquisite church featuring exposed concrete is already on the National Register of Historic Places.

Episcopal, Second Baptist, Calvary Baptist, Corinthian Baptist, the newer Chinese Community Church, St. Mary Mother of God, and St. Aloysius all continued to serve their congregations in the eastern part of Downtown. The New York Avenue Presbyterian Church, which had been rebuilt on Thirteenth Street in 1950, was still operating. There was even a new church in Downtown: on Sixteenth Street, a block north of St. John's Church, one of the many buildings that I. M. Pei designed for the Church of Christ, Scientist, was erected in 1971.

The remarkable existence of so many churches in Downtown is to a certain extent the work of the Downtown Cluster of Congregations, an ecumenical, nonprofit association of thirty-seven congregations founded in 1971. The group aims to meet human needs and to address the factors that create such needs. It has helped to establish the Downtown Cluster's Day Care Center, the New Community Land Trust (which assists low-income tenants in purchasing and owning their own houses as cooperatives), the Washington Area Community Investment Fund, and the Homeless Services Unit (a team of three full-time, bilingual outreach workers). The cluster, which has assisted in founding a number of other service programs, describes its key goal as "in addition to meeting desperate human needs...to help persons and communities achieve self-sufficiency, by assisting persons and neighborhoods to break the cycle of poverty."

Capitol Hill

In 1976, residents of Capitol Hill successfully petitioned to have a large western section near the Capitol designated a historic district. With more than eight thousand primary buildings, mostly modest row houses, it was in 2000 the second-largest historic district in the country (and one slated to be enlarged by about 25 percent). Yet despite its status, Capitol Hill welcomed elegant new buildings.

The neighborhood spawned some of the early citizen activists who defeated a federal attempt to turn East Capitol Street into a boulevard of federal offices before World War II, successfully resisted the city's plan to build an interstate freeway down East Eleventh Street along the edge of Lincoln Park in 1955, and defeated plans to construct the tallest private building in the city at Pennsylvania Avenue and Fourteenth Street SE. In 1957, the Capitol Hill Restoration Society established Washington's longest-running house and garden tour. The Capitol Hill Ministry has sponsored an annual Easter parade since the 1960s, and by the end of the century, more than fifty thousand people attended Market Day, sponsored by Friendship House, and the Octoberfest, organized by the Capitol Hill Association of Merchants and Professionals.

The Hill's Eastern Market, designed by Adolph Cluss in 1873, remained the only nineteenth-century market still in operation in 2000. It began to decline in the 1920s, due to competition from grocery stores; in the 1950s, competition from suburban malls forced it to shut down. In 1964, the Joint Landmarks Committee of the National Capital Planning Commission designated Eastern Market an "important living landmark," and it was eventually placed on the National

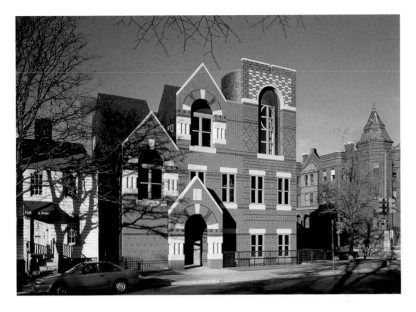

Office building in Capitol Hill Historic District, 1990. Designed by Amy Weinstein. *Max MacKenzie, AWA*

As with all new and remodeled buildings on Capitol Hill, this one was approved by the Historic Preservation Review Board and by Hill residents.

Townhomes on Capitol Hill, 1998. Designed by Weinstein Associates Architects, Oehme, van Sweden & Associates Landscape Architects, and Telesis Developers.

This project was initiated in 1989 by a small group of Capitol Hill citizens, including public housing residents, who formed the Ellen

Wilson Community Development Corporation. Replacing the Ellen Wilson Homes, which were troubled by crime, this 134-town-house cooperative was one of the first projects funded by a federal Department of Housing and Urban Development Hope VI program, with $2.6 million from HUD. One-fourth of the residents in 114 of the units earn less than 25 percent of the area's median income; one-fourth earn between 25 and 50 percent of the median; one-half earn between 50 and 80 percent of the median income; and twenty units are set aside for higher-income residents.

Shakespeare Theater, 1997. Renovated by Toby and Davis, Architects (original building, Independent Order of Odd Fellows Building, 1879).

Part of the neighborhood-based Eighth Street SE "main street" project, this building had served a variety of uses and was about to be abandoned in the early 1990s. The interior was gutted and rebuilt as offices and classrooms for the Shakespeare Theater group.

Bikeway on East Capitol Street, 1998.

In 1975, the D.C. Department of Transportation created a District of Columbia "bikeway" plan. With the support of residents, Capitol Hill became laced with bikeways, which continue to serve the Hill. The rest of the plan was never implemented, and the Department of Transportation was disbanded. Under Mayor Anthony Williams, the new Division of Transportation proposed bikeway plans for the remainder of the District of Columbia.

Second Empire Mansion on Logan Circle, c. 1875.

Queen Anne row house near Logan Circle, c. 1890, now restored.

Apartment hotel on Massachusetts Avenue at Thirteenth Street in Shaw, 1927, now restored.

Like many houses and apartments in Shaw, this historic residence has recently been restored.

Register of Historic Places. In response to a move to remodel it as an upscale retail location, Capitol Hill neighborhood groups working in tandem drafted legislation for strict preservation. In 1988, Council Member Sharon Ambrose sponsored the Eastern Market Real Property and Asset Management and Outdoor Vending Act. In 2000, community groups continued to act in an advisory role to Eastern Market management. *Washington at Home,* edited by Kathryn Schneider Smith, describes Capitol Hill in the late 1980s:

> Although the area of the Hill nearest the Capitol has become increasingly white and middle to upper-middle-class, the residents of the entire neighborhood represent every race and almost every nation. It is still a place where a U.S. senator, a former national president of the young Republicans, three generations of welfare recipi-

ents, a retired letter carrier, an electrician, an artist, attorneys, journalists, and Hill staffers all live on one block. It is a rare mixture of people with every local, as well as national and international, concern. It is in some ways an urban neighborhood like any other, except that the Capitol is just up the street.

Shaw

Since 1968, when the Department of Housing and Urban Development designated Shaw an urban renewal area, making it eligible for federal redevelopment funds, renewal in Shaw has combined new construction and rehabilitation. The redevelopment plans have tried to preserve space for low-income residents: Shaw Junior High School

African-American Civil War Memorial, 1998.
Designed by Ed Hamilton.

Dedicated to the 220,000 black soldiers who fought in the Civil War, the memorial is located on U Street near the site that was originally proposed shortly after the war but that failed to gain approval in the House of Representatives. The memorial is located next to a landmarked building by Albert Irvin Cassell, a distinguished African-American architect. In 2000, the city was making plans to convert the Cassell building into a visitors center, museum, and center for genealogical research.

Community Church Sanctuary, 1990. Designed by Suzanne Reatig. *Robert Lautman*

This modest structure is one of the most recent additions of religious architecture to Shaw, which contains more churches than any other neighborhood in the District of Columbia.

Row house in the Mount Vernon East Historic District, remodeled 1980. Redesign by Giorgio Forisio (original building, c. 1890).

The block of M Street between Fifth and Sixth Streets has been almost entirely renovated since the late 1980s. Despite gentrification, Shaw was still a racially integrated neighborhood in 2000.

was converted to apartments for the elderly, and a new school was built at Tenth Street and Rhode Island Avenue.

In the 1980s, James Adkins, an African-American developer, reopened the O Street Market, a landmarked building at O and Seventh Streets erected in 1886 but closed since the 1968 riots that followed the death of Martin Luther King Jr. In the traditional heart of the Shaw neighborhood, the Frank Reeves Center, a high-rise building dedicated in 1986 for the D.C. Department of Public Works, was constructed at U and Fourteenth Streets to spur revitalization of the local shopping area. The extension of the Metro Yellow Line to and beyond U Street was also aimed at helping U Street return to its early-twentieth-century vitality.

In 1998, when the District Council approved the plan to build the new convention center in Shaw, north of Mount Vernon Square, the council also approved two new historic districts, Mount Vernon West and Mount Vernon East. These new historic districts surround the convention center—it was the council's objective to prevent further commercial expansion into the Shaw residential neighborhood.

The quality of the late-nineteenth-century row houses in Shaw is comparable to the quality of houses in Dupont Circle. Through the end of the twentieth century, however, residents had not rallied behind historic designation. For a low-income family, the prospect of selling a residence at a large profit can be tempting. Whether Shaw will continue to be a racially integrated residential neighborhood or will become an extension of an already large Downtown remains to be settled.

Typical Queen Anne row houses, two blocks west of Dupont Circle, renovated c. 1985.

Except for the house still occupied by an early owner, these fine residences, dating from 1895, were gutted after World War II and turned into rooming houses. Since about 1985, the entire row has been renovated by new owners. Along with the modernized interiors, these now desirable and costly houses generally include a basement apartment.

Row house at 2114 O Street, remodeled 1985–87. Redesign by Joseph Passonneau (original building, 1892). *Robert Lautman*

This large row house, on a lot of twenty-two by ninety feet, is one of five built by a retired army officer, one for himself, four for speculation. The building now has a home office on the ground floor and two floors of living quarters including a kitchen, dining room, foyer-study, living room, three bedrooms, three baths, laundry, and small greenhouse, with a rental unit on the top floor. In the rear is a garden with a small pool and a deck over a two-car garage.

Dupont Circle

The blocks around Dupont Circle were developed in the late nineteenth century as a neighborhood of large Queen Anne row houses for an upper-class clientele, with mansions for the very wealthy on the circle itself and on the avenues. Many of the grand houses around Dupont Circle and on Connecticut and Massachusetts Avenues had been demolished by 1970 to make way for commercial buildings. Most of the residential blocks on the side streets, however, had survived, including modest residences on alley streets, such as Newport Place southwest of the circle and the streets east of Connecticut Avenue.

In 1976, citizens petitioned for a Dupont Circle Historic District designation. The application listed "over 100 notable buildings" and included the African-American neighborhood north of T Street. The primarily black Midway Civic Association and the mostly white Dupont Circle Citizens Association agreed on the boundaries. When the district was designated in 1978, the northeastern section surrounding the 1700 blocks of T and U Streets was not included. In 1985, however, this area, historically inhabited by African-Americans, was recognized as the Strivers Section Historic District. By the 1990s, many if not most of the Dupont and Strivers area row houses had been renovated, some by longtime residents, a large number by newcomers.

Most Dupont Circle houses are larger than the row houses typical of Capitol Hill, and even of Georgetown. Also, unlike Georgetown, which is zoned for single-family residences, Dupont Circle zoning permits row houses to be occupied by up to three apartments (including one home office). This provides for a rich mix of family types, income levels, and uses appropriate to a residential neighborhood that is an extension of Downtown. At the same time, historic zoning prevents any change in scale or building height, or commercial encroachment.

A number of houses built as showplaces, just before or after 1900, were still standing one hundred years later. The Townsend house (1904) at Massachusetts and Florida Avenues became the Cosmos Club. The Patterson house (1903) at 15 Dupont Circle became the home of the Washington Club, and the Wadsworth house (c. 1900) at 1801 Massachusetts Avenue became the Sulgrave Club; both front on Dupont Circle. The Walsh-McLean house (1903) at 2020 Massachusetts Avenue and the Boardman house (1893) at 1801 P Street, along with a number of other turn-of-the-century mansions, became embassies.

In contrast to other residential neighborhoods, Dupont Circle contains many multistory apartments located along the avenues on properties zoned for a building height of ninety feet. Here they take advantage of light and air in the wide rights-of-way and, by framing the avenues, create handsome public open spaces. Washington zoning allows bays to be extended from row houses into the public rights-of-way and permits multistory buildings to include balconies extending into the public space above the ground floor.

The Connecticut Avenue frontage, north and south of Dupont Circle, is almost entirely commercial, as is most of the area south of N

McCormick apartments, 1917–22. Designed by Jules Henri de Sibour, since 1996 the headquarters of the National Trust for Historic Preservation.

Stanley McCormick, heir to the McCormick reaper fortune, wanted and got the most luxurious apartment building in Washington. Each apartment covered an entire floor, over ten thousand square feet. Tenants included Lord Joseph Duveen, Andrew Mellon, and Perle Mesta. The Canadian government acquired the building in 1927 and used it as a chancery until 1988.

Typical new balcony apartment near Dupont Circle, c. 1990.

Because of the generous width of the L'Enfant streets, multistory buildings are permitted to have balconies extended above street level into the public rights-of-way.

Aerial view of Dupont Circle, looking south toward the Mall, 1996. *Jake McGuire, API*

This view shows a marked contrast to the devastation that had existed two and a half decades earlier.

Aerial view of Foggy Bottom, looking northwest from the Washington Monument, 2000.

A comparison with a view from the Washington Monument in 1901 (see page 104) suggests that of all the neighborhoods surrounding Downtown, Foggy Bottom changed the most during the twentieth century, with the exception of the urban-renewed Southwest.

Street. West of Sixteenth Street and south of Florida Avenue, however, there are almost fifty blocks of well-maintained residential buildings.

Dupont Circle adapted continuously for more than a century. In 2000, it was the most urban, and urbane, neighborhood in Washington. Its row house fabric had been modernized without losing its historic character; its grand mansions were now, in addition to embassies, social clubs and home to distinguished societies. Modern office buildings, apartments, and hotels lined the great avenues. The Phillips Collection, located just west of the circle in a private house turned into an art museum and opened to the public in 1921, stood out in a city of great museums. Besides area services, there were movie theaters and a variety of restaurants and shops within the neighborhood. Furthermore, Dupont Circle residents lived within walking distance of the center of the national capital.

Foggy Bottom

By 2000, all of Foggy Bottom east of Twentieth Street, south of E Street, and north of Pennsylvania Avenue was occupied by private office buildings and large institutions. These were mostly federal government buildings but also included the headquarters of the World Bank and the International Monetary Fund. The remainder of the Foggy Bottom neighborhood held George Washington University, high-rise apartments and hotels, a few office buildings, and a small residential historic district.

In 1940, George Washington University was contained within the one block bounded by G, H, Twentieth, and Twenty-first Streets, with minor extensions into surrounding blocks. By 1970, the university occupied most of the sixteen blocks bounded by Pennsylvania Avenue on the north, F Street on the south, Twentieth Street on the east, and Twenty-fourth Street on the west. About one-third of the land served as parking lots. By 2000, most of the property was occupied by university buildings or leased to other institutions.

An urban university can be a city's most important asset. Since World War II, however, research universities have continuously outgrown their campuses, creating friction between the schools and the surrounding neighborhoods. Since 1970, there has been a battle between George Washington University and developers on one side and residents and preservationists on the other. The university does not provide adequate student housing, which is one of the sources of friction with the remaining residential neighborhoods, and chafes at District of Columbia zoning requirements. Under pressure by residents, the city's Comprehensive Plan has gradually incorporated greater protection for residential neighborhoods, and the historic district constrains further commercial expansion.

Foggy Bottom west of Nineteenth Street and north of Virginia Avenue contained over fifty apartment buildings and almost three hundred row houses in 1940. In 2000, only a few dozen of Foggy Bottom's more modest row houses were still standing. Most inhabitants at the century's end lived in the several dozen fashionable multistory apartments and residential hotels. The brick laborers' houses near Twenty-fifth and I Street were now expensive town houses.

River Inn, 1978.

Erected in the 1950s as an apartment building on Twenty-fifth Street south of K Street, the structure was turned into a hotel in 1978, just before a 1980 zoning change prohibited such conversions. The inn became a destination for tour groups, complete with buses that clog the streets. Foggy Bottom residents persuaded the city to ban the buses on residential streets. The ban, which survived a court challenge, created a national precedent.

Griffin condominiums, 1990.

These condominiums replaced a group of row houses facing the I-66 interchange.

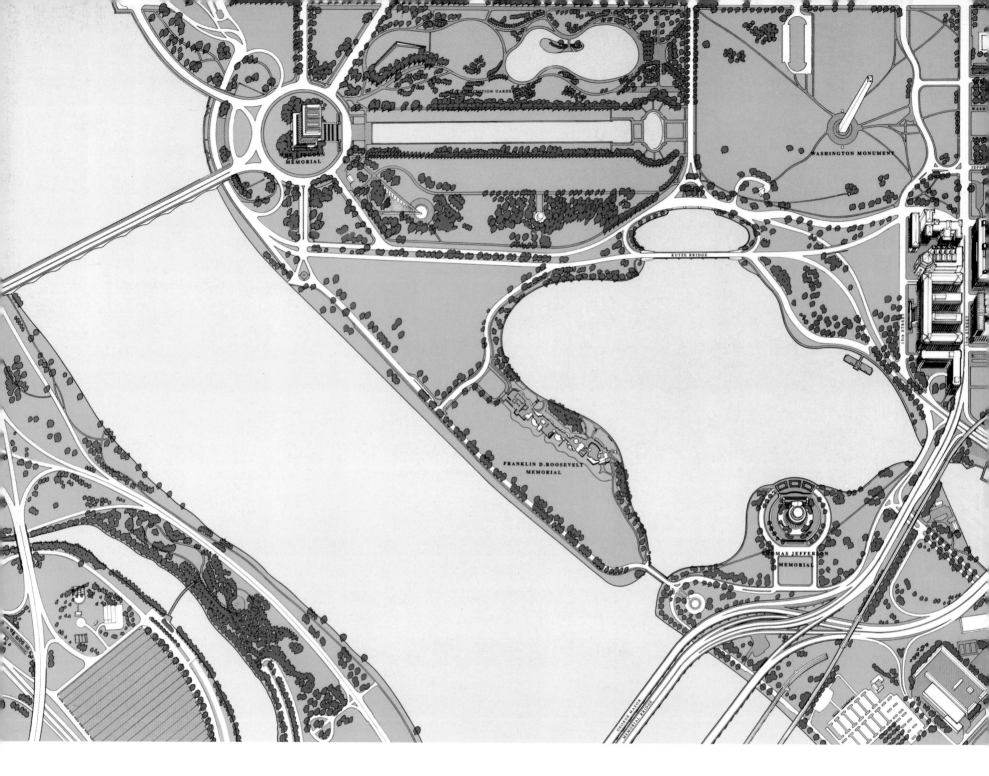

Southwest

During the two post–World War II decades, the Southwest neighborhood changed more drastically than any other area in Washington. In the last quarter of the twentieth century, however, with the exception of some infill of private buildings north of the Southwest Freeway, the neighborhood underwent few further alterations. In the 1990s, Southwest still retained some of the pre–urban renewal contrasts. East of Fourth Street, in the formerly segregated area occupied by black residents, African-Americans now lived in extensive blocks of public housing. West of Fourth Street stood residential towers and two- and three-story row houses, occupied by a largely white middle class. The *AIA Guide* (3rd ed., 1994) comments: "This is Washington's showplace of contemporary building, and perhaps will in the future constitute an outdoor museum of the architectural clichés of the two decades following World War II." While not entirely inaccurate, this remark misses the point most architecture critics would make—that the site plan is commendable and the individual building groups, by some of the most talented architects practicing in Washington after the war, are architecturally among the best large-scale, post–World War II public building projects in America.

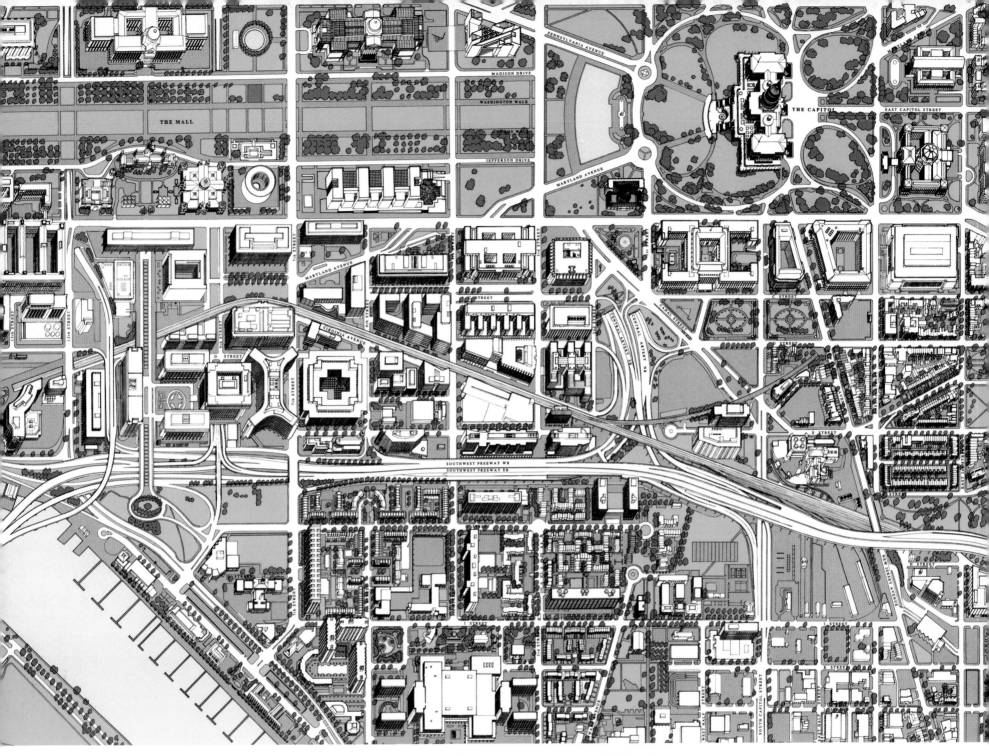

Southwest in 2000. *JRP*

1. **Franklin Delano Roosevelt Memorial**
2. **U.S. Holocaust Memorial Museum**
3. Thomas Jefferson Memorial
4. Tidal Basin
5. **James Madison Building, Library of Congress**
6. House of Representatives Office Buildings
7. Department of Health and Human Welfare
8. **Hubert Humphrey Building**
9. Department of Education
10. **National Aeronautics and Space Administration Building**
11. James Forrestal Building, Department of Energy
12. Department of Agriculture
13. Bureau of Engraving

14. L'Enfant Plaza
15. General Services Administration
16. Department of Housing and Urban Development
17. Department of Transportation
18. **U.S. Currency Building**
19. National Park Service
20. Railroad on embankment in Maryland Avenue
21. Railroad on embankment in Virginia Avenue
22. Passenger railroad in tunnel under East First Street
23. Southwest Freeway
24. Southeast Freeway

Buildings and public projects constructed after 1970
are listed in **bold** type.

Garden behind 3015 Q Street, 1975. Renovated by Joseph Passonneau.

The Cooke's Row houses built on Q Street in 1868 are on forty-two-foot lots—deep enough for large gardens and swimming pools.

Gardens in center of a typical Georgetown block, c. 1980.

Even Georgetown houses on more typical lots of twenty by about one hundred feet manage to provide outdoor space.

Georgetown Park, 1982. Designed by Alan J. Lockhart & Associates, with Chloethiel Woodard Smith & Associates, Clark Tribble Harris & Li, and Yah Lee & Associates.

This complex contains three stories of retail stores around an atrium and over a garage; on the roof is an expensive housing development. Part of the site, on the south side of M Street, was once at the hub of Washington's streetcar lines; the shell of the streetcar facility was retained.

Georgetown

While interiors had been remodeled and rear yards embellished with gardens and swimming pools, residential Georgetown was in 2000 almost unchanged since becoming a historic district in the 1950s. The late Colonel Robert Evans, president of the Citizens Association of Georgetown, expressed a widely shared opinion around 1980 : "I have a very parochial view of Georgetown; if I had my way the bridges would be drawbridges." The one significant change in residential Georgetown was the astronomical increase in property values.

Beyond the residential town, however, the changes in Georgetown in the decades since 1970 were even more radical than those in downtown Washington. In the 1970s, Georgetown still maintained the rich mix of urban activities characteristic of the earlier town. There were drugstores, hardware stores, groceries, bookstores, barbershops, shoe

repair shops, and a farmer's market. On the waterfront stood a lumberyard, a concrete-batch plant, and a blacksmith. During the 1970s, 1980s, and 1990s, however, the previously slow turnover of established names became more rapid. As the cost of overhead grew with the demand for commercial space, traditional businesses began to disappear. Weaver's Hardware, Doc's Drug Store (a favorite haunt of *Washington Post* feature writer Art Buchwald), and the Savile Book Store vanished. The farmer's market became Dean & DeLuca, a specialty grocer; Gallagher's Lumberyard was replaced by an office building; and the blacksmith was replaced by a small apartment building. The commercial area became a high-priced, specialized shopping center for the metropolitan area, with a myriad of restaurants that no longer served the rest of the Georgetown community. These changes dismayed many residents.

Canal Square, c. 1971. Renovated by Arthur Cotton Moore/Associates (original building, c. 1859).

One of the earliest renovations was Canal Square, on Thirty-first Street on the north side of the C & O Canal. The original, pre–Civil War building was the birthplace of Herman Hollerith's punch-card business, which eventually became IBM. Moore added a new wing, creating a handsome courtyard.

C & O Canal along the Georgetown waterfront, 1973.

After Supreme Court Justice William O. Douglas hiked up the canal towpath from Georgetown to Harpers Ferry, West Virginia, in 1956, he led the fight to have the canal transferred to the National Park Service and entered into the National Register of Historic Places. The canal has become the region's most popular trail for hiking, bicycle riding, and walking, and the section along the Georgetown waterfront is the most heavily used.

View of the Georgetown waterfront from Key Bridge, 2000.

Since the 1970s, the function and appearance of the Georgetown waterfront has changed drastically. The view from Key Bridge shows the Flour Mill built in 1848 by George Bomford and renovated and expanded by Peter Vercelli in 1980 as a large condominium complex; the Paper Mill built in the mid-nineteenth century and renovated in the early 1980s for offices and condominiums; Waterfront Center, 1980, by Hartman-Cox Architects; the Jefferson Court office building, 1984, by Skidmore, Owings & Merrill; and the mid-nineteenth century Foundry, renovated in 1977 by Arthur Cotton Moore/Associates for offices and retail shops. The smokestack of the abandoned district waste-disposal plant marks the location of the last major and largest addition to the waterfront, which was under construction in 2000.

The changes in building use started on M Street and Wisconsin Avenue and also on Prospect Street west of Wisconsin and, by 1970, began to affect structures along the Chesapeake & Ohio Canal. The canal—once an essential freight artery and source of water power, and later an open sewer—was rehabilitated by the National Park Service and became an attractive amenity.

In the early 1970s, the pressures for development already apparent north of the C & O Canal were beginning to have an impact on the waterfront south of the canal. Following a presidential directive, the National Capital Planning Commission and the D.C. Department of Highways sponsored a Georgetown waterfront area study. In January 1976, the consultant's final report recommended replacing the Whitehurst Freeway with an avenue above a depressed thoroughfare and called for an extension, down to the waterfront, of the traditional scale of Georgetown buildings north of M Street. Local disagreements prevented the study from being implemented, settling the future of the Georgetown waterfront.

In 1970, between the C & O Canal and the Potomac River, there was approximately 600,000 square feet of space, primarily in one- and two-story buildings (except for the massive General Services Administration heating plant and the partially vacant Flour Mill and Paper Mill). By 2000, there was more than 4,000,000 square feet of new space, about two-thirds of which was devoted to commercial purposes. In 1900, 150 row houses existed between the canal and the waterfront; by 1970, only 68 remained. These 68 row houses were still extant in 2000, although 6 had been converted to retail stores. There were now 68 new row houses—part of the Paper Mill redevelopment—and more than 200 new rental and condominium units, occupying five new apartment buildings.

While the uses of commercial buildings along Wisconsin Avenue and M Street changed, the building envelopes did not. Along the C & O Canal and between the canal and the Potomac waterfront, however, except for the 1946 General Services Administration heating plant on Rock Creek, almost every occupancy had changed; every building existing in 1970 had by 2000 been renovated; and almost every open space had been enclosed by a multistory building.

The detritus of the earlier industrial waterfront had been almost entirely removed by 2000. The railroad that brought coal to the GSA heating plant was replaced by trucks in 1990. In 2000, the GSA was using the heating plant only to back up power generated elsewhere and planned to eliminate the plant and its coal-handling facilities.

In the early 1980s, the D.C. Department of Public Works began a project to determine whether to eliminate or repair the Whitehurst Freeway. The work continued for more than a decade. The Whitehurst, which creates a discontinuity in the Georgetown street system, is not a true freeway; rather, it is an elevated arterial street with traffic controlled by signalized intersections at each end. The peak-hour delays had become some of the longest in the national capital region. The traffic problems created by the Whitehurst were never adequately explored, and in 2000, the freeway was still in place.

In the eighteenth century, waterfronts were not perceived as urban amenities and L'Enfant paid little attention to the relationship between his new city and the Potomac and Anacostia riverfronts. Historic maps suggest that this disregard continued through the nineteenth century. Even in 2000, Georgetown was one of the few parts of the city directly facing the Potomac River—and a precious historic resource. Only one building, however, Washington Harbor, had taken advantage of its riverfront location.

Like retail Georgetown and the neighborhood's waterfront, Georgetown University underwent change during the last quarter of the twentieth century. The university expanded rapidly, like George Washington University in Foggy Bottom, driven by increased enrollment and graduate research. Over many decades the school was transformed from a seminary in 1800 to an elite university in 2000 (with help from a spectacularly successful basketball program). Fortunately, Georgetown University had room for expansion to the west of its main campus and to the northwest, the location of its large medical center. It had also intruded somewhat into the residential neighborhood to the east.

Existing before the national capital was conceived and not part of the L'Enfant plan, Georgetown was in 2000 still an anomaly, unlike the rest of Washington. Throughout its history, until 1970, Georgetown was a complete town, with admirable residential neighborhoods. It was integrated racially, economically, ethnically, and politically. It was also

Washington Harbor, 1986. Designed by Arthur Cotton Moore/Associates. *Robert Lautman*

A large complex of shops, offices, and condominiums, Washington Harbor, the only building located directly on the waterfront, represents the kind of mixed-use development serious urbanists hope for in cities but seldom find in the national capital. The 1994 *AIA Guide* reports that the architect wanted his work "to reflect . . . the exuberant three-dimensional vocabulary of Georgetown in an abstract way, [simultaneously acknowledging] the monuments through a more classic, rhythmic, columnar quality."

integrated geographically: blacks and whites, rich and poor, Catholics and Protestants, new immigrants and old-family WASPS, left-wing Democrats and right-wing Republicans all lived side by side. Its varied housing stock harbored every type of urban citizen.

There were mansions such as Tudor Place, the Laird-Dunlop House, Evermay, and Dumbarton House (now the home of the Colonial Dames of America), upper-class residences such as Cooke's Row, a variety of middle-class row houses, tiny row houses for day laborers, and walk-up apartments of several kinds. Besides a mix of residential neighborhoods with shopping for residents, the town included an active industrial sector on the waterfront. It also included a major university, medical center, and religious community.

By the end of the twentieth century, the working-class population of Georgetown, white and black, had been forced out by the escalating cost of property. Georgetown consisted of four distinct, somewhat unrelated enclaves: residential neighborhoods for the rich and the very rich; a specialized regional shopping and entertainment center on M Street and Wisconsin Avenue; an extension of Washington's central business district on the waterfront; and the still expanding Georgetown University, hospital, and religious complex. In 2000, the four Georgetowns coexisted, albeit uncomfortably.

Georgetown in 2000

Residential Georgetown did not change between 1970 and 2000. Commercial Georgetown, on M Street and Wisconsin Avenue, changed slightly, but only in the use—not the form—of a few buildings. Georgetown University showed little alteration, although some important changes had occurred on the western and northwestern campus (not represented on the map). About half the buildings on the north edge of the C & O Canal were rebuilt or changed function, or both.

The most dramatic shift occurred between the canal and the Potomac River, where almost every building had been expanded and the use changed. Nearly every open space had been filled, except the large incinerator site between Thirty-first and M Streets and between K and South Streets. A massive building project, intended to fill the entire site, was under construction in 2000.

Key

- single-family residences
- walk-up residences
- elevator apartment
- hotel
- retail
- private offices
- federal offices
- federal institutions
- private & foreign institutions
- local institutions
- industrial
- warehouse
- transportation

1. Duke Ellington High School for the Performing Arts
2. Georgetown University and university playing fields and **hospital expansion**
3. **Georgetown University dormitories**: On and off campus.
4. Georgetown Park: Retail and apartments (remodeled).
5. Canal Square: Retail and offices (remodeled).
6. Flour Mill: Offices and condominiums (remodeled).
7. Paper Mill: Offices, apartments, and row houses (remodeled).
8. **Waterfront Center**: Offices.
9. **Jefferson Court**: Offices and retail.
10. The Foundry: Offices and retail (remodeled).
11. **Washington Harbor**: Offices, retail, and condominiums.
12. Former incinerator: Large mixed-use building under construction.

Buildings and public projects constructed or completed after 1970 are listed in **bold** type.

0 100   500   1000 ft

R Street

Dumbarton Oaks

Oak Hill Cemetery

Reservoir Road

1

Dent Place

R Street

Ivon Place

Dent Place

Cambridge Place

2

Tudor Place

Q Street

Dumbarton House

Q Street

Volta Place

Q Street

P Street

Wisconsin Avenue

P Street

P Street

O Street

Dumbarton Street

Georgetown University

3

37th Street

36th Street

35th Street

34th Street

33rd Street

Potomac Street

31st Street

30th Street

29th Street

28th Street

27th Street

Rock Creek Parkway

N Street

N Street

3

Olive Street

Prospect Street

26th Street

25th Street

24th Street

M Street

4

Pennsylvania Avenue

Chesapeake & Ohio Canal

5

10

6

Thomas Jefferson Street

9

Francis Scott Key Bridge

7

12

8

K Street

Whitehurst Freeway

11

Aerial view of the Mall, looking west past the Capitol, 1985. *Dennis Brack, NGA*

The Capitol and the Supreme Court are in the foreground. The East Building of the National Gallery of Art (1978) is on the right, and the National Air and Space Museum (1976) and the Hirshhorn Museum (1974) are on the left. Constitution Gardens lake (1976) can be seen in the distance on the right side of the Mall. The buildings for "scientific purposes and for the great museums" between the Capitol and the Washington Monument, as specified by the Senate Park Commission, were almost complete in 2000.

The Mall and Its Surroundings

The story of the Mall is the history of an odyssey that was almost complete in 2000. Only the site of the National Museum of the American Indian remained to be filled; the building is scheduled for completion in 2004. With the embellishment of Pennsylvania Avenue, the Ellipse still much as Andrew Jackson Downing had proposed it, and the Mall shaped as L'Enfant and the Senate Park Commission intended, the triangle of public spaces at the heart of L'Enfant's plan was in place.

The development of the Mall did not proceed along a straight path. It was, according to writer Joseph Varnum, a "mere cow-pasture" during much of the nineteenth century. Downing's "public museum of trees" lasted for over half a century. The trees disappeared only after the bitter controversy created by the plans of the Senate Park Commission. After the trees were banished, it was not until World War II that most of the commission's recommendations were implemented, and it took the remainder of the century to complete the majority of the commission's larger ambitions for the Mall.

The buildings lining the Mall are eight hundred feet apart, a dimension settled only after a long debate led by the Park Commission. The grassy carpet between Washington Walk and Adams Walk is two hundred feet in breadth and extends three hundred feet between the rows of elms bordering the two walkways. Threatened by Dutch elm disease, the trees are considered by the Commission of Fine Arts as essential to the character of the Mall. In 2000, the National Park Service had reduced the rate of tree loss significantly by developing methods of preservation. The Park Service was also in the process of nurturing two hundred elms of a disease-resistant strain, a worthy endeavor, since the zelkova, a tree of the elm family favored by commercial nurseries as a substitute for ailing elms, has none of the architectural qualities of the American elm.

The master plan of the Mall, begun by Skidmore, Owings & Merrill in the mid-1960s, had recommended that the double row of parking for cars be eliminated from what were Washington and Adams Drives, bordering the center greensward. The recommendation was enthusiastically supported by the Commission of Fine Arts, but it was contested for years by workers in the area. In the early 1970s, the Environmental Protection Act was marshaled, incongruously, in defense of parking. The proposal to replace the drives with a composite aggregate that would match the walks in the Tuileries Gardens in Paris—rather than with hard paved sidewalks—was opposed by the disabled. After tests with wheelchairs had been conducted, the composite aggregate was accepted, and the National Park Service was finally persuaded to eliminate parking from the center of the Mall. On the bicentennial of the Declaration of Independence, the Mall also celebrated the new design for its center.

Building on the Mall

The festering argument about the appropriate style for architecture on the Mall, which reached its peak of intensity immediately after World War II, had been settled during the 1960s when the firm of

The Mall, July 4, 1975.

The Mall, July 4, 1976.

Constitution Gardens, looking east to the Washington Monument, 1987.
Richard Longstreth

Constitution Gardens, proposed in the master plan for the Mall, replaced the temporary buildings still remaining from World War I. By the mid-1980s, the landscaping had matured.

Skidmore, Owings & Merrill was selected to develop the master plan, and I. M. Pei of I. M. Pei & Partners and Gyo Obata of Hellmuth, Obata + Kassabaum were chosen to design the East Building of the National Gallery of Art and the National Air and Space Museum, respectively. That the argument was made irrelevant may not have been recognized at the time: the works of John Russell Pope and his colleagues on the National Gallery of Art, Skidmore, Owings & Merrill on Constitution Gardens, Pei on the East Building, and Obata on the Air and Space Museum—in their quality as architecture and as elements in an urban mosaic—are now embedded in the history of architecture and transcend issues of style.

In his essay "High Noon on the Mall: Modernism versus Traditionalism, 1910–1970" in *The Mall in Washington 1791–1991*, edited by Richard Longstreth, historian Richard Guy Wilson argues

that modernism and traditionalism are not antitheses, that "a modernist myth was the escape from history, though proponents of such escape usually based their arguments on historical imperative ... For the traditional, or pre-modern, imagination only one history existed ... But the modern consciousness knows that history is imprecise, that the past is quicksand, constantly being revised and capable of being manufactured. Washington politics exemplifies this shifting history, for the past can be shredded, elaborated, forgotten, or declared inoperative."

The trapezoidal site for Pei's East Building was made more difficult by its location on the edge of the Mall, at the end of Pennsylvania Avenue. Off-center from the rigidly axial West Building, it posed additional formal problems for connecting the East and West Buildings.

Aerial view of the National Gallery's West and East Buildings, 1980. *NGA*

Essential to an understanding of the design of the East Building is its fundamental integration with the West Building.

The East Building, completed in 1978, was created to serve two basic functions. One purpose was as a center for advanced study, complete with a library, archives, and curators and an education department with administrators. Such an office building would clear the ground floor of the West Building, so that the great exhibition facility could become what it was intended to be. The second purpose was as space for temporary exhibitions and for the growing collection of twentieth-century art. A third function, which perhaps evolved and became the unifying element in the composition, was the need for a gathering place where donors, curators, artists, and the general public could meet and become acquainted with one another and with the museum.

The handsome east door of the West Building, previously unused, now opens directly onto the square connecting the two wings and onto

Central space in the East Building of the National Gallery. Designed by I. M. Pei & Partners, 1978.

The skylit central space serves as a dramatic exhibition area for sculpture and wall hangings and houses large plants. Along one side, a monumental stair and escalator connect the entrance level with the second-level exhibits and with a luncheon area that looks both in to the central space and out to the Mall.

Night view of National Air and Space Museum from the Mall, 1976.
Designed by Gyo Obata, Hellmuth, Obata + Kassabaum. *Robert Lautman*

Views of the Mall enhance the interior of the museum, and the museum enlivens the Mall. According to the architect, Gyo Obata, the museum staff insisted that "The building should be a place of excitement… celebrating an age that is still young, an age that we see not just as historians but as participants." The staff wanted the maximum volume of space devoted to housing as many examples of air and space vehicles as possible, an environment that would accommodate a variety of exhibits, from tiny models to large relics of the early air age.

the off-center entrance to the East Building, on axis with the East Building's central gallery. The central space, the most memorable part of the building, is covered with glazed tetrahedrons—what the museum's longest-serving director, J. Carter Brown, called "the leitmotif of triangles, based on L'Enfant's geometry of the intersection of Pennsylvania Avenue with the Mall," which is repeated in the reinforced concrete trusses, the marble floor slabs, and even the shape of the elevators.

Like the design of the East Building of the National Gallery, the design for the National Air and Space Museum, completed in 1976, was influenced by its location on the south side of the Mall facing Pope's National Gallery of Art. The Air and Space Museum's geometry and exterior materials, and probably its austere architectural expression, were inspired by the design of the National Gallery.

The narrow site set the dimensions of the building at 225 feet from north to south and 685 feet from east to west. The building is roughly the same size as the National Gallery and has a similar footprint. Four enclosed blocks flank three skylit blocks, glazed on the side facing the Mall. The south facade also reflects the interior spaces but turns away from the street and the sun.

The Air and Space Museum shares with the East Building of the National Gallery fine, elegantly detailed materials. Both contribute remarkable interior spaces to a city of exceptional interiors. The spaces could not be more different, however. The central atrium of the East Building is serene and encased in complex geometry; the simple geometry of the Air and Space Museum shares the Smithsonian's complexities, looking like an attic in a building long inhabited. Despite the jumble of exhibits, the museum is gloriously functional. A large glass-enclosed lunchroom was added in 1988 as an extension of the east end of the building. With twelve to fifteen million people entering its doors every year, the museum was one of the most visited spots in the world in 2000.

Important to building on the Mall, and a significant element of the L'Enfant plan, is the Eighth Street axis. L'Enfant had described Eighth Street as the location of three of the "Squares…proposed to be divided among the several states" and of the National Church, with a "grand fountain intended with a constant spout of water" at Pennsylvania Avenue. He proposed a water feature on the north edge of the Mall and the Naval Itinerary Column on the edge of the Potomac River, both on the Eighth Street axis, which created controversy, since it crosses the Mall.

In both L'Enfant's plan and that of the Senate Park Commission, the Eighth Street axis across the Mall is unobstructed. In 1966, Paul Mellon, serving as president of the National Gallery of Art, signed an agreement with Stewart Udall, secretary of the interior, stating that the site on the Eighth Street axis between the National Gallery and the National Museum of Natural History would become a national sculpture garden, operated by the National Gallery. When Joseph H. Hirshhorn, a successful speculator in metals, donated his art collection to the Smithsonian, he wanted it displayed at this site, next to the National Gallery. The gallery proposed an underground building,

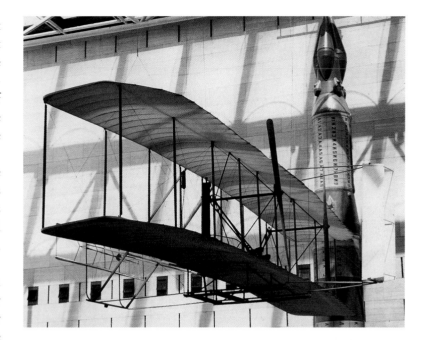

National Air and Space Museum, typical air-age exhibit.

National Air and Space Museum, typical space-age exhibit.

Hirshhorn Museum, looking across the Hirshhorn sculpture garden, 1974. Designed by Gordon Bunshaft, Skidmore, Owings & Merrill.

During the planning of the building that would hold Joseph Hirshhorn's collection of contemporary painting and sculpture, S. Dillon Ripley, secretary of the Smithsonian Institution, is reputed to have told the committee that if the building "were not controversial in almost every way, it would hardly qualify as a place to house contemporary art."

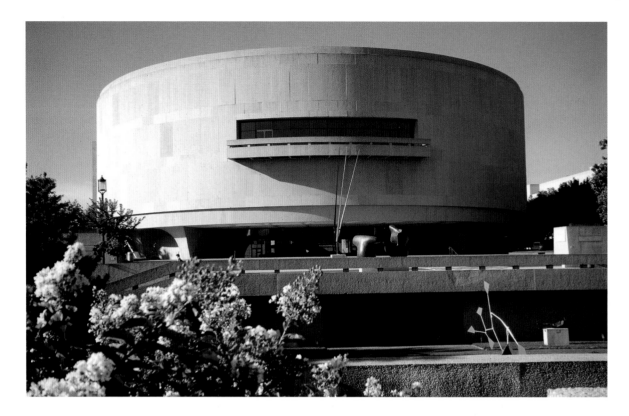

National Gallery of Art sculpture garden, completed 1999. Designed by Olin Partnership. *Laurie Olin*

In the center is a circular reflecting pool that becomes a skating rink in the winter.

U.S. Holocaust Memorial Museum, 1993. Designed by James Ingo Freed, Pei Cobb Freed & Partners, with Notter Finegold + Alexander Inc.

Located on Raoul Wallenberg Place and Fourteenth Street, between two Bureau of Engraving buildings, one Victorian and one neoclassical, the Holocaust Museum's brutal facade makes no concessions to either. Together with its interior of exposed steel and industrial brick and its moving and provocative exhibits, the museum creates a sinister reminder of the totalitarian state.

adjacent to the garden; Hirshhorn rejected the proposal, asserting that he could be buried but not his collection, and a new site was chosen.

The designer suggested to Hirshhorn was Gordon Bunshaft, senior partner at Skidmore, Owings & Merrill. Bunshaft reported later, "Joe and I hit it off right away . . . it was all settled in five minutes." Among other matters settled then or later was that the site, on the cross axis on the south side of the Mall, would be used for an aggressive, modernist building. A National Historic Landmark, the Army Medical Museum, was demolished to make room for the Hirshhorn Museum.

The National Capital Planning Commission suggested a circular structure, considering such a form less disruptive to the cross axis. Bunshaft designed a massive, round building, raised "to be seen through." He also proposed a sculpture garden, sunk eighteen feet deep and running five hundred feet across the Mall. The garden was eventually reduced to its more modest size in its present location, between Adams Walk and the Hirshhorn.

The National Gallery of Art sculpture garden, adjacent to the gallery's West Building on the Eighth Street axis, as arranged by Paul Mellon and Stewart Udall, finally opened to the public in 1999. It was designed by landscape architect Laurie Olin, of the Olin Partnership, to harmonize with the gallery. It is quite different from and more active than the Hirshhorn sculpture garden across the mall. The Hirshhorn garden, while not exactly buried, is below eye level when seen from the Mall and offers a quiet, contemplative setting.

Completed in 1993, the U.S. Holocaust Memorial Museum, designed by James Ingo Freed of Pei Cobb Freed & Partners, was built just off the Mall between Fourteenth and Fifteenth Streets SW. Visited by an overwhelming number of individuals and tour groups, exhibits include text, images, film, and objects from Nazi concentration camps and memorials to the Holocaust's victims, all presented in an emotionally jarring interior of exposed steel and industrial brick. The *AIA Guide* (3rd ed., 1994) quotes James Freed as commenting, "You can't deal with the Holocaust as a reasonable thing. This wholly un-American subject can only be treated in an emotional dimension."

Vietnam Veterans Memorial, 1982. Designed by Maya Lin, with Cooper-Lecky Architects. *NPS*

Sculpture at the entrance to the Vietnam Veterans Memorial, 1982. Designed by Frederick Hart.

Memorials and the Mall

L'Enfant was deeply concerned with memorials. In his August 1791 plan, he suggested that public open spaces "admit of Statues, Columns, Obelisks, and any other ornaments such as the different States may chose to erect; to perpetuate not only the memory of such individuals, whose Counsels, or military achievements, were conspicuous in giving liberty and independence to this Country; but also those whose usefulness hath rendered them worthy of general imitation; to invite the youths of succeeding generations to tread in the paths of those Sages or heroes, whom their country has thought proper to celebrate."

Since World War II, the demands for memorials, and for space on the Mall, have proliferated. The most controversial memorial honors veterans of the Vietnam War. It is also, along with the Lincoln Memorial, the most successful, in terms of numbers of visits by the public.

Legislation determined the location of the Vietnam Veterans Memorial, in the meadow of Constitution Gardens. The design was based on a competition held in 1981. In *The Mall in Washington 1791–1991,* J. Carter Brown, then chairman of the Commission of Fine Arts, describes the difficult process of memorializing an excruciating national experience:

> The greensward we [the Commission] were hoping to protect . . . could not remain completely open . . . We indicated that if anything were to be built, it ought not to extend vertically; the wonderful sense of meadow was to be respected. As it turned out, we got a masterwork.
>
> Paul Spreiregen conducted the competition, and the jurors had the wisdom to chose, of 1,421 entries, number 1,026, by Maya Lin, then an undergraduate student at the Yale School of Architecture. It was a brilliant leap of imagination to warp the ground plane down, to allow the meadow to remain open, and to orient the memorial's walls toward the two great monuments visible from there, the Lincoln and Washington Memorials, so that they are incorporated by reference, as

it were, allowing them to symbolize the great ideals and traditions for which those in Vietnam fought.

> The country, and Maya Lin, owe a debt of gratitude to a prescient jury; Lin's minimalist presentation was at first passed over, then resurrected by jurors who were moved by both her scripted statement of purpose and her simple sketch. Laymen had even more trouble visualizing Lin's plans. Brown continues:

> There was a tremendous reaction against the design in certain very conservative quarters. Senator John Warner proved adept at making peace . . . but part of the deal struck, without the Commission's involvement, was that the memorial could be realized only if sculpture and flagpole were added . . . the site was ready for ground breaking so that the memorial could open by November for Veteran's Day. Then the Secretary of the Interior informed me that unless the Commission could accept the idea of adding sculpture and a flagpole, work would not begin . . .
>
> In October of 1982 so many people signed up for the hearing on the proposed additions that it could not be held in our quarters . . . among them was Maya Lin who eloquently expressed why she designed the memorial as she did, so that the names would commemorate the fallen in the order that they fell—a brilliant aspect of the design . . . We approved the sculpture and the flagpole at that meeting, but not their proposed locations. Not until the following meeting, in February 1983, was the matter resolved.
>
> Interestingly enough, Spreiregen's jury for the original competition had awarded third place to Frederick Hart, who made the sculpture now in question. Hart understood that his new work should not take the central position, but have an adjunct relation to the wall. In the surrounding grove of trees, the sculpture, I believe, really works, engaging in a dialogue with the memorial, but not detracting from it when one reaches the wall itself.
>
> The whole experience brings people to tears.

Korean War Veterans Memorial, 1995. Designed by Cooper-Lecky Architects. *Carol M. Highsmith, CLA*

Franklin Delano Roosevelt Memorial, 1997. Designed by Lawrence Halprin.

An underappreciated memorial that had stood on the Mall since the 1920s honoring Ulysses S. Grant was finally given an appropriate setting when a reflecting basin, designed by Skidmore, Owings & Merrill, was added over the Center Leg Freeway in 1976. The statue of Grant on horseback is flanked by two three-quarter-sized ensembles of troopers and gunners charging toward battle and occupies a commanding position at the base of Jenkins Hill. The image of Grant slumped under his poncho is probably both more realistic and more properly symbolic than a Grant resplendent on a charger, with sword on high.

Another memorial, in which the Commission of Fine Arts was strongly involved, commemorates the veterans of the Korean War. Neither that war nor its memorial was as divisive as those of Vietnam. The 1995 Korean War Veterans Memorial by Cooper-Lecky Architects, located in a grove south of the Lincoln Memorial reflecting basin, features soldiers in battle fatigues moving toward an American flag.

The last major memorial of the twentieth century commemorates President Franklin D. Roosevelt. Like the memorial to President Thomas Jefferson, it is located just south of the Mall. Roosevelt once noted that he did not want an elaborate memorial, only a simply inscribed stone. The stone exists in front of the National Archives on Pennsylvania Avenue, but his larger wish was not honored. The Franklin Delano Roosevelt Memorial, in East Potomac Park, covers over two acres. On May 9, 1997, the following critique by columnist Charles Krauthammer appeared in the *Washington Post,* under the title "The FDR Memorial Scam":

> I was ready, very ready, to like the Franklin Delano Roosevelt memorial in Washington . . . It works mind you, as a public space. Families will frolic in its pools and waterfalls. Kids will ride the statue of Roosevelt's dog, Fala. Lovers will appreciate its nooks and crannies.
>
> As a memorial, however, it is an embarrassment. First, there is the question of scale. It is massive, grossly out of proportion . . . Then you read some of the selected writings on the walls, and your heart sinks at this memorial's "aching political correctness," to quote Mary McGrory . . .
>
> FDR revived a nation, reconceived its government, bequeathed a social safety net and then vanquished the most radical evil of this century. You would think the memorializers would be satisfied with so prodigious a legacy. They weren't. They felt compelled to make him an environmentalist, antiwar champion of civil rights. What a pity.

An earlier design featuring quotations from Roosevelt's speeches, selected in competition, was both more modest and more dignified. It was rejected because of opposition from Roosevelt's children, who considered it too "modern."

In 1993, Congress authorized construction of a World War II memorial, and in 1995, the National Capital Planning Commission approved a location for the memorial in Constitution Gardens, just off the Mall. A month later, the location was moved to the middle of the Mall, east of the Lincoln Memorial Reflecting Basin.

Reflecting pool in front of the Grant Memorial, 1976. Designed by Skidmore, Owings & Merrill.

The Grant Memorial was erected in 1922. The sculpture, by Henry M. Shrady, was completed by Edmond R. Amateis, with a pedestal by Edward Pearce Casey.

Proposal for World War II Memorial, 2000. Designed by Friedrich St. Florian. *Rendering: Joe McKendrey, FSF*

St. Florian was the winner of the competition to design the World War II Memorial. The selected design, after many modifications, repeats the stripped-down classicism favored in the 1930s by governmental bureaucracies in both Europe and America.

More than one hundred editorial and feature writers for newspapers from all parts of the country protested Friedrich St. Florian's design, selected in 2000 through a competition, and asserted that the location would damage the Mall. The opposition argued that eloquent memorials are about memory, that the design as it existed told little about the war, and that the only adequate memorial would be a World War II museum, similar to the Holocaust Museum but more expansive, perhaps located on the Anacostia River near the Navy Yard. Yet the design was developed according to St. Florian's competition scheme, and construction is scheduled for completion in 2004.

The Mall as Stage

While the Mall in most of its first century may have been a "mere cowpasture," during its second century it became far more. It has been the setting for great events that have acted as national catharses: the meeting of the Grand Army of the Republic in 1892; Marian Anderson's performance of the national anthem in 1939 at the invitation of Harold Ickes, after she was barred from Constitution Hall, and her performance at Ickes's funeral in 1952; Martin Luther King Jr.'s delivery of his "I have a dream" speech in 1963; the twenty-fifth anniversary of the Civil Rights March in 1988; and smaller but not unimportant events such as Hands across America in 1986 and the March for Children in

1996. There have also been regular events, such as the quadrennial inauguration of the president on the west front of the Capitol, fireworks every Fourth of July, and the spring kite "fly-off" on the grounds of the Washington Monument. Since 1970, the greensward has also been the stage for antiwar and presidential impeachment demonstrations, among others.

In 1946, a plan was prepared for the Board of Commissioners, the governing body of the District of Columbia, to build a grade-separated, limited-access expressway through the heart of the Mall, from the Lincoln Memorial to the Capitol and beyond. Such a proposal made in 2000 would have elicited a firestorm of disapproval. Public attitudes toward the Mall had changed, in particular, since the removal of the World War I and II temporary buildings in 1965 and the elimination of automobiles from the center of the Mall in 1976, and as immensely popular museums and memorials were added in the last three decades of the twentieth century.

By the end of the century, the Mall had become a special cultural and civic place for Americans and for visitors from around the world. It also had come to serve as a playground and sports field for Washington's citizens—for downtown office workers as well as neighborhood residents, who would crowd the Mall from morning to evening, workdays and weekends, year-round.

View of the Mall, looking east from the vicinity of Twelfth Street, 1989. *Richard Longstreth*

Cub Scouts visiting the Capitol, 1989.

View of the Mall, looking west from the vicinity of Seventh Street, 1989. *Robert Longstreth*

Sunday morning pedestrians on the Mall, 1980.

Tour d'Ellipse, 1980.

East forecourt of the Capitol, 1980s.

By 1990, Congress decided that a parking lot was not a good use of the approach to the Capitol.

Aerial sketch of the planned east forecourt to the Capitol, 1998.
Designed by RTKL Associates Inc.

The underground Capitol Visitor Center and one thousand parking spaces were planned to be added; it is anticipated that the ensemble will have little impact on Olmsted's Capitol grounds.

The Capitol

The Capitol and its grounds are an extension of the Mall. Until recently, the Capitol attracted more visitors than any other location in the country (in 2000, the Air and Space Museum and the Union Station visitors center both drew more people). The Capitol rotunda, however, continued to remain a favorite tourist destination in 2000.

The position of Architect of the Capitol was created in 1793, more than two decades before the first plan for the Capitol was executed. Appointed by Congress, the architect manages the Capitol, its

Expansion of the Capitol under the west front, 1993. Designed by Hugh Newell Jacobsen. *Robert Lautman*

New space, shown from above and below, was created without damaging the Capitol facade.

Watercolor sketch of the interior of the Capitol rotunda, 1998.

Sketch: Richard Chenoweth.

The character of the magnificent domed interior of the rotunda,

almost impossible to photograph, is suggested in this sketch. John Trumbull's history paintings are at eye level, and Constantino Brumidi's fresco *Apotheosis of Washington* is visible in the oculus.

grounds, and the surrounding buildings—a challenging task. The congressional need for space within the Capitol increases constantly. The assembly of the two branches of Congress must be contained within a building completed before the Civil War, without doing damage to the Capitol grounds laid out in 1874 by Frederick Law Olmsted. All this must be accomplished under the watchful eyes of the Advisory Neighborhood Commissions and without undue encroachment into the surrounding residential neighborhood.

The Senate offices north of Constitution Avenue, the House of Representatives offices south of Independence Avenue, and the Library of Congress east of East First Street each have added buildings three times, and their needs continue to grow. Requirements for parking and visitor services also increase each year.

In June 2000, ground was broken for the underground Capitol Visitor Center. Work on the modernization of the Dirksen Senate Office Building was under way. Security, always an urgent concern, is regularly upgraded. The Capitol dome is an internationally recognized symbol of representative democracy; in need of constant maintenance, the dome was in 2000 undergoing renovation unprecedented since its completion in 1866.

Morning visitors on Pennsylvania Avenue in front of the White House.

By the end of the twentieth century, this location was crowded with visitors from early morning until late at night. Frequent tours through the White House leave from the east entrance.

The White House and Its Surroundings

The challenge of management faced by the White House at the end of the twentieth century was similar to that faced by the Capitol: meeting the demands of a twenty-first-century institution housed in nineteenth-century buildings in a constricted historic landscape besieged by tourists. The presidency occupies the Old Executive Office Building (formerly the State, War and Navy Building), as well as the White House. President Harry S. Truman added a back porch to the White House—over outraged cries of protest—and low, inconspicuous buildings have since been added to the east (for tourist access) and to the west (including the Oval Office). As with the Capitol, future expansion for the White House is planned to be underground.

Early concept of the addition to the Corcoran Gallery of Art, 1998. Designed by Frank O. Gehry and Associates. *CGA*

The White House has the added problem of a domain that is located close to the center of the commercial downtown. In response to terrorist activities in the mid-1990s, vehicular traffic was removed from Pennsylvania Avenue in front of the White House and removed temporarily from part of E Street between the White House and the Ellipse. The days when friends freely visited Theodore Roosevelt's children, and when Harry Truman regularly sauntered through Downtown accompanied by a lone Secret Service agent, have disappeared, however.

Across Seventeenth Street from the White House is the Corcoran Gallery of Art and Corcoran School of Art, one of the oldest private institutions in Washington. After the Civil War, William Wilson Corcoran, a wealthy banker and philanthropist, supported a number of institutions including, in 1873, a foundation that established an art museum. The gallery is also a teaching institution for artists, art historians, and curators. By 1990, the Corcoran was running out of space, and its administration considered several noted architects as potential designers for its expansion. During the last decades, the national capital has been well served by many excellent buildings, but few can be described as adventurous. In contrast, the Corcoran's choice of Frank Gehry as the designer for its addition is daring and ambitious. Gehry's Guggenheim Museum, in Bilbao, Spain, was financed by the Basque and Spanish national governments with the objective of changing Bilbao's abandoned industrial riverfront into a tourist destination. A year after the museum was completed, visits had exceeded projections by over 100 percent.

Moscow Metro station, c. 1940. *VG*

The Moscow subway stations are famous for their elegance. Built partly as air-raid shelters and designed to be attractive and comfortable for crowds of people, their decor was influenced by the baroque designs of Italian architects working in Russia in the early eighteenth century.

Metro Center subway station, 1975.
Designed by Harry Weese Associates.

Washington's immaculate Metro stations, like Moscow's, are admired by visitors from all over the world. Their architectural antecedents include the coffered vaults of Roman baths.

Travel within and to the Center

The most important changes in travel within and to the center of Washington during the last quarter of the twentieth century occurred as a result of the construction of the Metrorail transit system. In 1966, after a more than decade-long series of political twists and turns, President Lyndon Johnson signed a bill creating the Washington Metropolitan Area Transit Authority (WMATA). In the spring of 1968, the WMATA Board adopted the name "Metro" and unanimously approved a 97.2-mile-long Metrorail system comprising 38.4 miles in the District of Columbia, 29.7 miles in Maryland, and 29.1 miles in Virginia.

On December 9, 1969, the WMATA broke ground at Judiciary Square. On March 27, 1976, opening day for Metrorail, five Red Line stations east of and including Farragut Square were put into service. By July 1977, the Dupont Circle Red Line Station was open, and the Blue Line was completed between the National Airport and the Stadium-Armory Stations. In April 1983, the Yellow Line began operating between Gallery Place–Chinatown and National Airport, crossing the Potomac River on the new Charles R. Fenwick Bridge and essentially completing the system within the center of the capital.

During the 1980s, the WMATA voted for a series of extensions, increasing the length of the system to 103 miles. In October 1990, Congress approved $1.3 billion in federal funding; with $770 million in local funds, completion of the system was assured. In December 1991, the WMATA board approved the schedule and funding of a fast-track program for finishing the remaining $13\frac{1}{2}$ miles of the entire 103-mile system by 2001.

Despite the emergence of Metrorail, in 2000 about 80,000 cars entered downtown Washington during the typical morning rush hour between 8:00 and 9:00 A.M. By way of comparison, the Los Angeles transportation agencies estimate that, in 1995, 151,000 vehicles entered downtown Los Angeles between 6:00 and 10:00 A.M., traveling on the nine freeways that provide access to the freeway ring encircling downtown Los Angeles. In 1996, the Washington Metropolitan Council of Governments reported that a total of 227,000 vehicles entered the Washington Metro "core" between 6:30 and 9:30 A.M., traveling primarily on local arterial streets.

While efficient, the Washington street system does have discontinuities that compromise its performance. A major problem exists at the Anacostia Freeway interchange with Pennsylvania Avenue; the interchange is incomplete, making it difficult for Maryland traffic to enter the center. The D.C. Department of Public Works (DPW) first proposed replacing the existing arrangement with a large, clover-leaf interchange. Because it displaced a number of homes and businesses, however, Anacostia citizens rejected the proposal and it was abandoned.

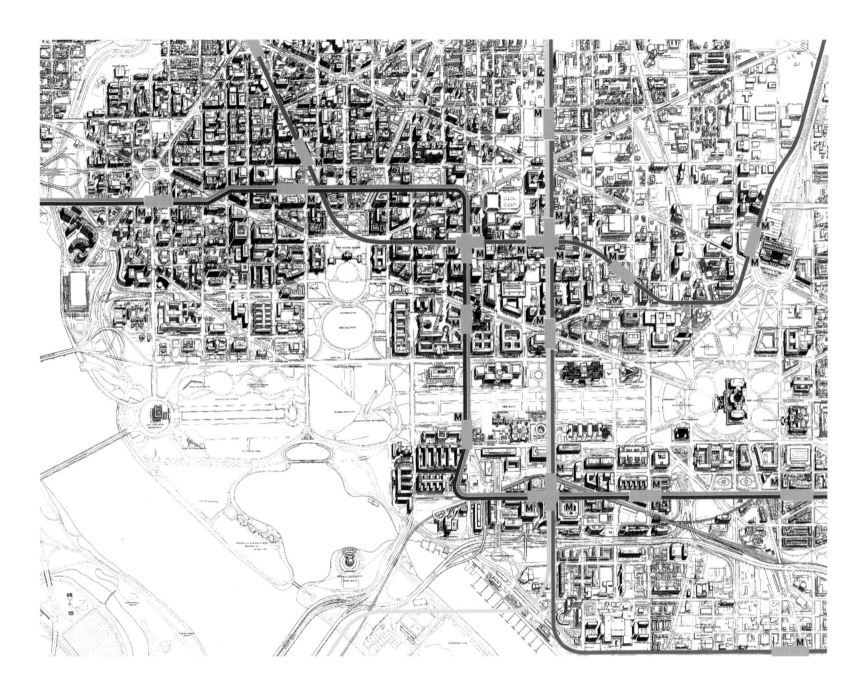

**Map of Metrorail subway system
in downtown Washington, 2000.** *JRP*

Metrorail is a combination commuter
rail and downtown circulation system.
Because travel time must be competi-
tive with other ways of traveling to the
center, stations are widely spaced, even
in the center. By 2000, ridership had
increased to a point at which expansion would become necessary—
at great expense. Unfortunately,
financial support for Metrorail, from
the municipalities it serves so well, was
still precarious at the end of the
twentieth century.

Ronald Reagan National Airport terminal expansion, 1997. Designed by Cesar Pelli & Associates. *CPA*

Interior of Ronald Reagan National Airport terminal expansion. *CPA*

The DPW then designed an alternative, an extension of the Southeast Freeway under Barney Circle to a new freeway bridge across the Anacostia River. The new bridge and freeway modification were approved by all the necessary local, state, and federal agencies, and federal financing was assured. An environmentally destructive proposal costing $200 million, it could have delivered another three thousand cars an hour to the center every morning.

While some Capitol Hill citizens supported the Barney Circle Freeway, a large group bitterly opposed it. In the late 1980s, the Committee of 100 on the Federal City developed an alternative that would complete the Anacostia Freeway/Pennsylvania Avenue interchange for about $30 million, with no displacements and no environmental problems. After a battle that lasted almost a decade, the D.C. City Council passed a bill in December 1996 entitled "Barney Circle Freeway Modification Contract Disapproval." District Representative Eleanor Holmes Norton arranged for the unspent part of the $200 million to be returned to the city for badly needed local transportation projects.

By 2000, the D.C. Office of Planning and the Division (soon to be Department) of Transportation were considering plans to eliminate or bury the freeways that cut off the Capitol Hill and Anacostia neighborhoods from the Anacostia River. If the new freeway bridge had been built, the neighborhoods would almost surely have continued to be isolated from the river well into the future.

While travel within the center was difficult and often unpleasant, travel to the center in 2000 was, for most travelers, rapid, efficient, and appealing. About 40 percent of commuters entering the center in 2000 traveled by public transit, approaching the 48 percent of commuters traveling by public transit in 1940. (Almost 90 percent of Manhattan commuters and 85 percent of Chicago commuters traveled by public transit in 2000.)

By the end of the twentieth century, Amtrak rail service and the region's three airports were bringing people to Washington from all over America and the world. Since they first opened, Washington's air terminals have had rapid, attractive parkway connections to the center of Washington, as does Baltimore/Washington International Airport. Ronald Reagan National Airport has efficient Metrorail connections to the center, and the Commonwealth of Virginia and the Washington Metropolitan Area Transit Authority were preparing to start construction of a continuation of the Metro Orange Line from Vienna, Virginia, to Dulles Airport, to be completed by 2010.

The transportation revolution that began—as did Washington—at the beginning of the nineteenth century continued to shape the city at the end of the twentieth century, pulling development toward the city's airports. The corridor between the Capital Beltway, Washington's heavily traveled circumferential freeway, and Dulles Airport had by 2000 become a twelve-mile-long linear city organized around a transportation spine that comprised an eight-lane high-speed freeway along with a four-lane freeway restricted to traffic between the Beltway and the airport, soon to be augmented

by Metrorail. Perhaps the fastest growing urban region in America, it represented the kind of city anticipated by visionary architects early in the twentieth century.

Traditionally, most great cities have been port cities; their ports have connected them, economically and politically, to the world beyond their boundaries. Among the essential ports to a modern city are its airports. Washington's airports now connect the national capital to the global economy and to the global political network, of which it has become a most important center.

Union Station, restored 1988. Restoration by Harry Weese Associates and Benjamin Thompson and Associates (original building, Daniel Burnham, 1908).

In the late 1960s, passenger railways operating along the Washington–New York–Boston corridor were losing riders and money. The National Park Service was charged with converting the little-used Union Station into a national visitors center. Consultants to the Park Service designed an unreasonably expensive parking garage and so damaged Union Station—by carving a large, ill-advised hole in the floor of the monumental lobby—that the project was abandoned. By 1980, ridership on Amtrak's passenger rail service from Washington to Boston was encouraging enough to refocus attention on the station. Daniel Burnham's design was restored, and by the end of the twentieth century, Union Station was an active passenger rail station with a functioning visitors center; its retail outlets generate a higher volume of sales per square foot than any other similar retail location in Washington.

Washington in 2000

- By 2000, the population of the District of Columbia had declined to five hundred thousand while the population of the urban region beyond the District had increased to more than three million.
- In 1974, the District of Columbia was granted "home rule." The city has struggled with pre–home rule problems, constraints placed on its independence, and persistent deficits. In 1995, Anthony Williams was appointed chief financial officer, and in 1998, he was elected mayor. In 2000, the District of Columbia was on sound financial footing for almost the first time in two hundred years.
- Beginning before World War I and accelerating after World War II, two "industries" grew in city centers—the office industry and the tourist industry. By 2000, the growth of these two industries had transformed the center of Washington.
- Washington's downtown, with about 450,000 jobs—and approximately another 100,000 jobs in Rosslyn and Crystal City across the Potomac River in Virginia—was in 2000 the second-largest employment center in America.
- Except for parts of the Shaw neighborhood, the late-nineteenth-century residential neighborhoods surrounding the center were protected by historic preservation statutes and politically sophisticated residents. With houses modernized in their interiors and rear gardens by owners who respected the historic character, these neighborhoods provide a living history of the city's first two centuries and assurance that the center will continue to be an attractive place in which to live.
- The Mall had become, functionally, ceremonially, and aesthetically, one of the most impressive and active public gathering places in the world. The Mall is managed by the National Park Service with oversight by the Commission of Fine Arts; the Smithsonian Institution and the National Gallery of Art developed and continue to manage the museums. These museums, and even more popular new additions, including the East Wing of the National Gallery of Art, the National Air and Space Museum, and the Hirshhorn Museum and, just off the Mall, the U.S. Holocaust Memorial Museum, continue to serve visitors from America and abroad.
- During the country's first century and a half, four memorials were constructed on or just off the Mall: L'Enfant located "the equestrian figure of George Washington," which became the Washington Monument; the Senate Park Commission added the Lincoln Memorial, the Grant Memorial, and the Jefferson Memorial. Four more memorials have been added since 1970: the Vietnam Veterans Memorial, the Korean War Veterans Memorial, the Franklin Delano Roosevelt Memorial, and in Constitution Gardens, the 56 Signers of the Declaration of Independence Memorial. The World War II Memorial will be the first added in the twenty-first century. An extraordinary affirmation of American ideals, and their history, is embedded in three dimensions at the center of L'Enfant's plan—in the Capitol, in the White House, and in the museums and memorials of the Mall and its surroundings.

- The Metrorail subway system had become a spectacularly successful public works project. By 2000, it was operating at close to capacity and was looking toward expanded service. Union Station, Ronald Reagan National Airport, and Washington Dulles International Airport provide efficient and elegant entrances to the capital.
- While much remained to be done, the monumental and commercial center—the L'Enfant city—had become the political and ceremonial center and, increasingly, a commercial and intellectual center of the nation and the world.

Key

- single-family residences
- walk-up residences
- elevator apartment
- hotel
- retail
- private offices
- federal offices
- federal institutions
- private & foreign institutions
- local institutions
- industrial
- warehouse
- transportation

0 100   500   1000 ft

1. Capitol
2. White House
3. Supreme Court
4. Senate Office Building
5. New Senate Office Building
6. **U.S. Judiciary Office Building**
7. Library of Congress
8. Union Station
9. Department of Labor
10. U.S. Courts Headquarters
11. Federal Trade Commission
12. National Archives
13. Department of Justice
14. Federal Bureau of Investigation
15. Internal Revenue Service
16. Postal Department
17. Interstate Commerce Commission
18. **Ronald Reagan Building**
19. Commerce Department
20. Treasury Department
21. Old Executive Office Building
22. General Services Administration
23. Office of Personnel Management
24. Department of the Interior
25. Bureau of Indian Affairs
26. Federal Reserve
27. Department of State
28. Bureau of Naval Medicine
29. Weather Bureau
30. Department of Agriculture
31. District Building
32. District Court
33. D.C. Court of Appeals
34. **D.C. Superior Court**
35. Martin Luther King Jr. Memorial Library
36. **D.C. Convention Center**
37. D.C. Municipal Offices

38. Washington Monument
39. Lincoln Memorial
40. **Vietnam Veterans Memorial**
41. Ulysses S. Grant Memorial
42. **Korean War Veterans Memorial**
43. National Museum of American History
44. National Museum of Natural History
45. National Gallery of Art, West Building
46. **National Gallery of Art, East Building**
47. Botanical Garden
48. Folger Shakespeare Library
49. **National Air and Space Museum**
50. **Hirshhorn Museum of Art and Sculpture Garden**
51. Museum of Arts and Industry
52. Smithsonian "Castle"
53. **Museum of African Art**
54. **Arthur M. Sackler Gallery**
55. Freer Gallery of Asian Art
56. Kennedy Center for the Performing Arts
57. Nancy Hanks Center/Old Post Office
58. National Museum of American Art
59. National Portrait Gallery
60. National Building Museum
61. George Washington University
62. Columbia Hospital for Women
63. National Geographic Society
64. National Theater
65. Ford's Theater
66. **Arena MCI Center**
67. **Shakespeare Theater**
68. **Navy Memorial**
69. **Postal Museum**
70. **56 Signers of the Declaration of Independence Memorial**
71. **Constitution Gardens**
72. **Freedom Plaza**
73. **Pershing Square**

74. **John Marshall Park**
75. **National Gallery of Art Sculpture Garden**
76. The Ellipse
77. Rawlins Park
78. Judiciary Square
79. Lafayette Square
80. Franklin Square
81. McPherson Square
82. Farragut Square
83. Washington Circle
84. Mount Vernon Square
85. Dupont Circle
86. Logan Circle
87. Scott Circle
88. Thomas Circle
89. Longfellow Square
90. Rock Creek Park
91. Chesapeake & Ohio Canal

Buildings and public projects constructed or completed after 1970 are listed in **bold** type.

0 100   500   1000 ft

Conclusion

The National Capital at the Beginning of the Twenty-first Century: Looking to the Future

The economic success of Washington's monumental and commercial center in the last three decades of the twentieth century has obscured problems that have been mounting, in the center and beyond, during the last half of the twentieth and first years of the twenty-first century. Despite the fact that the capital has one of the largest downtowns in America (in terms of area), it is running out of room to expand. Dependence on private automobiles for travel to and through the downtown area compromises the quality and efficiency of the center. The remnants of late-nineteenth-century railroad building and late-twentieth-century expressway building continue to cut off neighborhoods from one another and from the rivers, although the city's neglect of its rivers goes back to L'Enfant's original plan. In addition, while the new neighborhoods beyond the District of Columbia that have grown since World War II are functionally united with the center, they are politically—and in the minds of their citizens—separate communities. The planting and maintenance of trees, once the glory of the capital, has been drastically curtailed by the city's financial problems. Finally, since September 11, 2001, security against terrorist attack has become a new focus for design in the national capital.

Current Mayor Anthony Williams, with his background in city planning, has reinvigorated the Office of Planning and created a new Department of Transportation. These actions suggest that Washington's tradition of centennial planning—one that began with the L'Enfant plan at the turn of the nineteenth century and extended through the Senate Park Commission Plan at the turn of the twentieth century—can be continued.

Travel within Downtown

Downtown Washington's large concentration of employment is spread out over a vast area; within that area, people travel from place to place primarily in private automobiles. Travel by automobile in downtown Washington is defeated by its own congestion, by the complications of the L'Enfant street system, and by the sizable areas in the center where automobiles are banned.

The solution to this most troubling physical problem is simple. The Department of Public Works (now the D.C. Department of Transportation), in *A Transportation Vision, Strategy, and Action Plan*

Painting of a proposal for a typical riverfront development. From *Extending the Legacy: Planning America's Capital for the 21st Century*, National Capital Planning Commission, 1996.

Special Streets—Park System Plan.
From *The Regional Development Guide 1966–2000*, Metro-Center Policies Plan, National Capital Planning Commission. *NCPC*

The report states, "The proposed system shown here aims to establish a visual structure consistent with the complex functional requirements of today's Metro-Center. The connective tissue of 'open space' would ... link special areas visually and generally add a series of open spaces at a scale ranging from the grand monumentality of the Mall to the informality of special shopping streets and places. Such a system would serve as a constant source of orientation and delight."

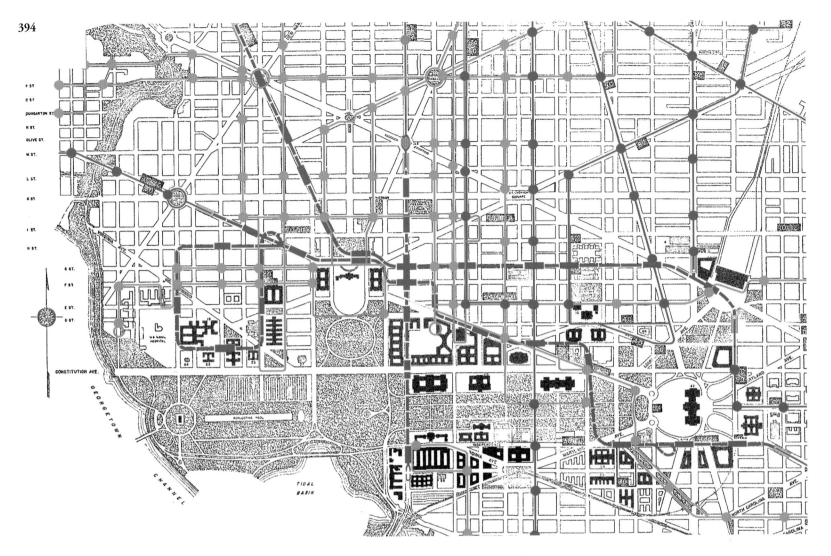

Pre–World War II downtown Washington public transit network, with proposed subway system.
From *A Transportation Survey and Plan for the Central Area of Washington, D.C.*, Commissioners of the District of Columbia, 1944.

Color has been added to this early public transit map; red designates streetcar lines, orange indicates bus lines. The wide red lines locate the proposed subway system.

for the Nation's Capital (1997), proposes that the city "focus transit improvements on internal circulation to provide city residents with improved alternatives to the private automobile . . . A set of improvements are recommended to promote a transportation system that connects roadways and parking facilities and other modes and facilities so that motorists can park once in the city and then travel around by transit, walking and bicycle for all internal trips in the City. Related to the 'park once' concept is a focus on internal transit circulation as a top transportation priority." This "vision" is unusual coming from a trans-portation agency, since it gives travel by public transit, bicycling, and walking parity with travel by private automobile.

There has been no lack of plans for central Washington since World War II, but there has been a lack of support for implementing them. *The Regional Development Guide 1966–2000,* created by the National Capital Planning Commission in 1966, includes "policies plans" for the region, the "Metro-Center," and the District. While the *Regional Development Guide* has been generally ignored, the Metro-Center Policies Plan should be reexamined. The Metro-Center section

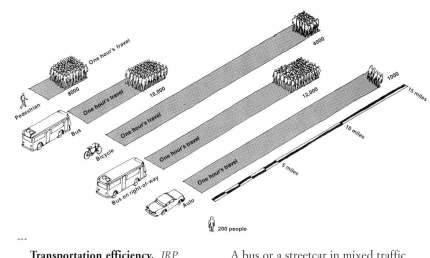

Transportation efficiency. *JRP*

A "travel mode" is not just a vehicle; it is a vehicle plus its travelway.

A bus or a streetcar in mixed traffic is a very different travel mode from a bus or a streetcar on its own travelway.

Streetcars on Bahnhofstrasse in Zurich.

Department stores are concentrated on this street. With the exception of service vehicles, private traffic is barred. Portland, Oregon, has a somewhat similar but more complicated arrangement, to serve its downtown.

"Woonerf" in Munich.

While the etymology of the term *woonerf* is obscure, the operation of such a street is not: on these streets pedestrians have absolute right-of-way. Both the Capitol Hill and Georgetown neighborhoods would be well served by woonerfs.

Reserved "contra flow" bus lanes in Paris.

On the wide boulevards of Paris, which are two-way streets, private vehicles travel in one direction only; buses travel in the opposite direction. Here, automobile drivers do not compete with buses.

Exclusive busways in Madrid.

On this Madrid street, the curb lanes are reserved for buses, taxis, and right-turning vehicles. The "headways" (distance between buses) are small, so automobile drivers are not tempted to intrude into the transit lanes—a problem where transitways are not occupied by buses.

Reserved lane for buses and bicycles on the Kurfurstendamm, Berlin.

When Otto von Bismarck returned from Paris in the 1870s, he decreed that the Kurfurstendamm should copy that conquered city's Champs-Elysées. With a right-of-way of approximately 160 feet, the same width as Washington's Pennsylvania Avenue, the Kurfurstendamm is one of Berlin's major shopping streets. Because buses and bicycles share the same right-of-way, buses have an advantage over tracked transit.

proposes a "Special Streets—Park System" that provides an urban design framework for the Department of Transportation's "park once" proposals. It describes the importance of the L'Enfant avenues as follows:

> One of the prominent features of the L'Enfant Plan was the series of broad avenues which focus on important buildings and monuments in the central area. These avenues have been greatly neglected since the eighteenth century and are distinguished primarily because of their great width in contrast to the gridiron street system . . . L'Enfant's avenues exist today as one of the greatest design potentials of the Metro-Center area. They are broad, with wide rights-of-way ranging up to 160 feet . . . It is proposed that these avenues be developed as opportunity allows as special boulevards, with generous sidewalks and park-like settings. Automobile traffic would not be eliminated, but in most cases would be minimized.

Before World War II, downtown Washington had one of the country's most efficient public transit systems. After the war, however, the capital's transportation agencies, convinced that automobiles needed more space, replaced the streetcars with buses mixed in with automobile traffic. European planners never made the same mistake. In the centers of large western European cities, where travel is even more congested than in American cities, streetcars and buses travel on exclusive transit lanes from which automobiles are banned.

The wide L'Enfant streets and avenues have the potential to provide the city's transportation redemption. This could be accomplished by replicating the pre–World War II public transportation network, with buses or streetcars assigned to travelways reserved for public transit. Within those streets and avenues, ample room exists for streetcars, buses, and bicycles—as well as for people to walk, leisurely—all shielded from automobile congestion. More space still would remain for automobiles and trucks than exists in the entire street systems of most American cities.

While the solution to downtown travel problems in Washington is simple technically, it will not be easy to implement politically. It is likely to be difficult to convince drivers to give up the convenience of private cars, but by putting in place the "park once" strategy, the city can provide travel through Downtown that is on average faster, more convenient (with no car to park), and less expensive, both to the individual and to the city, than travel by private automobile.

New Community Focus. From *The Regional Development Guide 1966–2000*, Metro-Center Policies Plan, National Capital Planning Commission. *NCPC*

The report notes, "The process of building subways and renewing older communities will afford the opportunity to create new community centers…These new centers of employment and shopping should establish pedestrian precincts. Housing should be available in the District, within the limits of economic feasibility, to all income groups. Most high density residential development should be located near…Metrorail transit stations, employment centers, and local open spaces."

The Future of Employment and Commercial Development in the Center of the National Capital

Downtown Washington is zoned primarily for commercial development, limited vertically by the 1910 Act to Regulate the Height of Buildings and horizontally by residential neighborhoods that are important to the success of Downtown. At the beginning of the twenty-first century, it is clear that this commercial space will soon be completely developed. It is also clear that the economic growth of the city, and of the region, will depend to a considerable extent on the continuing growth of employment within the District of Columbia. The city and the federal government have begun construction of the new southeast federal center and an expanded Navy Yard—once the city's major employer. Both are mixed-use developments that combine offices, retail space, and residences. Such actions are shifting development toward the Anacostia River, an underutilized resource, and toward the Anacostia neighborhood on the southeast side of the river, which stands to benefit from participating in the city's expanding job market. The National Capital Planning Commission, in its *Extending the Legacy: Planning America's Capital for the 21st Century*

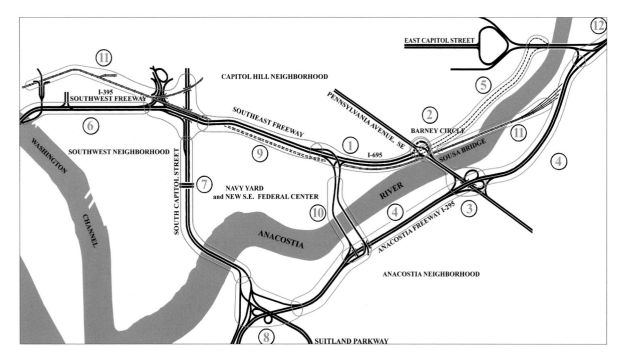

Anacostia waterfront and its environs, transportation problems, and opportunities, 2002. *JRP*

The diagram locates the many separate but related transportation issues addressed by the Anacostia Waterfront Initiative.

Industrial waterfront, where South Capitol Street meets the Anacostia River, 2000.

As the South Capitol Street corridor is redeveloped, parks, residences, retail stores, and office buildings can replace the waterfront industry.

Anacostia Freeway, looking northeast across the ramps to the Southeast Freeway, 2000.

This freeway, a substandard road, cuts off the Anacostia neighborhood

from the river. South of South Capitol Street, the freeway could be replaced by a parkway or signalized boulevard, providing vehicular access to the neighborhood and pedestrian access to the waterfront.

(1996), proposed one way to extend that space. The South Capitol Street corridor is underdeveloped because it is cut off from the rest of the center by the Southwest and Southeast Freeways and by railroads. In *Extending the Legacy,* the NCPC recommends that the freeways and railroads be eliminated or depressed, and that South Capitol Street and its surroundings be developed by the same kind of public-private partnership that created the present-day Pennsylvania Avenue.

Employment and Housing beyond the Center

American suburbs have developed in waves, according to *Black's Guide* (1996), a journal for developers. As each new wave of development has occurred farther from the center, older development closer to the center has decayed. *Black's* describes the growth of the national capital region as an exception, however. Where early suburbs close to

Southeast Freeway, looking north-west from Eleventh Street, 2000.

During the morning rush hour, about four thousand cars are delivered to the freeway by the Anacostia Freeway ramps, visible in the foreground. If this traffic were rerouted, Virginia Avenue could be re-created, and about nineteen acres of land would be returned to the Capitol Hill neighborhood.

Freight train on embankment in the middle of Virginia Avenue, 2000.

The railroad that intrudes on Virginia and Maryland Avenues is destructive functionally and aesthetically. The continuation of the freight railroad into an obsolete, turn-of-the-nineteenth-century tunnel east of South Capitol Street is dangerous. An obsolete marshaling yard occupying National Park Service land should be consolidated with the railroad yards north of New York Avenue.

Southeast Freeway between Barney Circle and Eleventh Street, 2000.

Here only about one-fourth of the three-hundred-foot freeway right-of-way is used. Virginia Avenue could be re-created at this location immediately, improving access to the downtown area and returning about eight acres of land to the neighborhood.

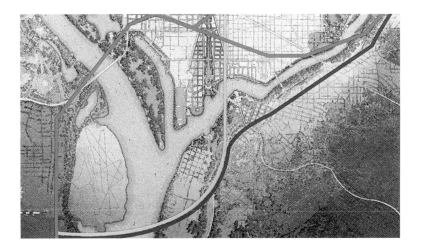

Railroad relocation proposal (modified), 2002. From *Extending the Legacy: Planning America's Capital for the 21st Century,* National Capital Planning Commission, 1996.

On the diagram, the yellow line indicates the NCPC's proposed relocation of passenger rail, and the blue line, the proposed freight rail location. The plan that freight rail diverge from passenger rail south of the Anacostia River, would be unacceptable to the Anacostia community. Both passenger and freight rail should continue north, together, as indicated by the broken blue line.

the center have rezoned space around Metrorail stations for dense residential and commercial development—as in Rockville, Bethesda, and Friendship Heights in Maryland, and Rosslyn, Ballston, and Alexandria in Virginia—they have prospered. One of the objectives of the Office of Planning is to create jobs throughout the city, close to workers' residences. Metrorail stations within the District hold the same potential to fulfill this goal as the stations in the suburbs just beyond the District line.

Reconnecting the City to Its Waterfronts

The Anacostia Waterfront Initiative (AWI), a District-federal community partnership managed by the city and including the National Capital Planning Commission and the National Park Service, was formed in 2000 to revitalize the neighborhoods on both sides of the Anacostia River and to reconnect South Capital Street to the center of the capital. The future quality of these neighborhoods and the future

Painting of the Capitol, looking north from South Capitol Street.
From *Extending the Legacy: Planning America's Capital for the 21st Century,* National Capital Planning Commission, 1996.

The report states, "Untangled from the maze of freeways and railroad tracks, South Capitol Street can become another Pennsylvania Avenue, an exciting mix of shops, housing and museums. The Capitol Dome is a stunning backdrop for night life on the new South Capitol Street."

View of the Capitol, looking north from South Capitol Street, 2000.

The Southeast Freeway, which dates from the 1960s, and the freight rail-road, dating from the nineteenth century, block access between the downtown and South Capitol Street. The passenger rail line can be seen in the distance.

character of South Capital Street will depend to a large extent on solutions to transportation infrastructure problems identified by the NCPC. In *Extending the Legacy,* the NCPC described "the highway programs of the 1950s and 1960s which created a moat around much of central Washington . . . Freeways have fractured neighborhoods and severed the city from its waterfronts. Undesirable in any city, such disruptions are intolerable in the Nation's Capital."

On the north side of the Anacostia River, the Southeast Freeway, an infamous elevated expressway that triggered citizen revolt against all expressways in the national capital, separates the Capitol Hill neighborhood from the river. As a result, much of the north riverbank is now industrial. South of the river, the Anacostia Freeway and the remnants of the abandoned Center Leg Freeway separate the Anacostia neighborhood from the river. A freight railroad north of the river in a turn-of-the-nineteenth-century tunnel and an abandoned railway right-of-way south of the river add to the separation.

In *Extending the Legacy,* the NCPC proposed that the Southeast Freeway be eliminated and that both passenger and freight rail lines approach the center through a tunnel under the Potomac River, south of Ronald Reagan National Airport, similar to the way railroads enter Manhattan under the Hudson River. Passenger rail lines would connect with the tunnel that had been constructed under East First Street for passenger rail by the Senate Park Commission.

The NCPC performed an important service by pointing out a number of problems in the Anacostia watershed—problems created by destructive railroad decisions made in the nineteenth century and

equally destructive highway decisions made toward the end of the twentieth. The NCPC, however, has no powers of implementation. The AWI, on the other hand, is led by the D.C. Office of Planning and the D.C. Department of Transportation; these District agencies can both plan for the future and realize their plans.

Maryland Representative Steny Hoyer initiated and funded a redesign of the South Capitol Street corridor to create a fitting ceremonial entrance from Maryland to the center of the capital. The design study (and ensuing construction contracts) will be managed by the D.C. Department of Transportation. But that ceremonial entrance cannot go forward, nor can South Capitol Street be reconnected to the commercial and monumental center, as long as the elevated freeway crosses South Capitol Street.

To untangle the thicket of problems along the Anacostia River, the elevated Southeast Freeway must first be removed from Virginia Avenue. A transportation planner in the Office of Planning has suggested that Southeast Freeway traffic be put in a tunnel under the South Capitol Street corridor, carrying the traffic from the Anacostia Freeway into the Center Leg Freeway tunnel under the Mall and to the Southwest Freeway. An ingenious idea, it is not an easy one to implement. Yet only when that is achieved can the rest of these otherwise intractable issues be resolved.

Accepting its charge broadly, the Anacostia Waterfront Initiative must do work at the scale as that of the Senate Park Commission. The commission's work, which was first attacked, was only partly accomplished when the Jefferson Memorial was installed, almost a half-century after the plan was made public. The commission's recommendations for the Mall will finally be completely realized when the National Museum of the American Indian opens, in the first decade of the twenty-first century.

The Anacostia Waterfront Initiative faces a number of daunting, expensive, but necessary tasks, which, like the work of the Senate Park Commission, may take a number of years to implement. In order to accomplish its goals, it will need the continuing financial support of the federal government, in much the same way that the government was active in seeing that the plans of the Senate Park Commission were carried out.

A City of Trees

Before World War II, Washington was known as a city of trees. Many citizens contributed to this reputation. Thomas Jefferson, who bemoaned the loss of "valuable groves" as the L'Enfant rights-of-way were cleared, had poplars planted on Pennsylvania Avenue. Andrew Jackson Downing landscaped the grounds south of the White House as they still exist. After the Civil War, Major Nathaniel Michler planted the Mall and Lafayette Square, and Alexander Robey Shepherd planted sixty thousand trees throughout the L'Enfant city. In 1912, flowering cherry trees, gifts from Japan, were planted around the new Tidal Basin; and in 1927, Congress authorized the National Arboretum. Since the beginning of the Great Depression, however, little has been added to Washington's parks, and in the city center, the street trees have been devastated.

By the early 1990s, the Department of Public Works, responsible for the city's trees, lacked funds and came close to shutting down its tree planting and maintenance programs. Those programs were resurrected by Mayor Anthony Williams soon after he was elected in 1998. In addition, the Casey Trees Endowment Fund, established in 2000 by Betty Brown Casey, a private citizen of the District, has helped ensure that Washington will soon be a city of trees once again. The interest from the endowment will be used to support tree programs for the District of Columbia in perpetuity. Further attention should be paid to this distinctive aspect of the capital.

The National Capital Region beyond the District of Columbia

During World War II, America was focused on the war, with little energy remaining for city building. After the war this changed, and building proliferated. When, in 1962, the National Capital Planning Commission was re-created by Congress, it was charged with preparing a "general plan for the National Capital Region." The plan that the NCPC created, *The Regional Development Guide 1966–2000,* signed in 1966 by President John F. Kennedy and intended to guide the growth of the region until the end of the twentieth century, is the only comprehensive plan ever created for the national capital region.

While the Metro-Center Policies Plan, part of the *Regional Development Guide,* has a renewed relevance, this is not true of the Regional Policies Plan, the major element in the *Guide.* In developing this latter section of the *Guide,* regional planners mapped seven possible suburban arrangements, including the Radial Corridor Plan, popularly called the "Wedges and Corridors Plan," which the *Guide* adopted.

The *Guide* had clearly stated development objectives, and it proposed a transportation network aimed at implementing those objectives. However, it assumed suburban lifestyles that even today, close to four decades after its publication, continue to be rejected by most people who live in the region beyond the District of Columbia. In addition, the development pattern that the *Guide* proposed was based on the radial travel patterns of late-nineteenth-century cities served by passenger and commuter rail and by streetcars at a time when it was already apparent that urban travel had become circumferential as well as radial.

Despite the strictures of the federally supported *Regional Development Guide,* and despite the elimination of the expressway system planned beyond the Capital Beltway and the completion of an expensive transit system aimed at concentrating development, the Washington region has continued to expand at increasingly lower densities. Since World War II, the way in which Washington, and American cities in general, have been planned and have grown has changed. Until that war, local city agencies laid out streets in order to create and channel city development. After the war, under the aegis of federal agencies, streets and suburban roads were laid out to accommodate travel by drivers of private automobiles. This practice and related federal policies, combined with a steady increase in private wealth, have made the country, for most—but not all—of its citizens, the best-housed society in history.

These public investments, and the pattern of development they have encouraged, have had other consequences. Unintentionally, the federal government has subsidized private land development in the suburbs, supported geographic segregation of the races and economic classes, and acquiesced in the devastation (evident since the early 1970s) of the centers of American cities. A large sector of American society approves of the lifestyle these investments have created. Another sector passionately disapproves of this lifestyle and its consequences. But about one consequence there can be no disagreement: by financing suburban road building, the federal government, through the Federal Highway Administration, has been building new cities. City building is too important to be left to highway engineers or, for that matter, to city planners or to any other profession. To be effective, it must be pursued—as in the L'Enfant center at critical times in the city's history—by the highest levels of government supported by a concerned citizenry.

Although development of the national capital region has not been shaped by the *Regional Development Guide,* and while there is no accepted regional plan, there has nevertheless been regional planning. Throughout the 1990s, the Metropolitan Washington Council of Governments (COG) conducted a series of "transportation visioning" sessions. While citizen participation has been exemplary and the

Wedges and Corridors Plan. From
The Regional Development Guide 1966–2000.

This diagram proposed "radial urbanized
corridors" separated by "wedges of controlled open space." The subway system
proposed by the *Regional Development
Guide* has been completed, but the *Guide*
has otherwise been ignored. An exception
is the Montgomery County, Maryland,
open-space program of parks and agricul-
tural preserves.

COG's technical staff is highly qualified, these "visions" have not produced a consensus. The reason is simple: how can a transportation
vision for the region be created before a vision for the region is created? Transportation does not exist for its own sake; it is a means, not
an end. What end is the transportation vision to serve? Whose vision
can this represent?

These are not easy questions to answer. A partial response is that
the region should be "sustainable." At a minimum, the region should
be efficient; it should husband scarce resources. Commitment to sus-
tainability is not a goal that is widely shared by a consumer society. Ove
Arup, one of the twentieth century's great engineers—responsible for
engineering marvels like the Opera House in Sydney and the

Pompidou Center in Paris—concluded a public address he gave late in his life with the following admonition:

Man's battle with nature has been won. Whether we like it or not, we are now burdened with the administration of the conquered territory. Nature reserves, landscapes, townscapes: they will all be wantonly destroyed, to the ultimate ruin of man, or they must be deliberately planned to serve his needs. Much has been destroyed already, and more will be destroyed, but the alarm has been sounded. Pollution, the population explosion, these things are news. The battle is on, and it is a crucial battle for mankind. Those who long for the good old days must be told that road is now closed . . .

[I]t is my conviction that whilst we have become very clever at doing almost anything we like, we are very backward in choosing the right thing to do.

In addition to the COG, other organizations have proposed visions for the region's future. In 1998, the Washington Board of Trade published a document arguing for a renewal of expressway building. In addition, there have been favorably received proposals for "growth boundaries" similar to those established in Portland, Oregon. Former Maryland Governor Parris Glendening's administration has a "smart growth" initiative that focuses on reinvestment in existing communities.

Many citizens are concerned about the future of the region. Assuming that the regional population will double (it has been doubling approximately every thirty years since 1800, although growth may be slowing down), the consequences, including economic and environmental ones, of three competing models of the future should be explored by the COG: "uncontrolled growth," with transportation investments and land-use decisions proceeding as at present; "growth boundaries," similar to those established by Portland; and development within the direction of the current leading edge—a draconian

version of Maryland's "smart growth" policy. This or similar work is a prerequisite for responsible action.

It is possible to create policies that provide better housing for more people without many of the destructive consequences for the national capital and American society beyond the capital. Like the policies that have, in one view, degraded American cities, these new policies must control transportation investments. By providing access to areas where development is needed and by denying access to areas that need to be protected, the arrangement of the region's activities can be reshaped almost completely—and more positively. Investments in roads and in public transportation are made primarily by state governments, using local funds and federal money provided through the federal Department of Transportation. Allocation of federal transportation money is made by state and local representatives acting through the Council of Governments. The process is political, as it should be, and any change in the present allocation of transportation funds must be enacted politically. An understanding of the consequences of alternative courses of action could help clarify the regional dialogue, leading to a conscious political choice and, in turn, to a twenty-first-century vision for the national capital region, one supported by the region's citizens. Given a regional agreement, the federal government would surely contribute financially, as it has in the past.

The capital has expanded far beyond the territory it encompassed during its first half century. The developed area of the capital now also includes the District of Columbia beyond the center and the region beyond the District of Columbia. Yet what is called the region is a single capital city, and the monumental and commercial center is still at the heart of the city, and at the heart of the nation. The quality of the city of Washington will continue to depend on the quality and character of its monumental and commercial center. The future quality of the center, in turn, will depend on the effectiveness of its relationship to the larger city of which it is a part.

Drawing of proposed regional community. From *A Better Way to Grow,* Chesapeake Bay Foundation, 1996. *CBF*

In 1996, the Chesapeake Bay Foundation, organized to re-create the original quality of the Chesapeake Bay area, issued *A Better Way to Grow,* Maryland's "smart growth" policy. Many architect-developers support such proposals, calling them New Urbanism—late-nineteenth-century urbanism with a twentieth-century name. Close to half of all new development in cities in the eastern United States is concentrated in "town houses," similar to nineteenth-century row houses. These developments, however, try to imitate typical suburbia as much as possible. The foundation and other New Urbanists argue for complete towns, with shopping, schools, and job locations as part of a compact development.

Acknowledgments

In the spring of 1998, the American Architectural Foundation mounted an exhibition at the Washington, D.C., headquarters of the American Institute of Architects entitled "Washington through Two Centuries in Maps and Images," which helped lead to this publication. The materials in the exhibition were prepared by Joseph Passonneau & Partners. Foundation members Eryl Platzer, Linnea Hammer, and Norman Koontz (now executive vice president and chief executive officer of the AIA) arranged for the exhibition.

Among the many books on which I have relied while preparing this text, six have been most important. Two works by John W. Reps, *Monumental Washington: The Planning and Development of the Capital Center* and *Washington on View: The Nation's Capital since 1790,* should be read by anyone who wants to delve into the planning history of the national capital. *Washington on View* is a wonderfully informative book, with gorgeous reproductions of early Washington paintings and planning documents, all in color. Many are reproduced here.

The degradation of historic Washington that began early in the twentieth century and accelerated after World War II is recorded in James M. Goode's accurately titled *Capital Losses: A Cultural History of Washington's Destroyed Buildings.* In Goode's book, photographs of each building accompany the history of the building and its owner. Fifty of these buildings, razed by 1970, appear on the axonometric map of Washington in 1940.

Much of the background on neighborhood history comes from *Washington at Home: An Illustrated History of Neighborhoods in the Nation's Capital,* edited by Kathryn Schneider Smith; this useful book is unfortunately out of print. The history of the Mall is described in *The Mall in Washington 1791–1991,* edited by Richard Longstreth. This documentation of the two-hundred-year development of the Mall includes essays on architecture, urban design, and the planning history of Washington. *The AIA Guide to the Architecture of Washington, D.C.,* third edition, edited by Christopher Weeks, has excellent essays on architecture and Washington, and thumbnail sketches on the architectural and social history of 341 buildings and places, most of which are located in the area covered by the maps in this book.

A number of other books have been helpful, particularly in providing access to the images so important in this history of physical change in Washington: *Bridges and the City of Washington,* by Donald Beekman Myer; *Cities and People: A Social and Architectural History,* by Mark Girouard; *The City of Washington: An Illustrated History,* by the Junior League of Washington; *The Federal City: Plans and Realities,* by Frederick Gutheim and Wilcomb E. Washburn; *Mr. Lincoln's City: An Illustrated Guide to the Civil War Sites of Washington,* by Richard M. Lee; *Old Washington, D.C., in Early Photographs, 1846–1932,* by Robert Reed; *The Outdoor Sculpture of Washington, D.C.: A Comprehensive Historical Guide,* by James M. Goode; *Port Town to Urban Neighborhood: The Georgetown Waterfront of Washington, D.C., 1880–1920,* by Kathryn Schneider Smith; *Washington, D.C., Then and Now: 69 Sites Photographed in the Past and Present,* by Charles Suddrath Kelly; and *Washington Seen: A Photographic History 1875–1965,* by Fredric M. Miller and Howard Gillette Jr.

Public and private agencies rain planning documents on the national capital. The following have been helpful: *A Transportation Survey and Plan for the Central Area of Washington, D.C.,* by the commissioners of the District of Columbia, October 1944; *The Regional Development Guide 1966–2000,* by the National Capital Planning Commission, 1966; *Extending the Legacy: Planning America's Capital for the 21st Century,* by the National Capital Planning Commission, draft issued March 1996, final report undated; *A Transportation Vision, Strategy, and Action Plan for the Nation's Capital,* by the District of Columbia Department of Public Works, 1997; and *Anacostia Waterfront Initiative: A District, Federal, and Community Partnership,* by the D.C. Office of Planning, 2000.

The discussion of the future of the city center is based on planning documents by public agencies; on the *Central Washington Transportation and Civic Design Study,* supported by a grant to my office from the National Endowment for the Arts; and on work with the Committee of 100 on the Federal City. The brief discussion of the future of the region grew out of work with the Metropolitan Washington Council of Governments and with a number of civic groups: the Piedmont Environmental Council, the Washington Regional Network for Livable Communities, and the Bypass Alternatives Review Committee.

Elliott Carroll FAIA reviewed an early draft of the text. Architectural historian Pamela Scott read the important section on the work of Peter Charles (Pierre) L'Enfant. David Maloney, on the staff of the D.C. Historic Preservation Office, read the material on Georgetown, and Ray Kukulski, chairman of the Citizens Association of Georgetown, also reviewed the discussion of present-day Georgetown. Kirkwood White, former trustee of the Committee of 100 on the Federal City, encouraged me in my writing related to the future of the monumental and commercial center. Leo Schefer, president of the Washington Airports Task Force, reviewed a draft of the material on the future of the region beyond the District of Columbia. Robert Lautman, besides providing many images of the city today, contributed encouragement and advice.

In addition to the many individuals who have loaned images and photographs, I am especially indebted to the Washington institutions that preserve in their archives the history of the national capital: the Historical Society of Washington, D.C., the Commission of Fine Arts, the Kiplinger Collection of the George Washington University library, the Martin Luther King Jr. Memorial Library Washingtoniana Division, the National Archives, the National Gallery of Art, the National Geographic Society, and the Smithsonian Institution. The staff of the King Memorial Library Washingtoniana Division assisted in retrieving old maps and newspaper descriptions of buildings and civic affairs. Susan Malbin, archivist of the Peabody Room of the Georgetown Branch Library (and then head of the Washingtoniana Division), was particularly helpful in unearthing background information about the first settlements in the area. The Geography and Map Division of the Library of Congress has been a continuing source of information and encouragement for the maps in this book. I am grateful in particular to Ralph Ehrenberg, John Hébert, and James Flatness.

My partner, David Akopian, has managed the exacting process of preparing and organizing digitized images and transmitting them between Washington and New York City. This book could not exist without his labor over the course of more than a decade.

Of the many people who have provided help and support for this book, two have been most important. Urban historian and scholar Sam Bass Warner, most recently professor in the Department of Urban Studies and Planning at the Massachusetts Institute of Technology, reviewed and contributed suggestions to a number of the many drafts. Janet Passonneau undertook much of the library research and prepared most of the Georgetown material.

The quality of this book owes an immeasurable debt to the dedication of its editor, Stephanie Salomon, and its designer, Abigail Sturges. While many people have helped me through the writing and publishing of this book, I am solely responsible for the accuracy of its contents.

Work on this book began with a grant from the Graham Foundation for Advanced Study in the Fine Arts. It was carried forward with help from the Kea Foundation and by a series of grants from the National Endowment for the Arts. The most significant financial support for this project has been supplied by what I affectionately describe as the Janet Vivian Passonneau Charitable Trust. Janet has retired as chief of the Laboratory of Cellular Neurochemistry at the National Institutes of Health, so the trust is out of business. But the work is done.

—J.R.P.

Photographic Sources

ACE   Army Corps of Engineers
ACIC   Aeronautical Chart Information Center
ACM   Arthur Cotton Moore/Associates
AFIP   Army Forces Institute of Pathology
AIAWC   American Institute of Architects, Washington Chapter
AOC   Architect of the Capitol
API   Autumn Publishing, Inc.
AWA   Amy Weinstein Architects
CBF   Chesapeake Bay Foundation
CCHS   Chevy Chase Historical Society
CFA   Commission of Fine Arts
CGA   Corcoran Gallery of Art
CHS   Columbia Historical Society
CLA   Cooper-Lecky Architects
CPA   Cesar Pelli & Associates
CUFAL   Cornell University Fine Arts Library
CUOL   Cornell University, Olin Library
DCDHT   D.C. Department of Highways and Traffic
DCDPL   D.C. Department of Public Works
DCDT   D.C. Department of Transportation
DCPL   D.C. Preservation League
DH   Don Hawkins Collection
FCC   Federal City Council
ES   *Evening Star*
FS   Frederick Schonbach
FSA   Frank Schlesinger Architects
FSF   Friedrich St. Florian
GGA   Graham Gund Architects
GWU   George Washington University
HABS   Historic American Buildings Survey
HC   Hartman-Cox Architects
HSW   Historical Society of Washington, D.C.
IMP   International Museum of Photography
JRP   Joseph R. Passonneau
JWR   John W. Reps Collection
KC   Kiplinger Collection
LBM   Landslides, Boston, Massachusetts
LCDH   Library of Congress, Don Hawkins
LCGM   Library of Congress Geography and Maps
LCM   Library of Congress Manuscripts
LCND   Library of Congress Newspaper Division
LCPP   Library of Congress Prints and Photographs
LCSC   Library of Congress Special Collections
LEG   Lawrence E. Geischner Collection
LOK   Leroy O. King Collection
MLKL   Martin Luther King Library

MMNN   Mariners' Museum, Newport News
NA   National Archives
NCPC   National Capital Planning Commission
NEA   National Educational Association
NGA   National Gallery of Art
NGS   National Geographic Society
NPS   National Park Service
NSCD   National Society of Colonial Dames
NYPL   New York Public Library
NZP   National Zoological Park
PAAAP   *Pennsylvania Avenue: An American Place*
PAP   Pennsylvania Avenue Plan
PC   Plan of Chicago
PCPA   President's Council on Pennsylvania Avenue
PEC   Potomac Electric Company
RAT   Robert A. Truax Collection
SI   Smithsonian Institution
SIA   Smithsonian Institution Archives
SOM   Skidmore, Owings & Merrill
SS   Scurlock Studios
SSC   Security Storage Corporation
VG   Vitali Gevorkian
VK   Vlastimil Koubek
WEB   William Edmund Barrett Collection
WGLC   Washington Gas Light Company
WP   *Washington Post*

Unless otherwise noted, all photographs are by Joseph R. Passonneau.

Bibliographic Sources

Anacostia Waterfront Initiative: A District, Federal, and Community Partnership. Washington, D.C.: D.C. Office of Planning, 2000.

Bergheim, Laura. *The Washington Historical Atlas: Who Did What When and Where in the Nation's Capital.* Rockville, Md.: Woodbine House, 1992.

A Better Way to Grow: For More Livable Communities and a Healthier Chesapeake Bay. Annapolis, Md.: Chesapeake Bay Foundation, 1996.

Choukas-Bradley, Melanie, and Polly Alexander. *City of Trees.* Rev. ed. Baltimore: Johns Hopkins University Press, 1987.

The Downtown Cluster of Congregations: Twenty Years of Working Together in Unity for a Better City. Washington, D.C.: Downtown Cluster of Congregations, 1992.

Extending the Legacy: Planning America's Capital for the 21st Century. Washington, D.C.: National Capital Planning Commission, 1996.

Georgetown Historic Waterfront, Washington, D.C.: A Review of Canal and Riverside Architecture. Washington, D.C.: United States Commission of Fine Arts and Office of Archeology and Historic Preservation, National Park Service, Department of the Interior, 1993.

Girouard, Mark. *Cities and People: A Social and Architectural History.* New Haven, Conn.: Yale University Press, 1985.

Goode, James M. *Capital Losses: A Cultural History of Washington's Destroyed Buildings.* Washington, D.C.: Smithsonian Institution Press, 1979.

———. *The Outdoor Sculpture of Washington, D.C.: A Comprehensive Historical Guide.* Washington, D.C.: Smithsonian Institution Press, 1974.

Green, Constance McLaughlin. *Washington Capital City, 1879–1950.* Princeton, N.J.: Princeton University Press, 1963.

———. *Washington Village and Capital, 1800–1878.* Princeton, N.J.: Princeton University Press, 1962.

Gutheim, Frederick, and Wilcomb E. Washburn. *The Federal City: Plans and Realities.* Washington, D.C.: Smithsonian Institution Press, in cooperation with the National Capital Planning Commission, 1976.

Highsmith, Carol M., and Ted Landphair. *Pennsylvania Avenue: America's Main Street.* Washington, D.C.: American Institute of Architects Press, 1988.

Junior League of Washington. *The City of Washington: An Illustrated History.* Ed. Thomas Froncek. New York: Alfred A. Knopf, 1977.

Kelly, Charles Suddrath. *Washington, D.C., Then and Now: 69 Sites Photographed in the Past and Present.* New York: Dover Publications, 1984.

King, LeRoy O., Jr. *100 Years of Capital Traction: The History of Streetcars in the Nation's Capital.* Dallas: Taylor Publishing Company, 1972.

Lee, Richard M. *Mr. Lincoln's City: An Illustrated Guide to the Civil War Sites of Washington.* McLean, Va.: EPM Publications, 1981.

Longstreth, Richard, ed. *The Mall in Washington 1791–1991.* Washington, D.C.: National Gallery of Art, 1991.

Miller, Fredric M., and Howard Gillette Jr. *Washington Seen: A Photographic History 1875–1965.* Baltimore: Johns Hopkins University Press, 1995.

Myer, Donald Beekman. *Bridges and the City of Washington.* Washington, D.C.: United States Commission of Fine Arts, 1992.

National Capital Planning Commission. Frederick Gutheim, consultant. *Worthy of the Nation: The History of Planning for the National Capital.* Washington, D.C.: Smithsonian Institution Press, 1977.

Passonneau, Joseph R. *Central Washington Transportation and Civic Design Study.* 1977.

Passonneau, Joseph R., and Richard Saul Wurman. *Urban Atlas: Twenty American Cities.* Cambridge, Mass.: MIT Press, 1966.

Reed, Robert. *Old Washington, D.C., in Early Photographs, 1846–1932.* New York: Dover Publications, 1980.

The Regional Development Guide 1966–2000. Washington, D.C.: National Capital Planning Commission, 1966.

Reps, John W. *Monumental Washington: The Planning and Development of the Capital Center.* Princeton, N.J.: Princeton University Press, 1967.

———. *Washington on View: The Nation's Capital since 1790.* Chapel Hill, N.C.: University of North Carolina Press, 1991.

Resources for the Future. *Cities and Space: The Future Use of Urban Land.* Ed. Lowdon Wingo. Baltimore: Johns Hopkins University Press, 1963.

Smith, Kathryn Schneider. *Port Town to Urban Neighborhood: The Georgetown Waterfront of Washington, D.C., 1880–1920.* Dubuque, Iowa: Kendall Hunt Publishing Company, 1989.

Smith, Kathryn Schneider, ed. *Washington at Home: An Illustrated History of Neighborhoods in the Nation's Capital.* Northridge, Calif.: Windsor Publications/Columbia Historical Society, Washington, D.C., 1988.

A Transportation Survey and Plan for the Central Area of Washington, D.C. Commissioners of the District of Columbia, 1944.

A Transportation Vision, Strategy, and Action Plan for the Nation's Capital. District of Columbia Department of Public Works, 1997.

Warner, Sam Bass. *Planning for a Nation of Cities.* Cambridge, Mass.: MIT Press, 1966.

———. *Streetcar Suburbs: The Process of Growth in Boston, 1870–1900.* First ed. Cambridge, Mass.: Harvard University Press/MIT Press, 1962.

———. *The Urban Wilderness: A History of the American City.* Berkeley, Calif.: University of California Press, 1972.

Washington's Three-Sisters Bridge and Inner Loop Freeway Controversies. Washington, D.C.: Committee of 100 on the Federal City, 1998.

Weeks, Christopher, ed. *The AIA Guide to the Architecture of Washington, D.C.* Third ed. Baltimore: Johns Hopkins University Press, 1994.

Index